All Balls and Glitter

My Life

CRAIG REVEL HORWOOD

with Alison Maloney

Michael O'Mara Books Limited

First published in Great Britain in 2008 by
Michael O'Mara Books Limited
9 Lion Yard
Tremadoc Road
London SW4 7NQ

Revised and updated paperback edition first published in 2009

Papers used by Michael O'Mara Books Limited are natural, recyclable
products made from wood grown in sustainable forests. The manufacturing
processes conform to the environmental regulations of the country of origin.

ISBN: 978-1-84317-388-5

1 3 5 7 9 10 8 6 4 2

Designed and typeset by E-Type

Plate section designed by www.envydesign.co.uk

Printed and bound in Great Britain by CPI Cox & Wyman, Reading, Berks

www.mombooks.com

Contents

Author's Acknowledgements

I'd really like to thank my family for being brave and supporting me in the content of this book. I know how hard it must have been to relive some of the experiences we have shared, both good and bad. The fact that there were incidents of which we were not all aware and have learned only through reading the book cannot have been easy.

I have not written *All Balls and Glitter* to offend anyone, but simply to explain how each and every person can touch your life, no matter how large or small the involvement or part they play in it.

I believe that you meet certain people at certain times for a reason – and that's to learn something more about yourself, so you can gain a better understanding, not only personally, but socially; how to respect the views and opinions of others to make the world in which we live a better place.

I'm grateful to everyone who has helped me to see me as I am. I pray that my honesty continues throughout my life – and doesn't get me into too much trouble!

Alison, without you, this book would be illiterate. Thank you for your organization skills.

To all the beautiful people I have mentioned in this tome, my sincere apologies, and thanks for making my life so special and rewarding. Life, it seems, really is what you make it and we continue to learn and grow every day.

A special thank you to Grant, the man I love: the poor bugger has been thrown in at the deep end!

Craig, 2008

CHAPTER 1 *A Lavish Life*

Lavish stood on the stage at the Comedy Club in Adelaide, exhausted but exhilarated. She'd been working at the theatre all day and gone on to the club afterwards, but her act had been amazing. The crowd had loved the tap, the trumpet and the fabulous voice, and had roared as the dancing diva went into 'Greatest Love of All'. Now they were screaming for more.

The gigs were getting increasingly frequent and the stage managers were willing to pay top whack for more songs, but somehow it wasn't enough. As she faced an adoring audience and delivered her finale, she lapped up the applause and smiled her most engaging smile. And all the time she was plotting her own demise.

Like many of the beautiful and talented, Lavish was always destined to die young. That moment had come. It was Craig's turn to shine.

By the time I decided to kill off Lavish, my glamorous alter ego, we had been together for two years.

As an aspiring and hugely ambitious twenty-year-old dancer, I soon got sick of being stuck in the chorus line where I felt my true potential was being missed. I was always the understudy to the leading characters, but I never got to play them straight off. I wanted to be different.

I had already seen myself in drag when I'd dressed up for the Miss Alternate pageant in Melbourne in 1982. I'd looked pretty hot. Never being one to set my sights too low, I now thought, 'Maybe I could be a drag pop princess or an androgynous singer like David Bowie.'

It was the eighties and Culture Club were huge, so being in drag didn't seem a big deal. I saw an interview on the telly with Boy George and he was so honest and open: a great inspiration. Unlike most people in the public eye, who appeared fake to me, he stood up for what he believed in and said, 'Yes, I like wearing lipstick. Yes, I look good.'

I decided to go for it. At the time, I was dancing every night in high heels in *La Cage aux Folles*, so I was halfway to being a drag act anyway. Creating an alter ego would be a fitting way of exposing my other talents. Lavish was born.

It was Danny La Rue who had nicknamed me Lavish when I was touring with him (which he and all my other friends frequently shortened to 'Lav'). That, naturally, became my drag name. The character was simple too. She was a glamour puss who couldn't stop singing and dancing, and she loved doing cover versions of Whitney Houston songs. I was never going to sing like Whitney, and I certainly couldn't look like her, so I had to develop my own style.

For the image, I didn't need to go far. This was the *Dynasty* era, so I set about recreating that Joan Collins allure: sparkle and extravagant fashion were a must. I copied Joan's make-up and found myself an emerald-green dress with the perfect design: long sleeves to cover my hairy arms, and massive eighties shoulder pads. I finished the look with open-toed courts complete with six-inch stiletto heels – fabulous! What a dazzling, talented creature I had created. She was nearly seven feet tall in those shoes, with wild auburn hair, and was extremely popular on the drag circuits.

Lavish didn't need much patter because she had a belter of a singing voice and always performed live. Drag queens were all the rage in Australia at the time, but they were all miming – it was like *The Adventures of Priscilla, Queen of the Desert* – so Lavish's version of 'Greatest Love of All' was legendary. Other favourites were 'I Am Woman', the Helen Reddy classic, and 'You Gotta Have a Gimmick', which is usually performed by three women, but Lavish did all the parts: playing the trumpet, tap-dancing and ending with a sprinkling of ballet into the splits. She would execute a series of dramatic *fouetté* turns and then, with a big bang, slide into the splits on the cymbal crash.

The act went down a storm and the clubs were clamouring to book her, for more money each time. At the end of every gig, they'd ask for more songs for more cash too, so, for a while, it was all going to plan.

By the time she really took off I was in a show called *Sugar Babies* in Perth, Western Australia. I'd perform until about 10.30 p.m., then I'd get dressed and leave the theatre as a woman, lugging my trumpet, my backing tracks, microphones and cables. I was dragging myself around in more ways than one!

Eventually, Lavish's popularity became the bane of my life. It was good experience, but she was so successful on the drag circuit that people only wanted me as her. The whole thing was becoming a chore.

Then came the clincher. After the act one night, an audience member came and knocked on my dressing-room door. I let him in.

'I saw you in *Sugar Babies* and I think you're wasting your time doing the drag thing,' he said bluntly. 'You were fantastic. You should be singing as a man, not a woman.'

I'd fallen in love with the adoration of the crowds and all the screaming, and had not really been contemplating what I was doing. This guy made me stop and think. Whoever you were, thank you – you were right. Lavish had to go.

Deep down inside, I had probably known for a long time that I couldn't keep trawling round these tragic clubs. I suppose I could have taken the character further, but I would have ended up doing it for a living, like Barry Humphries or Danny La Rue, having to put on all this clobber every time I wanted to perform.

As soon as my run in *Sugar Babies* finished, Lavish and I said goodbye. She was last seen at 7 a.m. on 1 November 1988, after an all-night Halloween bash, walking up the Champs-Elysées in Paris with her heels off and getting on the number 31 bus with Tina Turner (not the real one, of course). She ended up at *la Tour Eiffel* and was never seen again.

I miss her, from time to time, but Lavish was never destined to be old. I suppose I miss her youth and beauty most of all. If you paint your face, the canvas changes and moves with age and you can't achieve the same look, so she would have been a sad state now.

Years later, when I was in *Miss Saigon* in London, Lavish was invited to a birthday party, but I really didn't want to revive her. Instead, I went as Lavish's heroin-addict sister. She had beard growth, a messy blonde wig, the same green dress and hairy legs with no tights. The make-up was big dark circles round the eyes and smeared lipstick. She was rough as guts.

As the drugged-up sibling, I announced Lavish's untimely death to the gathered throng and so she was finally laid to rest.

The real roots of Lavish can probably be traced back to the small town of Ballarat, Victoria, in Australia, where I was born and where, after much moving about, my family finally settled.

In our dress-up box at home we had a synthetic platinum-blonde wig, which was actually not a wig at all, but one of those swimming caps for women with hair on it. I used to put that on all the time, along with various absurd outfits, and then I'd do a little show for everyone. There were frosted-glass, double sliding doors in our living room that created a perfect central entrance for me because I could start my act behind them, then dramatically slide them open for a tantalizing reveal.

At one cocktail party at our house on Ditchfield Road, when I was about seven years old, I thought I'd entertain the guests with a performance. After announcing my plan, I rushed up to my bedroom to get into my costume. Out came the famous blonde wig/ swimming cap, which had always had a dreadful stench of old musty rubber about it. I draped a bit of random fabric around me like a boa and slicked on some lipstick to complete my transformation.

Everyone was gathered in the living room. There was lots of shushing as I quite clearly got ready behind the glass doors. My sister Sue introduced me, and then I made my entrance in flamboyant fashion. I sang an original song I'd made up entitled 'A Pimple on Your Bum', which was my solo. It was a popular favourite at the Christmas concert that my cousins, the Lancasters, my siblings and I put on every year for the family in the front room at my nanna's house – so for me, it was a sure-fire bet. The lyrics went like this:

> A pimple on your bum,
> A pimple on your bum,
> It's not gonna do some good,
> A pimple on your bum,
> A pimple on your bum,
> It's not gonna do some good.
> Ah, with a pimple on your bottom you just can't stop,
> You go around town doing – a plop,
> Well, you're just smelly, unclean, and filthy too,
> And now I know I'm not marrying you,
> Now – I know – I'm not marrying you!

The act began well. The crowd was going wild and I started to get carried away. When the raunchy section of my song kicked in, I went crazy and began to perform a bastardized version of the cancan, only to misjudge one high kick that knocked the drink out of the hands of one of the guests. I was mortified, finished the show early and ran out of the room as fast as I could, crying my eyes out.

My father was not happy – in fact, he was furious, and I don't think it was the drink I'd upset that was the problem. Dad was embarrassed that his son had got up in drag. He chased me through the house, screaming at me for dressing up like a girl. He was really angry. I found a hiding spot under Sue's bed, which was at the far end of the house. He eventually came into the room, looking for me. I held my breath and was so quiet and still. But he knew I was there.

'If I ever see you dressed like that again,' he said, 'I swear I'll ...'

All went silent except for his heavy breathing. Then, to my relief, I heard him walk slowly away back down the hall. I couldn't return to the party all night from sheer humiliation. But I got over it and, clearly, the urge never left me.

My father was in the navy. He had enlisted at the age of eighteen, having seen an ad in the *Ballarat Courier*, and enjoyed a twenty-year career with a string of promotions. He served five tours of duty as part of the Far East Strategic Reserve, and saw active service during the Malaysian clash with Indonesia in the *Konfrontasi* from 1962. As Dad's job took him all over the world, my formative years were somewhat nomadic, with the family moving every few years. My father was frequently absent: in fact, it wasn't until March 1964, the month of my conception, that my dad finally met my older sister, Susan, who was already six months old. He'd left to go on duty when Mum was pregnant; the next time he got leave, he met his first child – and left Mum expecting number two!

I was born on 4 January 1965, in the middle of the Australian summer, the second child of Beverley June and Philip Revel Horwood. I made a late entrance, a week overdue, at 4.40 a.m., weighing in at 7 lb, 2 oz. Mum was delighted to have a little boy to go with Sue, who was just sixteen months old then. I gather that Sue was not so thrilled at the new arrival.

Just six weeks later, I was moving house for the first time, from Ballarat to Huskisson at Jervis Bay, New South Wales. My father was stationed at HMAS Albatross, a naval airbase near Nowra, NSW, where he was responsible for directing anti-submarine aircraft and tracking helicopters. After a few months at Jervis Bay, we moved to a house in the base.

My mother tells me I was a very placid baby, who was able to amuse myself quite well. She would put me in a bouncing cradle and carry me out to the grass while she hung the washing on the clothes line. Obligingly, I would kick one leg and bounce myself to keep amused, and I would often doze off as a result of the motion. I also know, from Mum's meticulous recording of memories, that I crawled on 22 September 1965 and walked on 3 December 1965, a month before my first birthday.

Mum always knew when I was going to sleep as I had a rubber toy, a farmer holding a pig, that had one of those squeaky things inside, which, when pressed, made a whistling noise. As I got older, I would put it underneath me, and rock back and forth to make it squeak, and at the same time, I would roll my head from side to side and make a sort of humming noise until I dropped off.

Throughout my childhood, I would rock myself to sleep for hours, and it drove Mum mad because she could hear my bed creaking. I had a blue pillow with a picture of an orange rocking horse on it, which I'd had since I was a baby in my cot, and I would clutch it while I rocked and sang. I did that until I was about thirteen.

I still have the pillow at home, along with my original teddy bear, which my sister Sue kindly mended over the years and put through much-needed washes, after which the fur always went a bit funny. But then, it was very old and I'm amazed it had any fur left on it anyway after all the torture it had to endure in my possession. Perhaps bizarrely, I was fonder of the pillow than I ever was of the teddy, which was never even named. It must have been the smell of it that made me feel secure, like a baby's comfort blanket. Even as an adult, I have woken up rocking, but only if

I'm alone. When I'm anxious, I will wake up with my head spinning and I know I've been rocking again. Writing this makes me think I should look into getting myself some help.

After Nowra, our next destination was the village of Fareham, near Portsmouth in England, where we stayed while Dad completed two years' officer training. He was commissioned a sub-lieutenant in March 1969. His ship, HMS *Eagle*, was a 55,000-ton aircraft carrier that hosted the first ever sea trials of the Harrier Jump Jet. It was at the height of the Cold War and Russian spy ships were constantly shadowing them. That was Dad's normal life at the time, but it reads like the plot of a thriller now.

We were put up in a tiny two-up two-down. I had to share a room with my five-year-old sister, Susan, and our new sibling Diane, born on 3 April 1967, who was by then a toddler.

Many years later, in 2003, my mum came over to visit me in England and we went to see the house. It was much, much smaller than I'd remembered, but I suppose when you're a kid, everything seems bigger.

One of my earliest memories, from around that time, is the night of 21 July 1969, when Mum dragged us out of bed to watch the first man walking on the moon. We watched it on our black-and-white telly and I thought it was incredible. It really stuck in my memory.

My education began at the small village school in Fareham when I was four years old. It felt really odd putting on my first uniform, which was a grey outfit that looked like a proper suit, with a little hat. I also carried a school bag that contained black plimsolls for PE.

The first day was awful. There were lots of people everywhere and loads of corridors, and I didn't like having to hang up my shoes. Everything was too regimented after the relative chaos of home and I felt completely alone. I suppose I must have had an Australian accent, but I don't remember anyone mentioning it or making an issue of it.

At lunchtimes, the school served hot meals, which I recall because in Australia that doesn't happen. Mum made us packed lunches on most days, but once a week, at the start of class, we were handed a brown paper lunch bag on which a menu was printed and we had to tick what we wanted. The food then came round at lunchtime in the bag. You could have a cream puff, a hot pie or pasty. I used to love filling out the form and the smell of the cooked pies and pasties was fantastic.

After my father's training had finished, we went back to Ballarat for a while, where I was sent to Queen Street primary school. The only thing I remember about my time there is my first ever attack of stage fright. I was in a nativity play and I didn't know what I was doing. I must have been one of the wise men, because I recall that I had to hand someone a present, but I was horribly nervous and I didn't want to go on. It was a feeling that came back to haunt me on the professional stage – but more on that later.

Every time we had to switch accommodation, we would temporarily stay with my nanna – my mum's mum – at her big old Edwardian house in Ballarat. One of my very first memories is of an incident that took place there when I was three, before we went to England. I was playing in the front garden with Sue and she ran through the gate, so I followed. It was one of those old-fashioned sprung iron gates and as soon as she'd passed through, my darling sister let go. It swung back and smacked me on the head. While Sue carried on running and disappeared inside the house, I staggered in after her, crying, with blood dripping down my face. I had to have stitches and I still have the scar.

I was comforted by Fluffy, the little kitten that Sue and I had adopted from a neighbour who kept loads of cats. Tragically, only eighteen months after Fluffy had wandered into our lives, she was hit by a car and died. Sue and I had to bury her under the petunias.

Most of my recollections about Nanna's house are fond ones, however. She kept chickens out the back, which we fed every day with scraps from the kitchen – vegetable peelings and the like – and the contents of the grain bin. We'd dip into it, scoop up some grain and scatter handfuls of cereal about the chook house for the birds to peck upon. That was so much fun. Then we'd collect the freshly laid eggs for breakfast each morning.

Nanna didn't have an inside loo, so we had to go to the outhouse. It was really scary, always full of cobwebs, and there was never any lighting. There were holes in the door where the eyes of the wood had come out. Sue and I suspected that people could perv through while you were on the lav, so we stuck toilet paper into the holes. It always smelt really musty because it was right next to the garage, which was full of old hoses and farmyard tools. The garage was a great playground for me, though, because I loved going through all the dusty old machinery and junk.

My grandfather on my mother's side, whom we called Da – mostly because we couldn't manage to say 'Grandpa' when we were little and the nickname stuck – passed away on 18 December 1970, when I was only five. I remember that we were told he had died and gone to heaven, and was happy. My only other memory of Da is of him pushing us on the swing that he'd made for us in the backyard of the house on Victoria Street.

It was while we were living in Ballarat, after the Fareham posting, that I managed to burn down the kitchen. In my defence, I was only trying to be helpful as Mum was pregnant at the time – but help like that she could have done without!

We had a wood-burning stove, which heated the house and the hot water, and every morning my mum would get up and light the fire. One morning in August 1972, when I was seven, I decided to do it myself. I got up early and beat Mum to it. I'd watched her do it hundreds of times, so I got the fire started without any problem.

Unfortunately, I forgot to close the stove door. The paper I had used for kindling then fell out. There were tea towels hanging nearby, which immediately caught light, and before long the flames had spread to the cupboard and the curtains. I have never been so scared in my life. I started screaming and ran for Mum, shouting, 'The kitchen's on fire!'

The poor woman was seven months pregnant, but she moved as fast as she could in her encumbered state. She raced to the kitchen, went to the fridge, grabbed some cordial and used it to douse the flames.

I was devastated, and plagued by worrying thoughts: 'What if Dad finds out? What's going to happen to me?'

Dad was quite strict about things around the house. He would decide when we could have the heater on and when we couldn't, so I was really frightened about how he might react.

Mum managed to cover up the damage using that awful seventies vinyl that looks like wood. She told me he never found out about the kitchen fire, but I'm sure he knew, because you could see the signs. He never challenged me about it though and I've not asked him about it since.

Sue, Diane and I were very excited about the upcoming addition to our family. We all used to dangle Mum's wedding ring on a length of cotton over her tummy to see if it was a boy or a girl. According to the old wives' tale, if the ring, when held very still over the bump, begins to spin round in a strong circular motion, it will be a girl; if it swings back and forth like a pendulum, it will be a boy. Just quite how that worked I have no clue, but it was an intrigue that kept us all interested and involved in the birth.

My sister Sue and I were that bit older than Diane and therefore able to appreciate the difference between having a brother or sister. I desperately wanted a brother as I already had two sisters and was surrounded by females. I thought it would be fun to do boy things, even though there would still have been a seven-year age gap, and I envisaged lots more boys' toys to play with in the house. It wasn't to be: on 29 October 1972, Mel was born.

Such a fuss was made of her when she arrived home, with the three older kids being told, 'Don't do this, don't do that.' I guess I was a little jealous, but I retreated to my room and managed to keep myself busy by making and painting models, which was an enthusiasm of mine. I would often be found there building things like miniature ships and aeroplanes. I was always crafty – and I don't mean sly. My parents encouraged me by buying arts and crafts kits for my birthday and Christmas, and I spent hours on the hobby. My aptitude would later prove to be a huge blessing when I was out of work and extremely low on cash.

We soon learned how to feed a baby and change nappies, which were the old terry towelling type with big metal safety pins that clip down and lock the pointed part in place so as not to stab the baby's skin. And that wasn't all: we discovered how to test the temperature of bathwater and bathe a baby without drowning her; how to put glycerine on the dummy to stop her crying; the trick of placing her in the baby bouncer to make her laugh and send her to sleep; how to warm up milk and test it on your wrist before feeding her; how to burp her after feeding, and where to place the towel for the inevitable vomit that would land on your shoulder. Mel's presence turned us into mini parents and it was just as well because when Mum had our final sibling a few years later, our knowledge was an unbelievable help. Sue and I were old hands at it by then.

Despite my initial jealousy, Melanie was so cute and cuddly that Sue and I couldn't stop kissing her. She was such a podgy baby and we loved playing with her ears because they were fat too.

Of all my siblings, Susan was the one with whom I got along best. Diane was always that third child who was destined to be the brunt of our teasing and pranks. We would put her in a pushchair and shove her down a hill, then watch her crash and burn, chortling all the time! But the three of us were our own little nucleus of a family until Mel came along and grabbed all the attention, and that's when Susan and I really went our own way.

Susan used to have a bitch fight with her hair every day. It was the seventies and everyone had those centre partings and flicks, à la *Charlie's Angels*. Susan just had to have that style, but her hair was auburn and wavy so she was always curling it. Once, she managed to electrocute herself and we all screamed with laughter. It was hilarious!

Susan wasn't always that kind to me either. On one occasion, when an older cousin was visiting, the two of them ran a bath of boiling hot water and persuaded me to get in it. I really scalded myself and she still feels guilty to this day.

We hadn't been in Ballarat long before Dad got a posting to Sydney. We moved there when I was in grade three, aged seven. The six years that we spent in that city were the longest stretch we spent anywhere, and they were the happiest in my childhood. It was the one time I was able to build friendships – only for them to be broken again when we returned to Ballarat when I was thirteen.

Our townhouse in Sydney was in a place called Auburn. It formed part of a group of quite small, semi-detached naval houses located around a central courtyard. There was a little, green, square park with a big rock, where we used to play in good weather, and a weeping willow tree, on which we would swing. Despite being a naval community, it was very suburban and there wasn't much to amuse us kids there. There were, however, loads of cockroaches, as Sydney was swarming with them in the summer, and cicada shells on the trees to pick off and play with.

There was also a mad woman who lived directly opposite us, who used to try to commit suicide approximately once a year. Each of the houses had a little triangular roof with a window leading out on to a balcony, and she would climb out there and threaten to jump. Looking back on it, it wasn't actually very high. I think if she had jumped she would have succeeded in breaking only her legs.

She loved to drink and smoked like a chimney. Whenever she

needed fags, she'd give me five bucks and I'd go round the corner on my scooter to buy them for her. This was long before any laws prohibiting children from purchasing cigarettes.

The courtyard had a lot to answer for, as it was the setting for my first ever punch in the face. My assailant lived in another townhouse there. I was always involved in some sort of altercation with him and his brothers as they were the tough boys, the bullies on the block, and they thought they were cool. This particular day, I was playing in the courtyard and my enemy, as usual, shouted 'Poofter!' at me as he cycled past. I answered back, as instructed by my father if it ever happened again. 'It takes one to know one,' I yelled, without really knowing what it meant.

In response, the thug proceeded to get off his Chopper bike and then hit me fair and square in the face. Naturally, being the insecure kid I was, I cried like a baby and ran home. Dad gave me a boxing lesson after that incident, which actually gave me a small amount of confidence – if not to fight, then at least to look like I could.

I was always a bit of a scaredy-cat. Between the ages of nine and twelve, I suffered from weird nightmares and phobias. I had a recurrent dream about being in this terrible tunnel that was spinning round so that the skin on my face was pulled back. I'd grind my teeth all night. I also had a phobia about vampires, so I had to sleep with the light on. Though I can't remember ever seeing a vampire movie, somewhere along the line I must have done as I suddenly became obsessed with the idea that they were going to come and get me. Consequently, I made a crucifix out of an old television aerial, with some of the bits taken off, which I put at the end of my bed, and I'd barricade myself inside the room when it was time to go to sleep.

It was just as well that, other than in Fareham, I never had to share a bedroom. Because I was the only boy in the family, I had my own room, while my sisters slept in bunk beds.

I used to sleepwalk as well, which freaked Mum out. One night, Mum tells me, I got ready for school. She came downstairs in the middle of the night and I was under the stairwell. She asked, 'What are you doing?' and apparently I replied, 'I'm looking for my pencil case!' She then said, 'Come back to bed,' and as I was a good little sleepwalker, I always did what I was told.

On another occasion, she found me banging on my door trying to get out, convinced I was locked in my bedroom. I did all kinds of strange things in my sleep. I was always scared that I was going to walk outside into the main street during these episodes, because as a somnambulist you don't have any control over what you're doing.

As an adult, I have only sleepwalked twice. Both times, I went to the loo in the wrong place! The first incident was during a holiday in the Canary Islands. I was there with Stewart, a work friend of mine who was the stage manager of *Crazy for You* in the West End. I walked into his room, opened the wardrobe, placed a towel meticulously on the floor of the wardrobe and then proceeded to pee on to it. Once finished, I shut the wardrobe and his bedroom door, and went back to my own bed. Stewart watched the whole thing and could not believe his eyes. He asked me what the hell I was doing, but I didn't wake up. In the morning, when he told me about it, I was mortified. I'd had a vague memory of getting out of bed and using the bathroom in the night, but had thought I'd dreamed it all.

The other occasion happened while a boyfriend, Lloyd, and I were living together. I got out of bed, walked round to Lloyd's side, pulled the drawer out of his bedside cabinet and sat down as if it were a toilet. Then I pissed all over his undies and T-shirts before climbing back between the sheets. How terrible!

I suppose Sydney is where I grew up the most because that's where I did the most schooling. At Auburn primary, which was co-ed, I played with the girls in the playground because I didn't like spending time with the boys. They would be at the south end of the school while the girls – and I – would be at the north, skipping and playing hopscotch. I got teased about it all the time, but I just didn't enjoy games with the lads. They were always too busy with handball competitions and the like, which never really interested me. I had only one male friend; luckily, he didn't like handball either.

In fourth grade, there was a big craze for Knitting Nancys, those wooden knitting spools with nails on the top that you turn and loop wool around to make various items, but mainly tea cosies. I used to borrow my sister Sue's and take it to school so that I could knit at play- and lunchtimes. It had a face like Betty Boo's painted on it, with a black bob, and wore a little blouse and a red dress. Apart from me, there was only one other guy who was into Knitting Nancys, but I loved them. No wonder I was mocked so mercilessly.

The only game I played with the boys was marbles. It was around the time I moved from infants to juniors, which was based in a different building, so it felt like going to big school.

Academically, I didn't shine at all. By grade three, I still couldn't tell the time. I had terrible trouble learning it and got so confused because I simply couldn't work out why it was 'quarter to' anything. There was something about the basic structure that baffled me.

Perhaps I had a form of dyslexia because I still can't tell my left from my right. If someone tells me to turn left, I turn right. It may sound odd for a choreographer not to know left from right, but if you say 'stage left' or 'stage right', I'm fine. I have to think in 'stage speak' – prompt or O.P. (off prompt). Prompt is generally stage left. I was bewildered before, but now I'm worse because, as a director, I have to flip my left and right in my mind when I'm talking to companies. I'm always giving taxi drivers the wrong directions.

I was caned by the headmaster three times for not learning to tell the time, but the more I was punished, the more I struggled with it. I remember standing with my hand held out waiting for the whack, my palm shiny with sweat, fingers trembling: a nervous wreck. Then the blow, the crack of the cane and the unbelievable burning sting. It hurt so much. But, surprisingly, the pain never seemed to last long and my hand just went a little numb.

There was another teacher who caned me in grade four, over my maths, because my arithmetic was terrible. I was always dreadful at numbers. He would put two rulers together and whack them on the desk as a threat, but one day, he grew tired of issuing warnings and went for the real thing.

In high school, one teacher would pull our pants down and paddle us with a table-tennis bat in front of the whole class. We just accepted it as a normal part of school life, but it was probably not allowed to happen for many more years.

Going up to secondary school is strange. You feel like a big kid in grade six and then, in year seven, you're suddenly the little pipsqueak again. (In Australia, 'grades' referred to your primary school classes, while secondary schools used the term 'year'.) Everyone at my new school seemed to be very grown up to me.

Additionally, it was a peculiar experience going from a co-ed school to Granville Boys' High. It was the first time I'd been to a school without my sisters, who went to the nearby Auburn Girls' High School. I also had to start walking from the house to the station before catching a train to school, which took some getting used to.

I started there in 1977, the year of the Granville rail disaster. In January, a morning commuter train went under the Granville bridge and derailed, hitting the supports, and the bridge fell down on top of it. In all, 83 people died and 210 were injured. It is still the worst train crash in Australia's history.

Under normal circumstances, it would have been the same train I caught to school. Luckily, we were on a break and all the kids who would usually have taken that service were at home. Instead, we watched the events unfold on television and were glued to the screen all day.

One particular friendship at Granville was with a boy in my class who was a little more worldly-wise than me. He proved a bad influence when he taught me how to shoplift. We used to go to Woolies after school and see what we could plunder. I'd come out with a pencil and ask, 'What have you got?' and my mate, being an old hand at swiping things, would pull jewellery from his pocket.

As always with me, it wasn't something I did by halves. One day, I went on a rampage and stole ten felt-tipped pens, a biro and a big pack of Nestlé condensed milk tubes (the same foodstuff as the condensed milk sold in tins, but back then it was a popular craze for kids to buy these to suck on, like yoghurt tubes). All these items were chosen specifically because I could get them up my sleeve. I also stole an identity bracelet, which was all very seventies.

Finally, I pushed my luck a little too far in a shop called Franklin's, which is like Kwik Save or Wilkinson's in the UK, selling all plain label, no-frills goods (cheap, cheap, cheap!). I tried to steal a pencil there and got sprung. As I left, I felt the classic tap on the shoulder and this lady security guard said, 'Excuse me. Have you taken anything that you haven't paid for?'

My career as a master criminal fell at the first hurdle and I cracked under pressure.

'Yes, yes, I have,' I spluttered, and confessed all. The guard took me to the back of the shop and handed me over to the store manager, who said he was going to call the police and have me arrested unless I apologized and wrote a letter to say how sorry I was, and told my parents what I had done.

Then he went through my school briefcase and took everything out, asking, 'Did you steal this?'

Every time I would say, 'Yes, stolen.'

I didn't have to admit to anything except the pencil, but once I was caught, I became a blubbering wreck and launched into a major confession. Why, I'll never know. If I'd had any sense, I would have said nothing. Perhaps it was an early manifestation of my now trademark honesty – I never have been able to keep my mouth shut.

The manager presented me with a letter to give to my mum and dad, and that was the worst bit. I was in tears. I sat in the back of the shop crying like a newborn babe. It was pathetic.

As well as breaking down, I also managed to turn Queen's evidence. I was asked for the names of any friends that I knew stole from the shopping centre and I blurted out, 'My mate steals all the time.' I was so upset, nervous and shaken that I'd grassed him without a second thought.

When I got home, I was in a terrible state, sobbing inconsolably. I handed Mum the letter and, after reading it, she asked, 'Have you given it all back? Will you promise me you won't do it again?'

Mum was disappointed in me, as any mother would be, but she didn't shout or scream at me. Instead, she gave me a hug and a kiss and said, 'It's all going to be all right, as long as you don't do it again.'

That was Mum all over. She could see that I'd been raked over the coals at the store and had tortured myself over the prospect of having to tell her, so I didn't need any further punishment. Thankfully, Dad was away working and I don't think she ever told him about it. She's wonderful, my mum.

When I was eleven, I started guitar lessons. My sister Sue used to play the piano and I'd wanted to learn an instrument too. I loved those sessions to begin with. My teacher made a mean hot chocolate in the microwave – that was rather special, as they had only just been invented. In truth, the tutor was really scary as his movement was slow, his speech was laboured and the teaching was delivered at a snail's pace. Eventually, I grew bored.

At Granville Boys' High, the staff really supported my music. There, everyone played the recorder, but a group of friends and I took this skill to new and fabulous heights by performing on that ubiquitous instrument alongside a seven-piece orchestra at the famous Sydney Opera House.

That unusual achievement was all due to my music teacher, Miss Shaw. She was an inspirational instructor, who gave me confidence and sincerely believed in my talent, and was extremely important in my musical development. Miss Shaw placed me in the recorder set that performed at Rotary Club meetings in the evenings. She also entered us into a competition that culminated with a concert at the Opera House.

Once I'd mastered the recorder, I moved on to my beloved French horn. I practised every day because I adored it. It was great to have a hobby that fulfilled and excited me. I also belonged to a gymnastics club at that time, which must have helped with my balance and strength when I eventually took up dancing, but it was never a passion for me. Nevertheless, I did rather well at it, receiving an award for best newcomer.

I was always jealous of Sue when she used to do jazz ballet classes next door. I was like Billy Elliot, peeping round the curtain that divided the boys' class from that of the girls. When 'Delta Dawn' by Helen Reddy came out in 1973, I can remember Susan doing this chassé backstep to the song and, naturally, I tried to copy her. It seemed more fun to do something like that to music rather than strength training and walking on your hands.

Like Billy, I would discover my dancing talent in due course. Until then, I just had to bide my time, silently watching from the sidelines.

W e didn't spend that much time with my dad's side of the family when we were growing up because they always lived in Western Australia, while we were generally based in New South Wales or Victoria, which are in south-eastern Australia.

The Horwood family were devout followers of the Seventh-day Adventist Church, a branch of the Christian religion that believes the Sabbath day falls on a Saturday and that it should be strictly observed. Most branches of the family, led by my grandmother Phyllis (whom we all called Phonse), would keep the Sabbath sacred from sunset on Friday night to sunset on Saturday night, so there was no television or radio and no secular work. That's the way my dad was brought up too, but he went so far the other way that we grew up watching him fight against religion, among other things.

Our family were removed from the religious influence of Phonse both by geography and Dad's resolute rejection of it. My sisters and I would attend the local Sunday school, but Dad never went to services himself. In contrast, his sisters, Lorraine and Julie, are still very active in the Church and Lorraine's eldest son, Paul, works at the Seventh-day Adventists' Australian headquarters.

We were raised in the equivalent of the Church of England, which in Australia was called the Church of Christ. I was never interested in religion, partly because I found some of the teaching at Sunday school too bizarre for words.

In one lesson, we were asked, 'What do you say if someone stops you and asks for directions?' Well, one would think that the polite response would be to tell them which way to go, but not according to my Sunday school tutor. He said that the correct answer is: 'There is only one way and that is to God.' I remember sitting there thinking, 'I can't say that!'

It stuck with me, though. Every time anyone asks me how to get anywhere, I always think, 'There is only one way and that is to God.'

The church-led Boys' Brigade was quite big in Sydney so I decided to join, although I didn't last very long there. Their motto was 'Steadfast and Sure' and the boys all wore a uniform and a cadet's cap. I had to give up my gymnastics class to attend, but in retrospect, I should have stayed with the rings and the vaulting. I liked dressing up for the sessions, getting ready and having to polish the uniform's buttons – the 'showbiz' side of it – but knuckling down to pitching tents and lighting fires wasn't my thing. On one occasion I remember going on a hike when I was so unfit that I came back half a stone lighter – so at least that was a bonus.

The favourite game there was British Bulldog, where you split up into two teams and each group goes to either end of the hall. Then you try to reach your opponent's side of the room, while they attempt to bring you down with a tackle. It's like war. You have to bulldoze your way through and it's basically an excuse for anyone who hates you to beat seven bells out of you.

One minute, we'd be knocking the crap out of each other and the next – because the Boys' Brigade was run by the church – having a scripture lesson. I really wasn't suited to either of those pursuits. The crunch came when I was supposed to be baptized. Beforehand, everyone was going up to the priest and receiving a blessing, but when it came to my turn, I got all nervous and freaked out. I refused to do it. Beside the pulpit there was a big stone bath with steps leading down to it. I thought you had to take off your clothes and climb into the bath in front of everyone and then commit your whole life to God. Believe me, I wasn't prepared to do either!

Religion is a strange thing because although people are often brought up with it, and every official form you fill in asks you to which religion you belong, many of us no longer know what we believe in. I've read lots of books on the subject, including *The Road Less Travelled* and *Conversations with God*, and I find them fascinating. It's nice to believe in something, as it gives people a sense of security, but I think you have to create your own path and make the right choices. I'm unclear as to what my religion is today and whether I actually believe in God or not. I'm still confused. You are taught to pray as a child and it never quite leaves you. I believe there is something else, but not one thing alone.

One day, I asked my grandmother, Phonse, what it meant to be a Seventh-day Adventist. She told me it meant that when you died, you would stay in the ground until Jesus came back to get you.

My grandmother's fervent faith had come about as a result of a terrible childhood, and her eventual redemption from it.

When Phonse was nine years old, her mother died in childbirth, and she was put into a Catholic orphanage in Armidale, New South Wales with three of her sisters. The baby stayed in Kalgoorlie, Western Australia, where the family had lived. Although Phonse's dad was still alive, he couldn't look after her and her siblings because he didn't have the resources. There was no other family to help out and he had to work away from home even more than my own dad had done with the navy. There was nowhere else for the girls to go.

The orphanage experience was abysmal. The food was shocking, and the girls had to get up at four in the morning to do the washing and hang it outside in all weathers, with no shoes to wear. They had to say a prayer when they got out of bed (which Phonse still does now) and go to Mass every morning, but in the midst of all that religion, no love or affection was ever shown to the children.

In 1932, seven years after Phonse had joined the orphanage, her two brothers, aged nineteen and twenty-one, were working at a gold mine out at Bendigo, Victoria, which belonged to Phonse's uncle. They promised each other that they would rescue their sisters as soon as they found their first big nugget.

Two weeks later, they discovered a huge one, bought an old Rugby car, and drove all the way to Armidale to collect their siblings. Phonse had been sent to work at a convent school at Gunnedah, NSW, so they picked her up on the way. When she met her brothers, she didn't know who they were. They drove on and met the other girls, and then their dad got in the car and they didn't recognize him either.

The last thing Phonse was told at the orphanage was: 'Don't forget you're Catholic; don't let them take away your religion.' It turned out to be somewhat prophetic.

The brothers took the girls back to Bendigo. En route, they stayed at a hotel and the sisters, not knowing what a hotel was, got up at 5 a.m. to make the bed and clean the room. The younger ones also embarrassed their brothers because they had no idea how to use a knife and fork.

At Bendigo, arrangements were made for the girls to be looked after by a kindly local woman. She had recently become a Seventh-day Adventist, so she wouldn't let the girls go to Mass and threw out their rosary beads. She had six grown sons of her own, but she doted on the girls. At last, they had a family and a lot of love and care. While the Catholic religion had, in their minds, brought them all that had been ghastly in their lives, the Seventh-day Adventist Church was where they received affection, compassion and attention.

For my father, the church was just another thing to rail against, but for Phonse it represented the best thing that had happened to her. It's easy to see why she remains so devout.

Although Phonse is committed to the church, she is never judgemental or pious. She loves everybody and everybody loves her. Everything revolves around family and the heart – even the special routine that she taught me for drying myself when I got out of the bath.

'Start with your feet and legs because they're a long way away from your heart,' she'd say. 'Then you do your back and your arms and the last part of your body that you dry is your heart, because that is the warmest part.'

I still dry myself that way even after all these years.

Phonse's cooking is amazing and she makes the best fishcakes in the world.

Phonse's husband was my grandfather Revielle, who died in 1985. His complicated name was later abbreviated to Revel, and both my dad and I inherited it as a middle name. Our namesake was more rebel than Revel, refusing to toe the family line on religion. Often, when Phonse turned off the TV on a Friday night, he would switch it straight back on again. He was also something of a gambler.

Revel, whom we called Mozza, taught me a lot of magic tricks. He used to tell me that if you placed your hands on someone's temples, you could read minds, and I was totally sucked in by this. He would say, 'Think of a number between one and ten,' and then guess what it was by putting his hands on our heads. I couldn't work out how he did it. Phonse confided the supposed secret: feel for the pulse and then count the beats. I was constantly putting my hands on people's temples, but all I could sense was a normal pulse. I never discovered the real trick, although I believe it had something to do with an accomplice.

Mozza had a huge costume box. He would dress up as a clown for children's parties, and then perform magic tricks. He had a penny-farthing that he used to ride around on. I used to borrow his clown outfit and dress up for parties in our naval unit in Sydney. I had a disappearing egg-cup trick, which I loved doing, and could also use the magic rings. Anything that was to do with magic, I was really into. Magic tricks taught me that things weren't always as they seemed and so I wanted to know more about the subject.

At family gatherings, such as Christmas, the kids always put on a concert – organized, naturally, by me. Christmases were generally spent with my mother's family, the Lancasters, and particularly my nanna, Constance, whose house in Ballarat was a second home to us all.

While the grown-ups talked in the living room, the children would go into the front room and rehearse. We made up songs and played instruments, and performed plays and sketches. Susan and I were always the leads and Diane would get a small role, with the younger kids running on occasionally in the latter years.

The cousins would all get involved as well. Peter sang 'Oh Currie Currie Ana, I Found a Squashed Banana' (a schoolyard parody of the traditional Maori love song 'Pokarekare Ana') and then my Auntie June would get in on the act with her rendition of 'Are You Lonesome Tonight?' At Christmas, we always finished with a festive carol, which everyone would sing.

Susan and I looked forward to our little productions with great excitement, but as we got older, the cousins lost interest one by one and the family gatherings got smaller and smaller. Inevitably, the Christmas shows stopped.

Perhaps what we loved most about those days was the charade of a happy, united family, which hid the horror of everyday life with my father.

My dad, Philip Revel Horwood, was (and still is) an alcoholic – and an abusive one at that. As soon as he started drinking, we knew we were in for it, but we got used to it. We learned to live with the shouting and screaming, and simply turned a blind eye to it. We all knew that he was going to get aggressive. As we were kids, we just had to deal with it.

His position of lieutenant commander meant that he was away most of the time in the early part of my childhood, sometimes for stretches of ten months, and they were happy times at home. Ironically, though, we looked forward to his return because he always brought us great presents when he'd been away. He would come back laden with bikes or expensive gifts from faraway places and, to start with, we'd be happy to see him. When he was sober, he was a wonderful, charming man – a completely different person. But when he'd had too much to drink, he was an absolute nightmare.

My sisters and I were always the ones sent to fetch the beers from the kitchen, take the tops off them and set them up for him because he wouldn't get out of his chair. We used to count how many he'd had because we always knew the seventh bottle was crucial. That's when we knew there would be trouble.

The stages of his daily descent into rage were predictable. The first few beers would lead to funny antics, then to nagging self-righteousness, ending with ugly, abusive outbursts. This was a pattern we kids grew used to. Sometimes, we took advantage of this knowledge by poking fun at him during the merry stage, then we would tease and confront him during the 'I love myself' stage, when he started going on and on about how marvellous and mightily important he was. During the scary stage, I would retreat to my room, but Susan was often braver, standing up to him before she hid herself away.

The aggressive phase would last for an hour or two and then he'd fall asleep. His chin would drop and his teeth would fall on to his chest, and then we knew we could all relax. Occasionally, for a laugh, we would hide his teeth.

The abuse was mostly verbal, directed at anyone in the house, but more often than not it was my mum who bore the brunt. If we were in the living room, sitting on beanbags, he would kick us as he walked past, but we soon learned not to get in the way. And we also learned to shut up, not to complain and not to open our mouths because that was asking for an earbashing. I spent a lot of time in my room when he was in this state, just avoiding him.

Although he rarely lashed out physically, he would look like he was about to and we were afraid of him, anyway. But once he was drunk, he never shut up! He would spout off about anything and everything and we could forget any plans we had to watch television, because he would always talk over it all the time.

All through the Sydney years, he would rant about politics; the Prime Minister, Edward Gough Whitlam, and nuclear war were particular favourites. He made us watch films about atomic bombs that were meant for naval training and were far too gory for children, so we were scared witless. We knew all there was to know about nuclear fallout: that we should go against the wind because the fallout goes with the wind; about not drinking water; the importance of getting underground; how we should eat only tinned food. It was all stuff that kids normally wouldn't have to listen to, but we were trained in the navy way.

Even so, his biggest rant was reserved for the navy. In 1975, he was posted to HMAS *Hobart*, the ship on which he achieved his highest seagoing rank, that of lieutenant. During his two years aboard the guided missile destroyer, he circumnavigated the globe, attending the American bicentennial celebrations in New York and sailing through the Panama Canal on the way out and the Suez Canal on the way home. He used to tell stories from this trip over and over again, always repeating the same old things. We never found out anything about him as an individual as the drink masked the real man. He blamed everything on the navy – his drinking, his temper, his whole life.

We didn't feel we could bring our friends home. The few times we did, we were so embarrassed by him that we stopped inviting them.

Dad hit me twice. The first time was for swearing when I was thirteen: we were in Sydney in the backyard and I told him to 'fuck off', which he richly deserved at the time, and he gave me a backhander across my face. The second occasion, a year later, was punishment for getting in his way and supposedly answering him back.

Mum was a very loving mother and she had a lot to do, bringing up such a large family. Most of the time she was at home with us, although she also had an occasional job working at a motel, laying tables and generally helping out. For a while, she was a telephonist, at one of those old-fashioned exchanges where they would plug little wires into sockets to put through a call from overseas or another state.

She always managed to have a tasty meal ready at 6 p.m. without fail, with dessert to follow. I don't know if any of us can recall our father actually eating at the table with us. He would rather sprawl in the lounge and get sozzled while we all ate in the kitchen. Sometimes he would sit with us, but he would keep a handy little 'behaviour-modification device' next to him that we called 'the strap'. If we laughed at the table, boy, would we get it. The tension made us even more prone to giggling, of course, because if we looked at each other we couldn't keep it in and the guffaws would burst out uncontrollably.

Even the girls couldn't escape the strap. Back in Fareham, at the age of six, Sue accidentally smashed a vase and got belted so hard that she couldn't breathe for sobbing. I think it's fair to say that we preferred dinner without Dad.

Sue and I, as the eldest siblings, tried to take on responsibility where we could. When we were old enough, we would babysit the younger kids so that Mum and Dad could go out together. They never really went anywhere romantic as I recall; it was always to do chores and errands. They never asked us to babysit so that they could go out for a nice meal. Mum was totally starved of that side of Dad. He preferred to buy a leg of lamb or a kilo of prawns and have them at home as a treat for Mum. She would get the choice of the biggest prawns, though, which always put a big smile on her face. She loved being fussed over, as it very rarely happened.

Dad's drinking kept him at home: he could then consume as much as he wanted – which was a lot – and for a good price.

To earn money, I would stack all his empty beer bottles in the shed; once a whole wall was lined with bottles, I could take them to the man at the local shop and exchange them for cash. Dad always let me keep the money so I didn't mind doing the stacking.

By necessity, Mum hid a lot of things from my dad. The running of the house and the care of the children were always her domain and I don't think she told him what we got up to when he wasn't there. In fact, we never really heard them having a proper conversation. The only communication between them was arguments.

It was an odd sort of household, and full of drama. One time, Dad was shouting at us all and my plucky little sister Mel, who was about nine, attacked him with an 'icy pole' (one of those long ice lollies). She jumped on his back and started hitting him on the head with it. Our house had loads of sliding doors inside and all of us ended up chasing him through these doors while she was on his back. It sounds funny now, but it wasn't at the time because he used to lay into Mum a lot, calling her a host of ugly names – 'cabbage' was an all-time favourite – and she didn't deserve that.

On another occasion, in Sydney, Dad decided to make some home brew. It was so strong that a single bottle was all it took to get him off his head. His parents, Phonse and Mozza, who were visiting us from Perth, were both horrified. Dad got very drunk, belittling Mum and talking absolute shite all night. He was shouting about every politician who came on TV, and banging on and on.

Mozza, who was never really a drinker himself – in fact, he loathed the booze – was the angriest he'd ever been. He went over to the home brew, which was fermenting in the kitchen and stank to high heaven, and tipped it all out. There was lots of yelling and screaming. Phonse is the most placid, loving person, and a really calming, soothing personality, but even she'd had enough. I've never seen her so animated and charged. Phonse seemed to take Dad's side, defending him, whereas Mozza was clearly championing Mum, so it felt as though the whole family was at war that night. But nothing could stop Dad drinking.

My parents are divorced now and, looking back, it's easy to think that Mum should have left him many years before. But times were very different then. There were us kids to think about and Mum didn't know how she would get on without the money that Dad was bringing in, so she was in a difficult position.

Then there was the self-esteem issue, which many a wife of an abusive man will recognize. Dad would taunt and chide with comments that were deliberately designed to make her feel worthless and useless. He did a good job of it, too. She took everything he said on board and started to believe that the hideous life with him was far better than a life without him. I also think she was desperately in love with him. I suspect she still is, to this day. We loved him too, when he was sober – but we hated him with a passion when he was drunk.

Living with my dad was never easy, but there were some good days, like the times when he'd take me on a ship or on an outing. When I was twelve, in Sydney, I helped to paint HMAS *Hobart*, which was the most sophisticated ship that Dad had ever served on. I really enjoyed the experience, but I think he was embarrassed because I had long hair and all the officers thought I was a girl. They said, 'There's some girl running around with a paintbrush, painting the ship.' And then Dad took me to the officers' mess and had to tell everyone, 'This is my son.'

Another time in Sydney, he showed me round a nuclear submarine. I couldn't imagine how people managed to live in those tiny little quarters. My father's cabin was miniscule and he also had to share with another lieutenant. Someone my size (I'm 6 foot 2) wouldn't fit in one at all; I would find it impossible.

The shore depot HMAS *Watson*, where my dad was based in the early seventies, was the site of some of my favourite memories of time spent with Dad. He used to take me to the naval base and buy me a raspberry fizzy drink as he mixed with the other officers at the bar. It was so exciting going through the front security gates and I felt special.

Dad also tried to teach me how to play cricket once, which was a huge failure. Mozza was a really keen cricketer and he forced Dad to play it, even though he wasn't really interested. Then, because I was his son, Dad thought he ought to introduce me to the sport – handing down the knowledge from one generation to the next, so to speak – but I hated it too.

Those were the only real things we did together. We never embarked on any other father-and-son activities, except going fishing occasionally, which was a nightmare. It was a six-hour drive in the blazing hot sunshine up to the Murray River, on the border of Victoria and New South Wales. We had to prepare food for ourselves and, although Dad was quite good at cooking, we would simply peel potatoes with a knife and carve them into chips and that was all we ate. He was too busy drinking to make anything else.

Perhaps because of Dad's alcoholism, we didn't go on many holidays. I do remember one family vacation at a place called Foster, though, which is a seaside resort in New South Wales.

Mum and Dad had hired a lovely house by the ocean and we were all really excited. On the very first day, my sister Diane cut her foot open, so she was bandaged up and out of action. She couldn't go swimming or play with us on the beach at all. Then I got sand rash from jumping on a blow-up boogie board, so I couldn't go in the sea either because it stung so much in the salt water. And by the end of the first day, we all had excruciating sunburn.

It wasn't great, but it was the only proper holiday we ever had. Mostly, we would go on trips to visit relatives.

Our family car was an old blue Holden. We used to take that on the long drive from Sydney to Ballarat, which took about twelve or thirteen hours. Once, when Phonse was with us, the car overheated and smoke started pouring from the engine. Phonse panicked and screamed, 'Get out! Get out of the car!' We all piled out and ran away as fast as we could.

This was before the days of highways, so we were in the middle of nowhere on a dusty old road in the heart of the bush. Apparently, there was no water in the radiator, which was why it had overheated. Dad had to walk miles to the nearest dam or waterhole to find more, while we just lay under a tree and waited.

Whenever we were due to drive to Ballarat to visit Nanna, Dad would rouse us at about 3.30 a.m. He and Mum used to make nests of bedding for us kids in the back of the car and we'd sleep on the way, but I hated being dragged out of bed in the early hours of the morning.

I have no idea how we all fitted into the car. In the end, we had to buy a combi van.

Our time in Sydney also saw a new, and final, addition to our family. My brother Trent, the youngest of the five of us, was born in Auburn Hospital in Sydney's western suburbs on 7 December 1977, when I was nearly thirteen.

We all went up to the hospital to see the baby, who was really ugly and red, but Mum looked surprisingly well. There were so many of us gathered round – Dad, me, my sisters Sue, Diane and Mel – it was certainly a momentous occasion.

Trent was destined to be spoilt by everyone, and indeed he was. He was such a gorgeous toddler with big brown eyes and a lovely nature: always a good little boy. He was a very late addition to the family and a mistake, or so we were told.

I was delighted I finally had a brother, but for me it was thirteen years too late. I always dreamed that when I was twenty-five and he was twelve I'd have a red MG sports car and I would pick him up from school in it, making all his classmates jealous.

Then I would take him for rides around Sydney, letting him take the steering wheel and beep the horn, and we would have a real brotherly relationship. It was all very clear to me how I would handle being his big brother. Sadly, that wasn't to be, as we moved back to Ballarat the following year and, to this day, I still don't have my driving licence.

I didn't really get to know my handsome little brother until recent years, as I left home early, when he was just a toddler. We didn't grow up together at all. Trent was raised the Ballarat way, loving Aussie Rules football, fast cars and motorbikes. He was also a keen drummer, which is what he now does professionally, playing in a band called Mushroom Giant. I know it's his passion, so we do at least have something in common – and that's rhythm. I just do it with my feet.

CHAPTER 3 *Ballarat Blues*

After Dad left the navy in 1978, we moved back to Ballarat for good. We stayed with Nanna for a short time, while Dad built an extension on our own house to accommodate the now seven-strong family.

Ballarat is Victoria's biggest inland city, but it's quite provincial nonetheless. In more recent years, a highway has been built so it's more commutable, but when I was growing up it was two-and-a-half hours to Melbourne on the old roads. Consequently, people worked locally and it had that small-town, country mentality.

The Sunshine biscuit factory had provided many jobs, but when that closed down, Mars came to town and a Mars factory was built. I remember my old man going for a couple of job interviews there once his naval career had ended. Other people worked in tourism or retail.

The town had originally sprung up around gold mines; a lot of the alluvial gold mined there built the city of Melbourne. The gold ran out, but a tourist attraction called Sovereign Hill now exists, where all the shacks have been rebuilt and you can see life as it was in the nineteenth century when the gold was discovered. Visitors dress up in period costume and there's a little old gaiety theatre, which plays host to end-of-the-pier-type shows, in which the cast sing 'I Do Like to Be Beside the Seaside' and suchlike. It's one of the major attractions in the area, so lots of people come on day trips to see it. When I got into amateur theatre as a teenager, I performed there a few times.

Two hundred years ago, there were 65,000 people living in Ballarat. Today, there are about 80,000, so it hasn't really grown much. It's become a lot more modern, but there are some classic buildings there – if you can call 150 years old 'classic', which you can in Australia. In the UK, that's almost a new build!

Sturt Street is the main road and there's also a lake, called Lake Wendouree, with big gardens all around it, which the posh people – doctors, lawyers and so on – live near by. The lake's all dried up now because of the drought, but it was once very beautiful. On family outings, we would feed the swans there and then have a picnic, or we would visit Hanging Rock, which wasn't far away. There are vineyards and wineries around Ballarat too; it's where Yellowglen makes its champagne.

All of us were excited about moving into the extended family home. It was a big house, with a tennis court and a swimming pool. Better still, we would each be getting a bedroom of our own.

Our upbringing in Ballarat was traditional on the whole. We always sat round the table at mealtimes, always said grace, and always had our chores to do. Chopping the wood was my responsibility because I was the only grown boy (Trent couldn't really be expected to help, aged nought), as was the weeding and pulling up the carrots.

When we wanted vegetables, we went out and got them from the earth, which looking back was a wonderful bonus, although I never gave it much thought back then. It was just another aspect of normal life. After Dad retired from his life on the sea, he wanted to get back to the soil. He spent all his time outside, digging, hoeing and growing various plants.

We had quite a lot of land around the house so, as well as cultivating the vegetable patch, Dad bought a goat to keep in the south paddock. We called him Snowy because he had a white hide – originality not being our strong point, obviously. He was a mad beast who used to ram anyone who got near him. I loved taking people down there because it would scare the pants off them when he started to run at them. He was on a chain, though, so he didn't often catch anyone, but it wasn't for the want of trying.

Snowy did escape once, and started eating Dad's broad beans. We all chased him round the paddock, trying to grab him before he could do too much damage, which must have looked hilarious.

Dad was very anti-pets, but he kept Snowy because he was a four-legged lawnmower. When he'd finished grazing one patch, we'd move him on to the next. It was a very funny sight as Snowy would 'mow' in circular patches, leaving what can only be described as crop circles in his wake.

The other 'pet' we had was a dog called Buddy, who was a stray that we had found and adopted. But he was just fed on leftovers and Dad wouldn't allow him in the house. He got in one day and we were all screaming and running after him to take him back outside.

There was also a cat in the neighbourhood, a stray that we called Mikie, but my sister Di later ran over it while backing out of the drive. Thankfully, she didn't kill it. That happened the following week when the poor thing was hit by a passing car.

When Mum and Dad were busy, our neighbour Corinne looked after us a lot. She was lovely and, because she wasn't married and didn't have any children, she treated us like her own. She used to take us on trips, including skiing or to the Brown Hill swimming pools when it was unbearably hot. We always loved going out in Corinne's car because she had air conditioning, which we didn't.

She took Sue and me to Thredbo once, an alpine village in the Snowy Mountains, which was amazing. It was the first time we'd ever tobogganed. I remember my legs stinging from getting wet with the snow. Afterwards, we sat in a warm cafe and drank hot chocolate with marshmallows till our jeans dried off. To savour any sort of foodstuff was a luxury. Because there were so many children in our family, you always had to finish your meals first if you wanted seconds, so we all ate really fast, and still do to this day. It's not that we ever starved, but there were seven mouths to feed and you had to grab what you could.

School in Ballarat was never a happy experience for me. Transferring in year nine, when I was thirteen, was hideous. I didn't know anyone and I had to introduce myself to the whole class. I remember thinking, 'I speak differently to them,' but I couldn't understand why. I suppose I just wasn't an ocker (an unrefined Aussie from the outback). The accents in Australia aren't necessarily regional, but you do have city folk and outback people, the real ockers, and that summed them up.

Ballarat East High was co-ed. As a teenager, I wasn't used to seeing girls in school, so I thought that was weird. And, believe me, the girls were tougher than any of the boys. They were rough as guts! They used to trip me over, block my way to the lockers and push me about. But they knew I couldn't lash out at them because you can't hit a girl, and if I retaliated at all, the boys ganged up on me. They were heinous.

I hated Ballarat East from day one. I felt like a total outsider and I didn't fit in at all.

I was fat and I was also really short, believe it or not, because everyone else had grown much more than I had. I was a late developer in everything and most of the class went through puberty a long time before I did.

I was picked on a lot – for my long eyelashes, for looking like a girl, for my weight. The girls at school would say I had mascara on, which I never did, and they said I should wear lipstick. They really gave me a hard time. The boys never stuck up for me because I didn't have any friends in the playground, so I used to hang around by myself, or sometimes with my sister and her friend. They never bullied me in front of Susan, only when I was on my own.

There was one male tormentor in particular who used to

torture me by saying, 'I'll be waiting behind the Caledonian Bridge. I'm gonna get you on your way home.' The only way I could get back to Ditchfield Road was under this bridge.

Soon after I joined the school, I managed to get two tickets for *Countdown*, which was like the Australian version of *Top of the Pops*. Everyone wanted to come. I decided to take Susan's friend Sharon Deacon, who was the most popular girl in the school. She looked exactly like Debbie Harry from Blondie, only with dark hair, and all the boys loved her. This bully was so put out by my choice of date that he said he was going to 'bash me up'. He had the hots for Sharon. That, combined with the fact that he didn't get to go to *Countdown* himself, was motive enough for wanting to hurt me.

My persecutor waited for me by the bridge, on and off, for ages before he got bored. Some days he was there and others he wasn't, but it didn't matter whether he showed up or not because the mere thought that he was around the corner frightened me enough.

Fortunately, I had a classmate called Steven Romeo, known only as Romeo, who used to defend me, and he became a friend. He was a big guy and he would walk me home because my tormentor couldn't touch me with him there. I couldn't protect myself at all. I was quite small and no threat to anyone.

It wasn't just the kids at school who bullied me. When we were staying at Nanna's, after we'd first moved back to Ballarat, but before our house was ready, we had to cycle to the high school on a path that went past a children's home. For some reason, the kids there decided they would pick on me too.

Every single morning, they would form a line across the road so that there was no way I could pass on my bike. They used to let my sister go through and then stop me, which was just bizarre. They didn't say much, just stood there in a long line and I would have to run the gauntlet to get to school. I didn't understand it. I never knew why I was being singled out.

It got to a point where I couldn't bear it any more, so I used the back route instead, which took three times as long. Luckily, all that came to an end when we moved to our own home and I went to school a different way.

The only thing I enjoyed about Ballarat East was the home economics class, in which I excelled. In all other academic disciplines, I was atrocious. I almost didn't pass year ten at all. I failed maths, geography and history because I just wasn't interested. My mind was forever elsewhere. I was good at art and music and that's what I loved, where my passion has always been.

Music was my escape, my way of getting away from everybody, so I spent every free moment practising. Unfortunately, there wasn't a French horn available, which was the instrument Miss Shaw had been teaching me in Sydney. My new school said I had to learn the trumpet instead, much to my disgust.

I was disappointed that I couldn't continue to study the French horn. Sometimes you don't get a choice in life. Given that I was stuck in a school I despised, I determined to make the most of a dispiriting situation. I simply had to learn to love the trumpet if I wanted to be in the school band.

All my practice paid off and I made the cut, in the position of second trumpet. I may have been compelled to master it, but in doing so and by accepting that, I actually grew and blossomed as a musician. And with the benefit of hindsight, Lavish wouldn't have been half the woman she was without the skilled trumpet toots that adorned her act.

Being in the school band was brilliant. You're at one with the instrument and the music, and you receive proper support, artistically, as well. For once, I wasn't being treated like a freak. Furthermore, thanks to the Ballarat Memorial Band – which was a community rather than a school venture – I was even able to keep up the French horn in my spare time, so all was not lost.

After the Easter holidays in 1978, when I was thirteen, came a moment that was to change my life. During the break, I'd won a colouring competition. I was at the very edge of the contest's age limit and to be entering colouring competitions at thirteen is a bit tragic. Anyway, I won it and I was invited to a department store called Myer, which is an Australian equivalent to Selfridges or John Lewis. When I got there, there was a big Easter bunny waiting to present me with a huge Easter egg. There was also a photographer from the *Ballarat Courier*, so I had my photo taken with this bunny and it ended up on the front page of the newspaper. At the time, I was doing a paper round, so, to my intense embarrassment, I had to deliver myself all around Ballarat.

After the Easter vacation, I walked to school feeling thoroughly sick. I knew everyone would know about my prize-winning exploits and that I'd be the focus of a fair amount of ridicule. Sure enough, everyone had seen my picture in the paper. It was a nightmare. I got mercilessly teased about it, to the point that I wanted to leave school. There wasn't anything I could do about it.

On top of this terrible shame came a new indignity. I had eaten the whole, massive chocolate egg myself, as well as numerous other Easter treats, and when I came back to school, I'd put on loads of weight. My PE teacher told me that I was fat, and that obviously Easter hadn't been kind to me. My body shape and size has been a constant battle throughout my life – more on that later – and his hurtful comments cut right to the bone.

Ballarat is known for its wet weather and that morning it was living up to its reputation. Nevertheless, my teacher made me take off my shirt and jog round the running track by myself, in front of the whole class.

I was the fattest in my year and all blubbery. My schoolmates stood there laughing as they watched me. It was total humiliation. I felt completely worthless.

From that moment on, I hated any physical activity at school, but I knew I had to do something about myself. Dance was to be my salvation.

After my teacher had made me so ashamed of my body, I

resolved to search out some exercise that I could enjoy. Shyly, I told Amanda, who sat next to me in the school band, that I needed to lose weight and she suggested I try classes, which I assumed were like Jane Fonda workouts or aerobics. Actually, they were dance classes – jazz, mostly – and I loved them. I started going once a week.

A few months before my fifteenth birthday, in 1979, the incomparable Bette Midler was responsible for a huge surge in my self-esteem. *The Rose* had just been released and I'd learned 'When a Man Loves a Woman' off by heart. All the other boys' voices had broken, but mine didn't break until the following year, so it was still really shrill, and I could do a perfect Bette impression.

For one school assignment, we all had to perform a song to boost our confidence. The first number I did was *The Mickey Mouse Club* anthem, in a really high-pitched voice, and then I went into *The Rose*.

Bette Midler did this whole spiel before beginning 'When a Man Loves a Woman'. It was called the 'Concert Monologue'. I was word-perfect. With a flawless Southern belle accent, I launched into the speech I'd been rehearsing in front of the mirror at home, part of which went something like, 'He comes home with the smell of another woman on him … I'm putting on my little waitress cap and my fancy high-heel shoes. I'm gonna go find me … a man to love me for sure!'

None of my classmates could believe it – but they all loved it. The funny thing was that it was all about sex, and from a woman's perspective, so I didn't really know what I was talking about. Nonetheless, I could take her off exactly as she did it.

It must have been so camp, but that never even occurred to me. You'd have thought that such a performance would have made the kids pick on me even more, but in fact it had the opposite effect. It somehow earned me respect because I'd made the whole class laugh and the teacher had adored it. Best of all, I had found a way to entertain.

It was in the wake of that turning point that an opportunity cropped up, which was to have a major impact on the rest of my life.

Somewhat unexpectedly, a girl called Angela asked me to be her partner at the debutante ball. Ballroom dancing was a normal part of the school curriculum in Australia then – but only if you were going to partner a debutante. As a result of her invitation, I took up ballroom lessons ... and found that I couldn't get enough.

My only previous experience of social dancing had been in Sydney, where the boys' school and the girls' school would come together for the occasional event. The boys would have to ask the girls to dance and I was so scared at the thought of approaching a member of the opposite sex that I'd hated every minute of it. That was my first impression and it wasn't a good one. The whole experience was ghastly.

Angela and I went to lessons after school, in a big church hall in Ballarat. Suddenly, I found that I was actually enjoying myself and, to my surprise, that I was rather good at it.

On the night of the ball, I hired a suit and we had our photos taken. Then the girls were paraded down the stairs one by one. It's all very American, a bit like a prom, except that you have to learn the dances beforehand and then you do them together.

That evening, I had a brilliant time. I loved the progressive routines, where you swapped partners and worked your way round the room, because everyone danced differently. Some were absolutely hopeless and I found that amusing. The dancing made me feel confident and all my self-consciousness disappeared. It was fine that other people were watching me because I had found something I could do and which, in fact, came so naturally to me that I found it odd others were having problems.

Given everything I'd endured at Ballarat East, it was an amazing night. I simply wanted it to go on forever. I was about to discover that, with the right training, I could make that dream a reality.

CHAPTER 4

Pirouettes and Pavlova

All this time, I kept up my weekly jazz classes with a zealous dedication. The man who led the sessions was a local TV personality called Fred Fargher, which added even more allure to my new vocation than the dancing itself, about which I was now passionate.

Fred was creative director of the TV station BTV6, which is now called Win TV, and he also had his own live variety programme, *Six Tonight*, on Channel Nine. Some great show-business names appeared on it, including Shirley Bassey, Neil Sedaka and Sophia Loren. Legend has it that all Fred offered them to secure their services was a limo ride to Ballarat and dinner.

Everyone in Ballarat watched the show. I remember one particular programme with Marcia Hines, the American singer who was hugely successful in Australia, which became her adopted homeland. She is now a judge on *Australian Idol*. In the 1970s, she was my absolute hero. I worshipped her. I used to chop the wood to her album. My mum was helping out at BTV6 that night and actually ironed Marcia's costume, which we all thought was the coolest thing in the world.

Around that time, I got to meet the Australian songwriter Peter Allen backstage at the TV station. He's written some extraordinary songs, including 'I'd Rather Leave While I'm in

Love', 'I Honestly Love You' and 'Don't Cry Out Loud'. Later, in 1982, he also won an Oscar, with his co-writers, for 'Arthur's Theme (Best That You Can Do)'. Seeing him was a life-changing experience because it was the first time I'd met anyone backstage in a dressing room. I was so excited, I couldn't speak. He was so nice and vivacious and he was asking me questions ... and I was speechless.

The Channel Nine crew used to come up every Saturday night to do the live show so, in Ballarat, Fred was famous. I was totally star-struck by this huge celebrity, and astounded when he took a shine to me and spurred me on. After my first class, he took me aside and said, 'Craig, you're very good at this. You have some natural ability. Would you like to take it further? Would you like to be in one of my shows?'

Fred starred in, directed and choreographed amateur productions for the Ballarat Lyric Theatre, which played at 'Hermaj' (Her Majesty's Theatre). He wanted me to appear in a revue he'd created called *Making Music*, which was to be my introduction to dance performance. I've still got pictures of myself after the show, pretending to sign autographs. How embarrassing.

It was a typical, although very good, am-dram production. I really enjoyed it. It wasn't just the dance – I found a whole new social crowd and established some real friendships for the first time in my life. The company had a lot of members who were older than me and I got on better with them than with my own peer group. They were interesting, they had cars and could drive me around, and they invited me to grown-up soirées. I started smoking Alpines because Margot Hood, one of the company, smoked them and she would say, 'Come on, let's have a fag.' I loved those parties.

I was relieved not to embarrass myself in front of Margot on the smoking front. By that time, I'd already experimented with cigarettes. I had my first fag aged about twelve, when I nicked a cigarette from Corinne. It was a menthol ciggie and I took it down to the garage. I couldn't draw it in; I just put it in my mouth and blew it out again.

The first time I did the drawback was with a friend with whom I occasionally played table tennis, who was a bit of a scallywag. He used to smoke regularly. We were standing at the bus stop near the old BP station in Ballarat when he handed me a cigarette and showed me how to inhale. Not wanting to appear uncool, I tried it. It made me feel violently ill. I felt sick, I felt dizzy, it was ghastly – but, by hook or by crook, I was determined to master it. By the time I was on to Alpines with the am-dram crew, I was a pro.

After *Making Music*, Fred suggested that I take the next step and study all the facets of theatre – acting, singing and dancing – properly. At that point, I had only learned ballroom in any depth, for my debutante date with Angela, but he encouraged me to train with local teacher Janet Brown.

'All dance is based on a good foundation and that, Craig, is classical ballet,' he told me. 'A friend of mine runs a school here in Ballarat and I urge you to go. You must have good technique, be like a tiger and have a killer instinct.'

Fred couldn't have been more right. But back then, I knew absolutely nothing about classical ballet – I couldn't even spell it. I just knew it was a girly thing to do that only weirdo boys did. Even so, I agreed to give it a try.

I started to train in Cecchetti, a classical ballet discipline, with an outrageous blonde woman – Janet Brown – who ran a dance school with her sister Cheryl. Those classes led to probably one of the biggest moments of my young life: putting on my first pair of tights.

The basic ballet uniform for boys was a white T-shirt, black tights, white socks and black ballet slippers. However, for my first two months with Janet, I just wore something I felt comfortable in: footy shorts and a singlet. The final ultimatum eventually came.

Janet said that if I didn't wear the right clothes in class, I would no longer be able to attend. After that session had finished, I met up with Fred and he took me to the dancewear shop, which was underneath the dance studio, to buy these horrific tights and the rest of the kit.

I took my purchases home, went to my room and shut the door before I tried them on. The tights were really thick and – to add insult to injury – I had to put on a dance support (a type of sports G-string) underneath, which was even worse. It was the most uncomfortable thing I'd ever experienced. It looked like something surgical and it went right up my jacksy, which was horrible. It is a necessary evil, though, because it gives you a neat package and protects the tackle when you're jumping about.

The first time I had to wear the tights in class was hideous. I pulled them on in the changing room and came out into the dance studio, where I was surrounded by mirrors. It was torture, especially as I was the only boy. You've got to be bloody brave and I wasn't feeling it at the time. The tights represented a commitment that, at fifteen, I wasn't sure I wanted to make. Did I want to go the whole way with dance, or was I becoming something I didn't want to be?

'Only poofs do ballet,' I was thinking as I walked out, 'and I don't want to be one of those.'

Obviously, I was still in denial.

As discomfited as I was to see myself in tights, there was no reaction at all from the rest of the class. It was normal uniform for them. I'd been thinking that the whole world was going to cave in and the floor would eat me up, but they totally ignored it.

Janet just said, 'At the barre! First position … Music!'

Then we started warm-up, the session went on as normal and my moment of excruciating embarrassment was over.

That first year I was studying ballet, I lost so much weight, I became extremely thin and really tall. It was bizarre. Within six months, I had grown from 5 foot 7 to about 6 foot 2 and lost every inch of fat. I remember putting on my jeans and saying, 'Mum, look,' because they didn't reach my ankles.

It was at this time that I left school to become an apprentice chef, having convinced myself that – whatever might be happening in the dance studio – my immediate future lay in a restaurant kitchen.

The reason for this insight was that I had recently won a prestigious culinary competition. Our home economics teacher wanted us all to enter a local contest to become the Sunbeam Junior Chef of the Year, so we all had to put together a dish that was entirely our own creation. I entered a recipe for Jellied Prawn Cocktail and won the Ballarat heat, so BTV6 came round and filmed me. (For readers who may wish to try my concoction, the recipe is as follows: blend together lemon jelly crystals, prawns, mayonnaise and fresh parsley, and put into a cocktail glass. It sounds awful, but it was really tasty.)

My triumph gained me some anomalous popularity at school because I had a TV crew following me round lessons for one day. I was going to be on the news that evening and people were really excited. Suddenly, everyone wanted to be my friend. That finally made up for the mortification of the colouring competition.

After the local heat, I had to attend an annual event called the Melbourne Show, where the provincial winners came together to compete for the state title. Here, I was on a stall and people gathered round to watch the contestants as they cooked, like chefs do in supermarkets. I heard someone in the crowd say, 'Look how much he's shaking!' I had to cut something up really finely and I was wobbling like a jelly. Years later, I was to react in the exact same way in a famously humiliating moment on *Celebrity Masterchef*.

Somehow, I got through my shakes and emerged triumphant, which meant I was representing Victoria in the finals of the Junior Chef of the Year contest in Sydney. Mum bought me some new clothes for the event, including a white calico shirt, which I loved, though it was so stiff that it scratched my nipples like hell.

On the day we left, I packed all my knives in my hand luggage and, not surprisingly, they were taken away from me at the airport and put into the hold.

Mum and I travelled together and we had a wonderful trip. It was a real adventure for us because we were flown to Sydney and put up in a fancy hotel, then taken on a Captain Cook cruise around Sydney Harbour. It was a beautiful day and I thought it was the poshest thing. It was fantastic.

Mum loved it because it was a weekend away and everything was laid on for us, including breakfast, lunch and dinner. She could really relax and we had a great time together. In a large family, the chance to be away with your mum by yourself is a rare treat, so it was lovely for me. For once, I didn't have to share her.

On the day of the show, I was just as nervous as before and, this time, I didn't win. I was runner-up, but apparently it was very close and the guy who did come first was already in his second year of a chef's apprenticeship, so I didn't do too badly.

The whole escapade convinced me that I had fallen in love with cooking – when, actually, I could make only one dish. I had no idea what it was really like to be a chef. I imagined it was rather easy and that this pleasant lifestyle went with it, so when I got back to Ballarat, that was what I had decided to do with my life. Needless to say, the experience of working in the kitchen of the local restaurant was not quite the same.

However, an apprenticeship was the only way to get out of school early. If you didn't have one, you had to finish. That was impetus enough for me.

I had undertaken two previous work experience stints in professional kitchens before I left school. The first was in Sydney, in year eight at Granville Boys' High, when I spent a week in the catering department at Auburn Hospital, where Trent was born. All I did that week was eat cheese toasties with lashings of butter, because we only ever had margarine at home, and mix up masses of 'deb' potato (instant, dried, mashed-potato mix).

The second was in year nine at Ballarat East High, when I helped out at Dyer's Steak Stable. Mum said I always came home reeking of garlic and stunk the car out. She never used to cook with garlic or strong spices much when we were growing up, so she was sensitive to the smell. During that work placement, I probably peeled and crushed enough garlic to sink a battleship. Garlic prawns were also very big on the menu, so the smell permeated my clothing and skin.

Actually, the apprenticeship that enabled me to leave school was secured through sheer maternal force. I was sent for the interview, but when I got there, they said the job had already gone. Mum went straight for the jugular and said, 'How can the vacancy be filled when we've only just been dispatched here for an interview?' Faced with the wrath of my mother, they decided to give me a trial.

The hours were dreadful. We'd finish the lunch shift and go home, then we'd have to go back again for dinner, and all I did was prep, prep, prep. I was always the last one in the kitchen doing the desserts, but I used to get migraines and faint sometimes, which at least got me out of work.

The head chef was such an arse. He called me every name under the sun, including 'poofter' and 'gay boy' and told me I was as thick as pig shit. He screamed at me all the time, saying things like, 'That's the fucking wrong sauce, you stupid c**t! How can you not know that's a white sauce? It's white!'

In my defence, there were, of course, two white sauces in the fridge. I chose one of them and, naturally, it had to be the wrong one. The béchamel sauce was white and the fish sauce was also white. He dragged me by the scruff of the neck into the fridge, shouting and screaming and generally being a dick, and rubbed my face in the fish sauce, saying, 'That's the fish sauce, you stupid little poofter and this is the white sauce. Don't fuck it up again!'

The abuse continued as I was left in the fridge with sauce all over my face. I was still confused and was even more nervous about getting mixed up, so really I learned nothing except to hate him. Every single thing I did was flawed. That job left me so stressed.

The one highlight of my spell as a trainee cook was making a dessert for Suzi Quatro. At the time, preparing her pudding was the biggest thing that had ever happened to me. I dined out on that story all my life – until September 2007, when, bizarrely enough, I ended up working with her on *The World's Greatest Elvis*, where she and I were judges in a contest to find the best Elvis impersonator.

Suddenly, there I was sitting next to Suzi on a BBC1 programme. I couldn't resist. I leaned over and said to her, 'You probably won't remember this, but you once performed in my home town of Ballarat and I was doing an apprenticeship as a chef, so I made your dessert.'

It was wonderful meeting Suzi and relating that coincidence, which she thought was hilarious. She's a total star.

My career in the catering industry lasted just three months, and then Fred Fargher rescued me from a future of kitchen serfdom. It wasn't until the 'tights' episode at ballet that I had seriously considered dance as a career, but after that it became my dream. I just couldn't work out how to combine my study of the art with a paid job. Fortunately, Fred gave me the opportunity to make that happen, and he also made me believe in myself. For that, I will always be grateful.

One day, he came into the restaurant and said, 'You should work at the TV station while you're training. I'll get you an interview.' True to his word, he arranged a meeting with Gavin Disney, the head of BTV6, and I got the job. I was to start as a cable boy and trainee cameraman under the tuition of the great Neil Sloan, one of BTV6's best cameramen.

On my first day at the station, I didn't do very much. I was shown around and met people, and then I was taught how to roll up cables. Later, they trained me to drive a forklift truck, so that I could move sets around. I was basically the odd-job man and I didn't get near a camera for ages, but I enjoyed it because it didn't feel like work. It was shifting and building scenery, which was fun. It was so exciting to be part of the studio that I would have laboured for nothing in all honesty.

One of my responsibilities was to feed the autocue to the newsreader, whose name was Craig Campbell. It was a Jurassic piece of machinery: pieces of A4 paper, Sellotaped neatly together, had to be fed by hand into an overhead projector that placed the script in front of the camera. Half the time my pages would get all scrambled and mulched up, and I'd be panicking horribly while Craig struggled to read the words.

I also worked as a sound recordist on the news team, which was fascinating. I moved around all the different departments, doing whatever was needed. All in all, it gave me a fantastic grounding in the business.

Even though I was just sixteen, I left home and moved to Black Hill, where the TV station was based. I shared a flat with two girls, one of whom also worked at BTV6. I was slowly finding my feet as a grown-up: earning a wage, creating a home, striving to achieve my goals. In addition – and not before time – I was about to experience a sexual revolution of my very own.

CHAPTER 5 *A Whole New World*

From quite an early age, probably about nine or ten, I knew that I was different, but I didn't know exactly what it was, or why. I tried to avoid it and convince myself nothing was wrong, so I still had girlfriends at school.

In grade five of primary school, I had a crush on a girl called Mary, but she was really mean to me. I found a gem and I stuck it on one of those rings you get in craft sets, then I put it in a little case and gave it to her, but she made fun of it, so that was clearly not a match made in heaven.

In grade six, aged eleven, I was supposedly 'going out' with Margaret Yellowchef, mainly because everyone said we were together and I went along with it. It was one of those 'Margaret Yellowchef – she's your girlfriend' taunts in the playground and I'd just say, 'Oh, all right.'

Unexpected drama arose from my 'relationship' with Margaret, though. Another girl, Lorna, imagined *she* was going out with me, so when she found out about Margaret, she attacked me in the playground and dug her nails right into my hand. I still have the scars. She scarred me for life!

Lorna wasn't the most attractive girl in school, while Margaret had a nice face, but was a little on the weighty side of thin. Mary was most definitely the prettiest girl I knew and that's why I went for her. Not that I ever really felt anything, deep inside. I just thought I should.

In later years, my debutante date Angela might have thought that I was her boyfriend, but we never became an item. I used to go round to her house and roller-skate, but nothing ever happened between us, although I think she may have wanted it to.

Instead, I went out with Christine, the girl next door, whom I cruelly finished with when I realized it wasn't working for me. We used to kiss and pet, but we never went further than that, except one time when I fondled her left breast. We would sit on the fence under the pine tree in the south paddock, where we kept Snowy the pet goat, and we'd snog for hours.

Christine went to a different school, but as she was our neighbour, we used to play together as children and things kind of progressed from there. She was quite short and of solid build, and she had massive boobs. It lasted about eight months and then we had an argument over something, I don't remember what, and I said, 'Right, you're dumped!' She was very upset, but that was it for me.

After Christine, I went out with a girl from school and it was the first time I'd ever been on a proper date. I took her to the pictures and, in the classic scenario, tried to pluck up the courage to put my arm round her. I was terrified. I have no idea what the film was about because I was concentrating so hard on getting my arm around her shoulders. It took me roughly an hour.

Although snogging Christine had taken up a lot of my time at the age of fourteen, the earth had never really moved. By the time I was sixteen, I'd worked out why.

After I started work at the TV station, I met an older man – let's call him Mr X. He made it clear he fancied me, but although I enjoyed his company, initially I kept him at arm's length. Instead, I fell straight into the arms of a young, good-looking colleague called 'Eric'.

The result, unbeknownst to me, was a love triangle going on between Mr X, Eric and myself. I had no idea that Eric was having a sexual relationship with Mr X when I started dating him, but then, we weren't betrothed to each other. We were just having fun. I was sixteen and he was eighteen, and he became my first lover.

It all started when his parents were away and he invited me over to his place. We began playing a game of strip poker, led by Eric. We both ended up in our underwear – and then I lost the next game and had to be the first to get naked.

Eric then removed all his clothes too and began to masturbate. I was in such a nervous state that I couldn't get an erection, but I was so highly charged that when he touched me, I prematurely ejaculated. That was the most embarrassing thing that has ever happened to me. I was mortified beyond belief. He said it was OK and then, on my recovery, we were at it all night. On the stairs, the couch, the floor, the bed – all over his parents' home. It was amazing! I was in love!

I fell madly and deeply, only to discover that he and Mr X had something going on. That was the end of us. I'd wanted Eric and me to be exclusive. In truth, I felt totally betrayed by the both of them, and the thought of Eric with Mr X made me sick to my stomach. I felt stupid, used and worthless.

Although I'd known that Eric was bisexual and could cope with him being with girls, the idea of him with Mr X was somehow a different matter. I think I felt that his sleeping with women would be all right because I believed that, in contrast, what we had was special, untouchable, unconditional love, both sharing a deep dark secret. With hindsight, that perceived clandestinity probably made our relationship that much more exciting.

It was my first experience of heartbreak and I became quite bitter about it. Little did I know that by no means would it be my last.

At this time, Mr X was still pursuing me, but I kept refusing him. We began to see more of each other, but only on a platonic level. The first time I got really drunk, I was with him. We were in Melbourne to see the Australian Ballet perform. I drank two large glasses of wine at dinner before the show and, after those, I could hardly walk! I had to be taken back to the hotel before the curtain even rose and I was throwing up the whole night.

I was only sixteen, and I wasn't used to drinking at all. As kids, Sue, Di and I would have a glass of spumante, but no more than that. We used to think we were off our heads on Brandavino (a foul wine that cost A$1.99 a bottle) after one swig, but I was probably just pretending to be drunk.

This time, it felt like I hadn't drunk anything and then suddenly it hit me and I couldn't stand up. It was really frightening because I didn't know what it was. I thought I'd been drunk before, but this was horrendous.

Of course, these days, it takes two bottles!

As my friendship with Mr X progressed, it became clear that he wasn't taking no for an answer. He was determined to have me. One day, when a group of us had gone out for a meal, Mr X took me to one side and told me he had a proposition for me.

'Craig, I want you to travel the world,' he said. 'I know you want to be a professional dancer. I want to take you to see the best theatre this planet has to offer, so that you can appreciate exactly what you're aspiring to.'

He told me he would buy two tickets for a six-week trip to America and London and pay for everything, but there was a catch. 'The only thing is that you need to sleep with me before we go,' he said, adding, 'I want to take you over the top.' I knew what *that* meant.

I must have had my head screwed on, even then, because I replied, 'No. I'll come away with you, but I will only sleep with you once we get there.'

When I told Eric about it, he said, 'Oh, it was meant to be me who was going. Why's he offered it to you?'

Obviously, I suspected that Mr X had already got what he wanted from Eric and although he'd promised him this adventure, he dumped him and now planned to go with me instead. Unlike

Eric, though, I had learned to hold out. I also laid down some ground rules there and then and told Mr X there were things I would do and things I wouldn't. It was a proposition and I saw it entirely as a business deal, so I negotiated my own terms.

For a start, I couldn't go away for a while. Spurred on by the increasing confidence that my ballet classes had given me, I'd recently attended my first audition. At the TV studio, there was a troupe called the Channel 7 Dancers, who performed on all the programmes. I'd heard that they were auditioning for new members, so I took myself along to the try-outs. Unfortunately, I believed I was a lot better than I actually was. In fact, I thought I was fantastic!

When I turned up at this audition, my first professional one, I walked in and just breathed, 'Oh. My. God.' There were dancers doing all these incredible turns and steps, and I thought, 'This is unbelievable. I am so out of my league. How did I ever think I could do it?'

After the humiliation was over, I came out to the car, where my mum was waiting, and I was so disappointed. I told her, 'That was shit. I was shit. I'm going to have to train much harder.'

Fred Fargher, who had taken such an interest in my early career, kindly paid for my first year at Tony Bartuccio's, a new theatre school that had recently started up in Prahran, Melbourne. I adored going there. I was one of the first students after it opened.

Tony was married to Caroline Gillmer, an actress from *Prisoner: Cell Block H*, and he managed the Channel 7 Dancers. That's how Fred knew him, and about his school. Fred thought it would provide a good all-round education in dancing and theatre, so that I wasn't putting all my eggs in one basket and limiting myself to Latin, ballroom or ballet.

At Bartuccio's, I learned classical, tap, modern, jazz, drama and singing, so it was similar to stage school in the UK, but that broad curriculum was a relatively new thing in Australia at that time. There was a major dance craze exploding across the country because of films such as *Saturday Night Fever* (1977) and that made such opportunities slowly more accessible – even more so now because of shows like *Strictly Come Dancing*. It's come completely full circle.

Bartuccio's was a full-time college, but because I was working at the TV station during the week, I had to take the part-time course on a Saturday. I travelled down there by train every weekend, a two-hour trip each way. Every Friday and Saturday night, I stayed with a guy called John Link. He'd been in *Making Music* with me in Ballarat and, fortuitously, lived round the corner from the school.

Staying with him was beneficial to me in many ways, but the fact he was openly gay was an unexpected inspiration. By this time, I was leaning that way too. I'd been with Eric, of course, and I was prepared to agree some sort of deal with Mr X, but I was still quite confused about my sexuality, so it was a long time before I fully came out.

I loved Bartuccio's. It was brilliant working with all these inspiring people who could drive me forward. The singer Toni Basil led a class there soon after the success of her hit song 'Hey Mickey', while cast members from *Prisoner* taught drama. My teachers included Val Lehman (Bea Smith) and Maggie Kirkpatrick (Joan 'The Freak' Ferguson); Caroline Gillmer, who played Helen Smart, was my main acting coach.

The school had a great canteen, which the Channel 7 Dancers used, so I was constantly star-struck. The college environment made me feel up there and on it, fierce and fashionable and involved, and that really drove me to want to turn professional.

In those days, they often used dancers for catwalk work. Bartuccio's was an agency as well as a school, and I was lucky enough to land a modelling job soon after I turned seventeen. It was a fabulous gig. Surrounded by gorgeous dancers and models, I travelled for two weeks up and down the east coast of Australia in a Learjet, modelling the Najee spring/summer collection. A typical day would involve rolling up on the Learjet and slipping into the clothes, then we'd disembark on to a red carpet, model the collection on the runway, get back on the plane, change and travel to the next destination, pose on the tarmac again, and so on. It was really weird.

I was also building on my performance experience. After *Making Music*, I starred in another of Fred Fargher's revues, *Rockin' the Town*. Unfortunately, this was where I suffered my first real dance injury.

One of my routines was to 'Johnny B. Goode'. I would come downstage and do a series of jumps in second position and then drop into the splits. One time when I did the splits, I ripped my hamstrings, completely, and had to limp off stage. The incident was in the local newspaper the next day and BTV6 came round to interview me about it – all publicity orchestrated by Fred to put bums on seats.

There was only a week's run left, so I still went back on stage. I showcased a ballet piece set to the Neil Diamond classic 'Love on the Rocks' – which incidentally was my first ever *pas de deux* – but I couldn't dance the 'Johnny B. Goode' number for the remaining performances.

Naturally, I went to a sports therapist about the injury, but even with the best care available, the setback took me a good nine months to get over.

It seemed a timely moment to accept Mr X's proposition of travelling the globe. I was seventeen and he was forty-two. He was a nice guy, and remains so. We are still friends, but I wouldn't ever have described us as lovers because it didn't feel like that to me.

Because I was under eighteen, Mum had to sign a document to say that it was all right for me to go with him as my guardian. Neither of my parents suspected that anything was going on between Mr X and me at the time. As far as they were concerned, Mr X was taking me overseas because he wanted to show me the world and demonstrate how talented I would have to be in order to become a dancer.

I knew exactly what I was doing, though. I was a rent boy, I suppose, but it was a means to an end. I saw him in our relationship more as a sugar daddy. I got to see the world and paid for it the only way I could, so I didn't owe anyone anything.

In September 1982, I left the TV station and Mr X and I set off on our grand adventure.

Our first destination was the UK, where we stayed at his sister's place in Dorking, Surrey. It was really hot and quite muggy that autumn. I remember being struck by how cheap everything was. You could buy a music cassette for 99p, which was incredible.

The first night we were together, I was a bit nervous. I didn't fancy him, but I wasn't dreading it. Boys of seventeen are pretty sexually charged – you're turned on easily and it's over relatively quickly! We got through the first time and I thought, 'That wasn't too bad.' There was no kissing, ever, because I wouldn't let him. All he did was go down on me.

The next day, Mr X took me to London to see *Cats* and I nearly exploded in my seat. Wow! I had never seen anything like it in my life. The singing, the dancing, the flashing eyes, the revolving stage – it was awe-inspiring. I sat, wide-eyed, in the audience, with butterflies whizzing around my stomach.

I couldn't believe that dancers could move *and* sing so well, that there were such multi-talented performers out there. I knew then that I would have to work really hard to achieve my ambition. It was a vital eye-opener.

'This is what I want to do,' I said to myself. 'One day, I'll be one of those amazing people.'

The next show we went to see was *Barnum*, starring Michael Crawford, which I also loved. I was having the most unbelievable time, travelling up from Dorking on the train, seeing the sights of London and then watching West End musicals. It was magnificent.

After England, we flew to New York, where we went to the opening night of *Cats* at the Winter Garden Theater. Goldie Hawn was there and I was so excited. The press were shouting, 'Miss Hawn, Miss Hawn, this way!' I came down the stairs behind her and there were photographers' flashes going off all over the place. I absolutely adored it.

After the spectacular show in London, I couldn't wait to see *Cats* again and the American production seemed much glossier. However, it was our first night in the States and I was so jet-lagged that I fell asleep during the second act and missed most of it.

While we were in the Big Apple, we saw the Broadway version of *Dreamgirls* with the original cast – Jennifer Holliday, Sheryl Lee Ralph and Loretta Devine. Who could have predicted that, twenty years on, I would be dining with Jennifer Holliday at an Angela Lansbury tribute in New York? Life has a funny way of joining up the dots.

Mr X and I stayed at the Hilton, which was more luxurious than anywhere I'd ever been before. It was beautiful. One twilit evening, I decided to go out on the roof and I set the alarm off. Very embarrassing.

While we were there, Mr X would ask me to pose in certain positions or to get down on all fours while he masturbated, but it never progressed any further than that. It was all on my terms and led by me, and he never forced me into anything. I made all my own decisions. He'd request particular things from me and it was entirely up to me as to whether or not I obliged.

Then, one night, he took off and left me. I had no idea where he was. I started planning what I was going to do if he didn't come back. We had intended to go to Florida and New Orleans, then Las Vegas and San Francisco, and finally to Hawaii, Sydney and Melbourne. I still had my plane ticket, passport and A$300 (£140), kindly donated by my parents. I decided that if Mr X didn't return, I would go to San Francisco and then home.

Before Mr X had vanished, we hadn't fallen out as such, but something unspoken had passed between us that had, perhaps, upset him, so I wasn't sure if he'd gone for good. While I was waiting to find out, I explored New York on my own.

I was quite happy. I'd travelled so much in my life, and changed schools so often, that new places never scared me. Back in the hotel, I had a facial, because I was quite spotty as a teenager, and then I had highlights put in my hair. When Mr X finally reappeared, two days later, I was covered in a rash and had a completely different hairstyle.

'Where have you been?' I asked him, more than a little miffed.

'I needed to get away for a couple of days' was the only explanation I received.

After that, we went to Florida, where we visited Disney World. By the time we got there, the whole set-up was wearing a bit thin. I just didn't fancy playing the rent boy any more.

Las Vegas was amazing, though. Walking around, I was totally absorbed because it was all so showbiz, with the flashing lights and the glitz. We played the casinos, and although I was underage, I was tall and could get away with it. I got a real buzz at the tables.

In San Francisco, we rode the cable cars and went to a cinema at a place that was appropriately named Nob Hill. It was a dirty old man's cinema. I sat in the middle of the seats and refused to do anything. So Mr X went off on his own and did whatever he had to do. Then we left, me none the wiser and him, well, probably satisfied.

Hawaii was our final destination before we were due to go back to Australia. I got so sunburned there, I couldn't be touched, which was a bonus. Every time Mr X came anywhere near me, I screamed, 'Don't touch me! Aaah!'

We still had a good time though. We walked around and strolled on Waikiki Beach, just like in all the movies, but we were winding down and getting ready to go home.

As soon as the plane landed in Melbourne, I saw my family waiting for me. I said goodbye to Mr X and it was all over. That was the last I saw of him for about a year.

I never fancied Mr X. It was a business arrangement, pure and simple. I was callous about it and, I can honestly say, totally unaffected by it all.

Mr X was quite a gentle man, very creative, not pushy at all. He was a very genuine and honest guy, but I didn't feel anything for him. I could switch myself off from the situation completely and it was surprisingly easy. We were travelling for about six weeks and that's as long as our sexual relationship lasted.

Looking back on it, I suppose it's slightly odd that a forty-two-year-old man would want to take a seventeen-year-old boy abroad, but I didn't think of it like that at the time. I just saw it as a way of achieving something, of getting what I wanted. I was quite level-headed and I felt very grown-up. My family never asked me about that side of things and I never told them. They didn't need to know.

It was strange being a kept man, but Mr X introduced me to quite some life, so it had an inspiring effect. It opened my eyes and that was what the whole trip was about.

By seventeen, I was terribly assertive and knew exactly what I wanted. It was a huge leap from the boy I'd been two years before, but the change happened almost overnight. I don't recall the actual moment, but it must have been partly influenced by my rapid growth spurt. As soon as I started towering over other people my age, I gained confidence.

But it was the dancing that really did it. At last, I could do something I was good at, that made me feel attractive, and that people liked to watch. I was becoming outstanding at something for the first time. I looked around at others in my peer group and determined, 'I can dance better than them. I can do this.'

When you find something you're good at, you don't want to let it go. I just wanted to get better and better. Becoming a professional dancer was the ultimate challenge, but I've always prided myself on seeing something through to the end. Too many people start this and that, but don't complete the journey. I think if you set your sights on a goal, you should stay committed to it, however slim the chances of success.

So upon my return from my trip with Mr X, with the *Cats* score still ringing in my ears and the world's rhythms pounding in my heart, I took the plunge and moved to Melbourne to pursue my daunting ambition.

CHAPTER 6 *Kick Ball Change*

My partner in audacity was Deanne. We met at Janet Brown's ballet class, and conspired to get together, move to the big city and 'just do it', as the slogan says.

The whole experience abroad with Mr X turned me off men for a while, and I started dating Deanne instead. We were the classic young lovers – impetuous, impassioned and full of dreams.

When we first arrived in Melbourne, we weren't skilled enough to get theatre jobs. We had to find supplementary work during the day and continue our dance training in the evening. That was our big plan.

At the time, my dad was working in the State Emergency Service (SES) in Melbourne during the week, and going home to the house on Ditchfield Road in Ballarat at weekends. He agreed to put us up in his flat, but made it clear that I would have to move back to Ballarat if I didn't get a job by the weekend. I couldn't even afford to pay for electricity or anything like that, so I was desperate.

Then I spotted an advert in the paper for a hairdressing apprenticeship. I went to the library and borrowed a book on the subject, which I read before going for the interview. Unbelievably, on the basis of that research, I landed the job. I signed a three-year indenture with the hairdressers, which meant I was contracted to Ulms for Hair in Camberwell and Dzintra, my boss. Deanne started working in the council offices, and we were away.

Convinced my name would one day be in lights, I decided to adopt an assumed name for my hairdressing 'career'. My family weren't too pleased about it because, in a moment of madness, I chose my little brother's name. The real Trent was only about three at the time. With two Trents now in the family, no one was thrilled.

Dad helped us to secure a flat of our own by paying the deposit, as I was earning only A$91 (£42) a week on my apprenticeship. Initially, I worked hard and I was really good at it. But there was a hitch. I had to attend hairdressing school as well as working in the salon, and there was so much initiation involved that I wasn't getting enough time to dance.

Deanne and I had intended to train in the evenings but, with all that snipping, perm winding and colouring, I could only manage two nights a week. Deanne had more time, but, disappointingly, she was slowly going off the idea of becoming a professional dancer.

At one point, I joined an amateur company in Melbourne and I had to ask Dzintra if that was OK because of my hectic hairdressing schedule. Luckily, she was understanding, and together we came up with the idea of reducing my practical coaching to a Wednesday evening only while I was in rehearsals for the group. I still had to ensure that I kept up with my homework – which entailed practising perm winding on a model head that was checked daily for flaws such as fish hooks, even winding and sectioning – and learning all the technical and scientific side of the business, which was extensive to say the least. On the other weekday evenings, and on Saturdays, I would be free to dance.

The Melbourne am-dram company cast me in a show called *Little Me*, alongside Maggie Kirkpatrick from *Prisoner*. That was a real turning point. It finally proved to me how much I loved performing, and convinced me that I could do it professionally, so I threw my all into my evening training sessions. The problem was that, as a result, I was showing up at the salon later and later. At one point, I completely overslept and missed about three perms.

It was obvious that my heart wasn't in hairdressing. Eventually, I rang Dzintra and said, 'I need to talk to you.' I asked to be released from my indenture. I had no idea what I was going to do instead, but I knew that I had to move on. Trent 2 was no longer.

During my time as a crimper, Deanne fell for another man and left me. She suddenly took off for three weeks without warning. When she came back, she knocked on the door and announced: 'Our relationship's over. I'm in love with someone I work with. I'm going to be living here, but I'll be in the spare room and that's how it is.' So I said, 'Fine.'

I was slowly becoming the real me. It was a bit like in *Muriel's Wedding*, where she goes back to being Muriel after living her life as someone else. I changed my name back to Craig and got a boyfriend for the first time, although the relationship only survived for a month. At long last, I could be openly gay.

Deanne wasn't surprised that I went from her to a man because I never lied to her about my bisexuality; we discussed everything. The big hurdle was breaking the news to my family, but that turned out to be remarkably easy. I told my sister, Susan, and she told Diane, who told Mel, and they all told Mum.

Shortly afterwards, I went back to Ballarat to do Mum's hair. (As I had been training to be a hairdresser, everyone expected free haircuts, naturally, so whenever I was at home, I would do my sisters, my mum and my brother. Even the aunties and uncles would pop round for a trim! Of course, I never minded, as it was actually a lot of fun – and the perfect way to indulge in a decent chinwag with them and catch up on their news. We all know how hairdressers like to talk.)

I was in the middle of giving my mum a perm, which was all the rage at the time, when she said, 'I know you're a bit "that way".'

I replied, 'Yes, I am.'

Nothing else needed to be said. It was totally accepted.

Later, I told my dad in the car, on the way back from Melbourne to Ballarat one weekend. I had been quite worried about informing him, because he was a navy man, and I didn't expect him to take it well. He did give me a little speech, along the lines of, 'You know, you can get court-martialled in the navy for that sort of thing,' but on the whole he coped very well.

Coming out can be a horrendous experience for some, but sometimes the fear of the family's reaction can be a lot worse than the reaction itself. It certainly was in my case.

As soon as I ditched the hairdressing and decided to focus all my energies on becoming a dancer, I needed to find a quick-fix job. I had to move out of the flat I shared with Deanne, too, because with no real money coming in I couldn't possibly afford it.

John Link, my friend from the Ballarat amateur company, was now living in Melbourne, so I rang him and asked if he knew of anywhere I could stay. Thankfully, he had a room going spare in his new pad so he let me reside awhile at his place again. It was quite a big house, but the only room vacant was a box room. At times there, I felt like I was sleeping in a cupboard.

One of John's flatmates was a girl called Cecily Grant. One day, she announced, 'Craig, I'm moving out of here. Do you want to come and live with me?'

She offered me my own double room for the same rent, so we moved up the road to a house in Dow Street, Port Melbourne. Cecily was a delight and we had a totally crazy time when we were living together – including my first experience of hard drugs.

We were in a bar with some of Cecily's mad friends and one of them offered me a line. So, I tried a snort of cocaine. It didn't have a good effect on me. First, I fell backwards off my chair and then I spent the rest of the night sitting beside the toilet, thinking I was about to croak. I wasn't actually sick, but I felt like I could vomit at any second.

It was the one and only time I tried charlie and it put me right off. Looking back on it now, it's quite embarrassing. Cecily and her friends had to look after me because I was lying on the floor morbidly saying, 'I'm going to die,' over and over again.

Cecily and I seemed to attract drama wherever we went together. She taught me such a lot and tirelessly encouraged me in my career. I have so much to be grateful to her for. We're great friends to this day, although she's in Australia and happily married to a charming and highly successful international businessman now, so I don't get to see her as often as I'd like. When we do meet up, whether it be in New York, Paris or Rome, there's never a dull moment.

Cecily had been a dancer in the United States, in European television and theatre productions, and in Paris at all of the major shows, including the Crazy Horse, the famous topless cabaret house. The girls there are chosen for their perfection: they're all the same size, height, weight and bust size, and all of them are amazing dancers. She'd had to give up her dance career because of injury, which is why she'd moved to Melbourne. It must have been fate – because she was about to change my life completely and forever.

Living with Cecily gave me total independence. I finally knew who I was. I wasn't scared of being out and everyone knowing I was gay. And she provided me with a job. She trained me as a fitness instructor and I taught aerobics to businessmen at 6.30 every morning, under the name of Craig Stevens.

It might seem bonkers that I kept changing my name, but I was so determined to be a successful dancer that I didn't want any other profession to be associated with it.

The fees from those aerobics sessions covered my rent, my food and my dance classes. What the sessions couldn't do was persuade me that I had an acceptable body shape; despite the punishing schedule I was forcing it to submit to day after day. My tendency to put on weight has always been the bane of my life.

When I lived in Melbourne, my obsession with losing fat left me with serious food issues.

Many people think that this is more of a woman's problem, but a lot of men battle with their weight too, and I've struggled with it all my life. I was always prone to chubbiness as a child. At ten, I was slightly porky and had little, fat boy boobs. My Auntie Mavis used to call me Tits, which I hated. I got bigger at twelve and even fatter at thirteen, much to the disgust of my unsympathetic PE teacher. It wasn't until my overnight growth spurt that the plumpness left me. When I started dancing, I began building muscle. I was still developing physically, which was a good thing because it enabled me to get a decent bone structure for a dance body.

In the six weeks I was away with Mr X, I didn't do any exercise or dancing at all. Walking up Sturt Street in Ballarat one day, after my return, I happened to glance at my reflection in a shop window. The sun was shining, making the likeness crystal clear, and I received quite a shock. 'My arse has dropped!' I thought. It had fallen, literally, by about an inch. Due to sheer lack of exercise, my whole body had sagged. I couldn't get back to the dance class quick enough.

By the time I took up aerobics alongside the dance, I was really just bones, but I still thought I had all this body fat, because I wasn't toned enough. I used the gym instructor job to try to create my perfect shape, but it soon became an unhealthy fixation. I was actually really thin, and had lost far too much weight, but I always thought I was tubby. When I looked at myself in the mirror, I saw my skin and anything that wasn't rock-solid muscle as fat.

Looking back, I now know that I was suffering from a severe eating disorder. I would starve myself and eat only lettuce for lunch and dinner for two weeks at a time. I was paranoid about every ounce of fat on my body, but I wasn't helping myself because I wasn't eating protein, so my energy levels were plummeting too.

There were times when I would go on a drink binge, and then pig out on ridiculous food like pizzas and burgers. I had no energy for dancing because I was either drinking and gorging on rubbish, or eating nothing at all. It was an awful time.

Although I hid my food issues from Cecily as much as possible, she proved a wonderful support, particularly with regard to my dance ambitions, which was my ultimate focus in life. She put me in touch with a wonderful Russian ballet teacher, Miss Golding, and forced me to go to her classical Russian ballet class at 9.30 every morning, making sure I was up and out the door and at the class on time. The cast of *West Side Story*, which was on at the Princess Theatre at that time, attended the same class, so I was training with professionals.

I'd been to see that production loads of times. Cecily used to take me because I couldn't afford the tickets, but she loved it as well because of her dance background. I can still remember sitting in the audience thinking, 'This is phenomenal.'

The classes were making me stronger and stronger. When an open audition came up for *West Side Story*, I thought I'd give it a go, just for the experience.

I was still in the relatively early stages of training and I didn't imagine for one moment that I was ready yet, dance-wise. The last audition I had been to, for the Channel 7 Dancers, had been a disaster, so I was apprehensive about going to this one. Nonetheless, Cecily persuaded me that it would be a good opportunity to face my fear and gain practical knowledge at the same time.

On the day, I wasn't nervous, just very excited. I'd seen the show three times by then and I was a bit starry-eyed about it. For the try-outs, we were asked to learn a routine from *A Chorus Line*, which had lots of high kicks, pirouettes and double turns to the knee in it: steps for which the choreographer was famous. I walked on the stage and performed it with all the other auditionees. Then we were broken down into groups of three and I danced again and again and then again.

The auditions were in the actual theatre, so to step out on to the set of *West Side Story* was frightening. I was terrified. If I didn't get the part, I told myself, at least I would have danced on that stage. Leigh Chambers, the choreographer, watched us intently. He was very camp, but I had to be as butch as possible because the role required it.

After I'd finished, Leigh said, 'Thank you very much,' and it was all over. As far as I was concerned, I hadn't got the part. I didn't know anything about auditions. I assumed that if you weren't hired on the spot, that was it.

Two days later, the phone rang and I was asked to join the company in the role of Pepe. I couldn't believe it! Little ol' me, the boy from Ballarat, was going to be in a professional show in the big smoke, with Philip Gould and Caroline O'Connor (who later performed the famous 'Roxanne' tango in *Moulin Rouge*) playing the leads.

Before rehearsals began, I was invited by a group of pals to a Miss Alternate beauty pageant, a drag queen extravaganza where all the participants get frocked up in the most outrageous costumes. One friend convinced me to drag up for the night.

When I got there, attired in all my finery, I happened upon some of the cast from *West Side Story*. It was the first time I'd met the company and I was introduced to them all as the new 'Shark' boy. Those of you who know the musical will remember that the Sharks are tough little Puerto Ricans. There I was, 6 foot 2 tall, skinny as a rake and in full make-up and high heels. God knows what they thought!

That was the first time I'd been in drag properly. I was quite taken aback at my transformation. A female friend had said, 'I'll do your make-up.' So I let her paint my face and put false eyelashes on me, then I slipped into a tiny snap-crotch teddy with stockings and suspenders, and squeezed my feet into a pair of platform shoes.

Finally, I steeled myself to look in the mirror. What a shock. 'Wow, that's amazing,' was my initial reaction. Scanning the photo I took of myself on that night from the distance of twenty-odd years, I demur – I look tragic – but at the time I thought I looked fantastic.

After that, I learned how to apply professional make-up so that I could paint my own face, sculpting the eyebrows and so on. Up close, it's frightful, like it's been laid on with a trowel; but on stage, under a spotlight, it looks great.

That night was also the first time I met Stuart McGhee (aka Magatha), who was in *West Side Story* in the swing position (which is not as rude as it sounds!). The swing is essentially the understudy to all roles: the cast member who goes on in the place of anyone who's sick or injured. Magatha was to become one of my closest friends. He would later prove instrumental in my move to Europe.

The *West Side Story* rehearsal period was about two weeks. Jane Beckett, who played a Jet girl, Velma, in the show and was one of my favourite dancers at the time, had the job of teaching me the routines, as she was the dance captain. I was in awe of her, and I never thought I was good enough next to her.

She taught me how to dance on a rake, which is the slope of the stage, as it changes your centre of balance when you're turning. There were about twenty triple pirouettes to the knee in that show, so you absolutely had to know where your centre was, otherwise you'd take out all the other dancers. When I got on stage to rehearse, I kept on turning down the rake and she'd scream at me, 'Change your centre!' over and over again. What a frustration I must have been for her, especially when she was really tired at ten in the morning, having danced in the show the evening before. It's a skill you really can't learn in a studio, though, where the floors are generally flat.

Plus, there are varying degrees of rakes, as each theatre requires different levels to enable the audience to see the stage from their seats. I learned so much in such a very short space of time thanks to Jane's patience and persistence.

My first time meeting the full cast was one of the scariest moments of my performing career, especially as I'd seen all of them on stage and knew them only as their characters: rough, tough fighting machines who would stab you in a millisecond. The company manager took me round the dressing rooms to introduce me.

I was full of admiration and completely star-struck. As I undertook my meet-and-greet, most of my new colleagues looked distracted and busy, getting ready for the performance ahead. They each possessed this intense confidence.

They had been on the road as a company for a year, so they knew one another intimately and had formed very tight, strong friendships – and enmities – with each other already. When I was introduced to them, some seemed not to care or just grunted at me. It felt quite awkward, as if I was in the way. They had nicknames for each other, and the mucking around and play fights were all too much to take in. It felt hostile, and I was completely overwhelmed by the amount of testosterone pumping through the backstage corridors. I was both unnerved and thrilled by it.

Some of the cast, of course, I had met a week or so previously at the Miss Alternate pageant. Word had naturally spread about my appearance in drag – so I was ribbed viciously for that during the introductions. It was an assault course, but I loved it.

Once the hideousness of the initial meetings was over, it was down to dancing for the first time with the company. I was about to be put into the show: another scary day in paradise. I never really believed that I was good enough to be dancing alongside such legends, but there I was, finally doing what I had always wanted and adoring every second.

I was rehearsed into the show with the full company – and then, that very same evening, it was my opening night.

I can't tell you how nervous I was when the overture began. It was happening; no turning back. I would leave the darkness of the wings and burst on to the stage for the first time as a professional. I was so pumped up with adrenalin, I didn't really contemplate that I was doing the show. It was just happening, and I had no time to think about it.

At the end of the performance, everything was a blur. It wasn't until after the bows had ended that I realized, 'Oh my God, I just performed in *West Side Story* in front of thousands of people and got paid for it. I am a professional dancer.'

My joy at landing the job was, unfortunately, short-lived. On my first day of performance, a notice went up on the board to say that the production was closing in two weeks. Even so, I was pleased to have got the job at all and thrilled that anyone would consider paying me for doing what I loved the most. Craig Stevens was no more. Craig Horwood's theatrical career was finally underway!

As the countdown to the end of the show began, I determined to enjoy the whole experience as much as I could. One night, Leigh, the choreographer, came up to me before the warm-up and said, 'I'm going to be watching you for another gig.' I had no idea what it was.

The *West Side Story* warm-up was a dance routine with turns and a whole jazz combination. We'd perform in groups, dancing in rows, then each row would split in the middle and the next row would come down the stage. Feeling Leigh's eyes on me, I danced my heart out.

After studying me for a while, Leigh then announced, 'I'd like to offer you a job. It starts the week after *West Side* finishes.'

Of course, I immediately enthused, 'Great!'

It turned out to be a touring production of *The Black and White Minstrel Show*, which meant a year on the road, living on a bus and trucking around Australia.

As usual, I turned to Cecily for help. She bought me the luggage I needed, taught me how to pack and which things to keep on the top, such as underwear and toiletries, so that I didn't need to unpack at every stop. She told me that I should always have one bag only, and that if I added anything to it, I should take something else away.

She also prepared me mentally with her stories of touring from her own dancing days, for which I was thankful once the production began. Touring is a strange experience because you don't remember where you've been half the time. *The Black and White Minstrel Show* played in these tiny outback towns with no facilities at all, like Mount Isa, Ayr, and all sorts of weird and wonderful places. In one town, Mackay in Queensland, we had to clean all the black make-up off our faces in a horse trough behind a tin shed. I'm not kidding. The audience could see us all scrubbing away as they walked back to their cars after the performance.

Of course, *The Black and White Minstrel Show* these days is not at all PC and I think is perhaps even outlawed in most countries. When I was in it, I never thought of it politically. It wasn't until after I had left the show and people began to protest their objections outside the front of theatres that I started to consider it in a negative way.

At the time, I simply saw it as a traditional entertainment and, of course, a job – and a laboured and messy one at that. Putting on all that black make-up anywhere there's a hint of skin, and wearing long white gloves and long black socks, was not my idea of fun. In fact, I went temporarily deaf due to the build-up of make-up in my ears: I had to have them syringed by a doctor.

We travelled all over Queensland, often enduring eighteen-hour bus trips. We'd get off the bus, black up, put on a curly wig and a hot velvet suit from London (which is where all the costumes came from), and dance. Then we'd get back on the bus to travel to the next place. It was mad.

It taught me how to be responsible for my own well-being, psychologically. People get on your nerves to a marked extent when you are living out of one suitcase, and you see only the same faces. On the bus, in the hotel, on stage – always the same faces. It's the same choreography in every venue. You just want to scream sometimes.

People deal with the close proximity in different ways. Some go very quiet, like one girl on tour, Kate Wilson (who later married and became Katie Kermond), who was in *West Side* with me playing Riff's girlfriend Graziella. She just went silent, completely introverted, which was quite the opposite to her natural character. Some find God. Others steep themselves in books.

I coped with it by turning a critical eye on myself. I thought about what I needed to work on, what I needed to improve. On *The Black and White Minstrel Show* tour, I was working on my voice, because the show was pre-recorded so I wasn't using it. I spent my spare time practising my scales.

The show was bizarre – and bad. It was mimed and even the leads were on tape, so there were many hilarious moments. They'd run two tapes concurrently because sometimes one got stretched and it would suddenly start sounding really slow, so they'd go to the other tape. On one occasion, the back-up tape snapped halfway through, which meant there was nothing going on at all.

We played every Returned and Services League (RSL) club in the country. Mainly grotty joints with pool tables and cheap beer, like working men's clubs in the UK, they were the tiniest little venues and most of them were half empty. The choreography included some sit lifts with the girls (where the male dancer lifts the female up to sit on his shoulder) and the ceilings of the RSL clubs were often too low to accommodate them. In many of the venues, we were dancing on carpet as well. It was ludicrous. I'm surprised we didn't all go insane.

The smallest thing would crack us up. There was one guy called Peter who, dressed as a bull, once fell down the stairs and, because his arms were inside his costume, couldn't get up again. He was wearing white tights and a hat, which fell off, and his face was blacked up. He just lay there waving his white legs in the air, with his blacked-up face and blond hair, while we fell about laughing.

We became so used to the steps that you could draft a shopping list on stage while you were dancing, or chat about what you were going to have for dinner.

The tour went on for a year and I hated it towards the end. It was hard going. I was so desperate to get out of it that I told the producers my mother was having a nervous breakdown and I had to go home. They were happy to release me from the contract as it helped them to save money on the New Zealand leg of the tour, thus it worked out amicably for both parties. I later found out through Magatha that, on the NZ tour, anti-racist groups picketed the theatres with slogans and chants such as 'Being black is not an act, racist shows don't go!' Eventually, the production had to close down.

When I left Melbourne to embark on the tour, I had been seeing a guy with whom I thought I was in love. I kissed him goodbye and went on the road, believing that even while you're apart, you remain monogamous and that, when you come back, your boyfriend will be waiting. I soon discovered that he had other ideas. The month before I came home, he had gone a bit weird on me, and stopped calling. The next time I saw him was when I bumped into him at a club called Pokies in St Kilda, Melbourne – with his new boyfriend. He was my Superman (he looked devastatingly like Clark Kent with his glasses on); I was heartbroken.

Lovelorn and between jobs, I began to brood over my appearance. At nineteen, I hated my nose with a passion. I didn't mind it from the front – in fact it was better than it is now – but I hated the profile. It didn't grow big until I was sixteen, or at least I hadn't noticed it till then, but after that, whenever I had photographs taken, it drove me nuts. It made me look as though I had no chin and I was all beak. I had major acne too, which didn't help.

One day, I was whinging about my nose to Cecily and she commented simply, 'I know a doctor who could fix that.' I went to see the surgeon on Thursday; by the weekend, I had a new nose.

They wouldn't make it as small as I wanted because the consultant said that, when I grew older, it would look ridiculous. When you see your nose as huge, you take it to extremes and yearn for a really tiny button one. The last thing I said before the anaesthetic took hold was, 'Please make it small. Please make it small.'

It's quite a nasty operation. (Look away now if you're squeamish.) The surgeon makes an incision on the inside of the nose and then cuts the cartilage away, quite roughly, with something like pinking shears. Afterwards, the nose is stuffed with swabs, which collect the blood and congeal. It's revolting. The doctor gave me a nose-cleaning kit, to help me to pull all the scabs out from inside my nose. Hideous. But I was young and fit, so it healed quite quickly.

It cost A\$1,500 (£700), which I didn't have, so I put it all on my credit card. Luckily, I got A\$990 (£465) back from Medicare Australia, which meant it only cost me about A\$500 (£235) all in, for the drugs involved and the time spent in hospital. I checked out after just one day because I couldn't afford another A\$500. The staff told me I could go home as long as I cleaned everything properly and came back for check-ups.

It was incredibly painful to begin with. I had to sleep bolt upright for two weeks and I looked a complete fright, with black eyes and a big plaster across my face. There was only one thing for it – I threw a hospital party!

It was fantastic. Everyone came with bandaged limbs, on crutches, or in doctors' and nurses' outfits, and we had such a fun time.

Even before the plaster came off, I could tell that I was going to love it. Ever after, I always made a point of looking away from the camera so it would capture my profile. In truth, hardly anyone else noticed the difference, but to me it was a massive improvement. It was something I did on a whim, but it changed my life enormously. It gave me so much more confidence that I haven't regretted it for a second.

After I'd recovered from the operation, I went into rehearsals for *The Danny La Rue Show*, which was another touring production. In one number, we had to roll our hats down off our heads. About a month after the nose job, I was practising this routine when the hat hit my conk. The pain nearly killed me. It was *so* sore.

In the show, I was one of four boys singing and dancing with Danny, and feeding him lines for his jokes. What I remember most about the experience – and it makes me shudder to this day to think of it – was an attack of the most awful stage fright. It was a horrible incident that has haunted my entire career.

I was on stage in Perth when it struck. For the life of me, I couldn't remember the script. I just went into a total panic because I was the last boy to deliver the feed line for a joke. The lad before me said, 'How many boyfriends have you had?' and all I had to say was, 'How many husbands have you had?' Not a lot to memorize at all.

I walked up to the front alongside Danny and I just stood there. All I could think was, 'What's my feed line?' I went totally lifeless, to the point where he had to turn me and push me off stage. I don't know what happened. There was nothing going on in my head at all.

Afterwards, I went backstage and knocked on Danny's door. I blurted out, 'Dan, I have to talk to you about this. I'm so, so sorry. I was blank.'

But the next night, the same thing happened. And the next night. On the fourth night, I put huge cue cards in the wings that said: 'HOW MANY HUSBANDS HAVE YOU HAD?'

By this time, Danny was getting pissed off with it,

understandably, because I only had one bloody line and I couldn't say it. The third boy went up, said his piece and went off. I walked on, went blank, walked off, read the cue card and came back on. Then I said the line that the guy before had just delivered.

After that, I was scared to death of going on stage. On the fifth night, I just kept looking at the cue card until it was time for my entrance and, when I opened my mouth to speak, luckily it came out.

From then on, I didn't freeze again – until we were live on national television. Then it happened once more, in front of millions. It is the most cringeworthy thing.

I don't really know how I got over it, but it has always worried me that it might come back. Stage fright has ruined many a promising career.

Sadly, while we were on the Australian and New Zealand tour, Danny's manager, Jack Hanson, died. He had a cerebral haemorrhage at the bar one night and just dropped to the ground, dead. He was Danny's life partner and Danny was understandably devastated, so it ended the tour.

We were in New Zealand by then and we got a note sent to our hotel rooms, saying, 'Tour's been cancelled,' and explaining that Jack had passed away. Jack was Danny's right-hand man and he found it very difficult to carry on without him. It was a big moment for us, and a traumatic time for Danny, who went back to London after that.

For me, it was back to the audition circuit.

CHAPTER 7 *High Heels and High Living*

I t may be my job to dish out the criticism these days, but as a young dancer, I faced my fair share of put-downs. In 1985, after *The Danny La Rue Show*, I flew to Sydney to try out for *La Cage aux Folles*, where I was told that my arms were way too wild. The producers asked me to come back for the next audition, but said they wanted to see that I could keep my extremities in check.

They were right, of course: I wasn't finishing my lines properly. It's one of the many things I look out for on *Strictly*. I always say to people like Zoë Ball, 'You have long arms so they need to be controlled.' The longer the arm, the further it has to go; every flaw is magnified and more obvious.

You have no choice but to listen to that sort of criticism as a dancer because it could mean the difference between getting the job or not. After the producers' feedback, I danced in front of a mirror every day and, as part of the show requires the chorus to be in drag, I even commandeered a pair of high heels to practise in, so that I grew used to balancing on them while I moved. They were a pair of strappy sandals – not ideal for dancing as they had absolutely no ankle or heel support, but they were the best I could get to squeeze my size 11 feet into at the time.

You can buy size 11 women's shoes at specialist shops for tall ladies – because they tend to have pretty large feet too. The problem is that they rarely stock high heels, because generally women that tall don't want to be any taller. Back then, in Australia, it was odd for a man to buy a pair of strappy heels – it probably still is, for that matter – so trying to get dance shoes was tough. All the ones in *La Cage aux Folles* had to be made specially. The first pair I practised in, I borrowed from a friend.

The auditions for the show dragged on for weeks and weeks. The final one lasted three days – eight hours a day – because I had to be made up. I learned to walk in the heels and wear leotards on stage, and I was tested to within an inch of my life. I memorized the script for five different characters: the songs, the jazz, the cancan, tap, classical, character combinations, everything. It was a major audition and I put my heart and soul into it. Then I heard absolutely nothing.

My first thought was that I just wasn't good enough for the part and they didn't want me. I decided I needed to get back to Melbourne, back to classes and intense training. I was upset because other people I knew were offered roles in the show, and I thought I was a better dancer, but I hadn't received the phone call I'd been waiting for. As soon as I returned to Melbourne, that call finally came. I'd landed the job. It had been an agonizing wait, but I was over the moon.

For the rehearsals, we were issued with our custom-made heels. It is absolutely essential to practise in heels because if you're not used to dancing in them, they kill. After the first two days, we were all screaming in agony. I don't know how girls cope! It's torture. Tap-dancing in a pair of heels felt almost impossible. You miss so many beats because you are already up on *relevé* (on the tips of your toes), so I missed all my shuffles to begin with. It was so frustrating.

The girls on *Strictly Come Dancing* wear four-and-a-half-inch heels, which are high for a dance shoe, but it's not the six-inch stiletto we had in *La Cage*. The professionals are used to dancing in the Latin heels and literally grow up in them, but contemporary and classical dancers are used to flat shoes, so as soon as they put high heels on, they can't dance any more.

In *La Cage*, the boys had to dance as boys *and* as girls, so we were always hurting our Achilles tendons. It was great fun, though. Bizarrely, the straight boys were the campiest. They loved dressing up. The whole atmosphere was so alive that it was a joy to sign in every night at the stage door. My old friend Magatha, of *West Side Story* and *The Black and White Minstrel Show* fame, had also been cast, playing Hanna from Hamburg, one of the lead Cagelles (the name for the drag queens in the club), and we had a riot together.

There was one section where we slid down fireman's poles from the fly floor (a narrow raised platform very high above the stage) in drag, wearing white heels, white leotards, glitter skullcaps and white satin tails. After making our dramatic entrance, we formed a line of high-kicking gals. One night, I landed badly at the base of the pole and felt something snap in my ankle. I continued with the show to the end of the kick line, fuelled by adrenalin, with my foot just feeling numb.

After I'd limped off stage, I went into the office and my whole foot ballooned up to twice its normal size. I'd ruptured a vein. I had to rest it for two days, but I carried on with the 'man' part of the show; I just couldn't dance in high heels until the swelling went down.

When I wasn't on stage, I was a booth singer, providing backing vocals while sitting in a booth wearing headphones. A lot of shows, including *Cats*, use live booth singers instead of backing tracks, mainly to beef up the sound in the big choral numbers when the dancers on stage have been dancing their hearts out and have no breath left with which to sing.

My dad adored *La Cage* and would come up as often as he could to see it. It was somewhat bizarre that he loved it so much, given his negative reaction to my dressing up as a child. Things changed after I moved out of home and started performing. He began to accept my passion for dance and the theatre.

He first saw me in proper drag in Melbourne, when I was living with Cecily. I was kitted out to go to a fancy-dress party when he popped round for a visit. He told me he thought I looked spectacular. When *La Cage* was on, he watched it at every opportunity – even if he just ended up getting drunk and falling asleep in the audience, as he once did. Everyone had cleared out one night when I heard a knock on my dressing-room door, and someone from front of house said, 'Your father's asleep in the auditorium.'

It was one of those unfortunate moments, but, of course, the next day he couldn't remember a thing.

Another night, he picked up Jon Ewing, the star of the show, and dragged him out of the toilet over his shoulder in a strange sort of celebration because he thought he was wonderful. He was captivated by that musical and so proud of me.

It was at this time that Lavish hit the circuit and began whoring herself about. Dad fell in love with the character. He would come to see the act all the time and even travelled all the way from Ballarat to Adelaide, South Australia to see Lavish in a comedy club there. I slid down the banister and went into 'Greatest Love of All' – and there he was in the audience. It shocked me, but he got such a kick out of watching her in action.

It was interesting having his support, particularly as my mum didn't like the idea of me being a drag queen. She eventually accepted that it was a theatrical outlet and not a life choice, and then she was happy to celebrate it. At the time, I think maybe she feared I would go the whole hog and become a transsexual or something. She certainly didn't think it was a great career choice. At that point, of course, nobody else predicted that it wouldn't be. The character was so popular that everyone addressed me as Lavish, even when I wasn't in drag. My dad, to this day, still calls me Lavish and writes 'Dear Lavish' in cards, which Mum hates.

I have the most beautiful picture of my alter ego painted by Keith Michell, the wonderful actor who starred as Heathcliff in

BBC TV's 1962 adaptation of *Wuthering Heights*, and who led the cast of *Man of La Mancha* in its first London production, among many other achievements. Keith is an accomplished artist in his spare time. He was in *La Cage aux Folles* with me and we did a private sitting as part of his *La Cage aux Folles* collection. I had a photo of the portrait enlarged and it now takes pride of place in the sitting room of Mum's home.

Despite my success, I got really paranoid about my body shape during the run of *La Cage* because people were making fun of my protruding hips. They have always been quite large in proportion to my torso and legs, and I felt that they were about an inch too wide.

So, I went to a doctor and asked him if it was surgically possible to remove part of my hips to make them smaller. I hated them, and the thinner I got, the more they stuck out. What I should have been doing was building up my shoulders to balance out my hips, and strengthening my abdominals and pectorals. Instead, I begged the consultant to take an inch off each side.

'That's impossible,' he said. 'Don't be so stupid!'

I didn't think it was such a wild idea. People were having sex changes, so I hadn't anticipated that an inch from each hip would be a problem!

While I was in *La Cage*, I dated the Cherry Ripe man, who was my first proper boyfriend on the gay scene. He was a model in the Cherry Ripe ad – Cherry Ripes were chocolate bars that were hugely popular in Australia in the 1980s.

I met him when I was dancing in a club. We only went out for about three weeks, but I sent him a huge bunch of flowers that was so big he couldn't get it through his front door. In return, he taught me how to wet shave, because I'd only used an electric razor up until then.

He came to see me in the show and Magatha and the cast ribbed me about him something rotten. We deliberately put him in an aisle seat because the drag queens come screaming down the aisle, and then we bought a load of Cherry Ripe bars and threw them at him as we passed.

La Cage ran for six months in Sydney and three months in Melbourne, where it was suddenly cut short by the arrival of AIDS. This terrible killer disease had just hit the headlines and nobody knew what it was. Some believed that *La Cage aux Folles* was propagating it because the show was about two gay guys and it was full of drag queens. The fear of the unknown caused homophobia to take over and people seriously thought that if they were even touched by a drag queen, they would get AIDS. It was really bad, totally ridiculous, but it caused the production to close early. In fact, most of the boys in the show were straight, so it was doubly stupid.

Like most gay men, I was scared to death by the spread of AIDS. Everyone was hearing that a friend of a friend had died, or someone you vaguely knew had passed on. People started hiding themselves away, particularly the guys with Kaposi's sarcoma, which is a skin cancer that comes up in big black patches. Once you had that, there was nothing anyone could do, so you had to start saying goodbye.

While I was doing *La Cage* in Sydney, everyone was talking about how you could catch it, questioning whether you might contract AIDS from kissing and so on. The topic cropped up again one day when a group of us were in the kitchen at my digs. One of the guys in the room, a friend of my landlord, was wearing a polo-neck sweater, despite it being the middle of summer. Partway through this conversation, he pulled up his sleeve to show me what Kaposi's sarcoma looked like and he said, 'This is all over my body.' They were huge black lesions and I thought, 'Oh my God. This is just horrific.' Everyone was being really cautious, and it did change everything.

In those days, once you were diagnosed, it was pretty much a death sentence. Even in 1993, when I was appearing in *Crazy for You*, a good friend of mine from the production, Colin John-Bell, died from AIDS. I remember how he used to try to keep his weight up by eating fish and chips and really high-fat foods.

In the end, he decided that he'd had enough, so he retreated to a darkened room and burned candles. It was really difficult for him because he was very young, only twenty-five. His life had just begun and his showbiz career was taking off. He was so in love with tap-dancing and so in love with the show because he'd created the character of Moose, which was a fantastic achievement.

I saw him at the theatre in the very last stage of his illness. He was completely ashen and looked awful, but the light behind his eyes was still there because he was watching the musical. Colin was such a lovely guy, great to be around, with the capacity to make people laugh every minute of the day. It was so sad to see such a talented, fun, young man die from this dreadful disease.

Now combination therapy has changed everything for the better, but back in the eighties it was a very different story, which I saw played out time and time again among the people I knew. If you were diagnosed with AIDS back then, that was it. There was no hope. It was a frightening fact for a young man coming out into the gay world and we were all really afraid. Not only was it fatal, but it also had this horrendous stigma attached to it that I don't believe the youth of today understand. It's not seen as much of a threat now, because of the life-saving drugs, but it is, and should be treated with all the seriousness that such a devastating disease can command.

I was lucky because, by the time it had become a recognized danger, I was in a long-term relationship with someone and I felt very secure in that. His name was Mark Gogoll. He was very good for me because he was a bit older and more experienced, and he gave me some excellent advice. He's now an agent in Melbourne, but he was an actor at the time.

Mark and I met as a result of a bet. Magatha was acquainted with him and dared me to go and ask him out. Never one to resist a challenge, I did just that and we stayed together for almost three years. He was the first boyfriend I brought home to meet Mum. The whole family loved him and they still do. Mark is now with a long-term partner called Darren, and they see my family to this day.

We lived together in Sydney for a little while and we were quite a romantic couple. One Valentine's Day, I bought 101 red roses and two white parakeets in a big, ornate cage, and had them delivered to Mark in Queensland, where he was working with the Victoria State Opera. He kept those birds for years. The gift cost me a fortune; I was totally broke, but I put it all on my credit card.

Being poor has never stopped me from making extravagant gestures towards the people I love. On Mother's Day 1985, when I was twenty and penniless, I splashed out and bought Mum a complete outfit from Myer in Melbourne. It cost me A$800 (£375), which was a huge amount of money to me at the time, but she still wears those clothes today and the look on her face back then was worth every cent. I bought Mel and Trent a trampoline as well. I was touring all the time, and hardly ever got to see them, so I wanted to do things for them when I could.

My credit card was maxed beyond belief, but I never minded debt. Somehow, I always knew I'd be able to pay it back some day.

After *La Cage* finished, I had a brief run in *Me and My Girl* in Melbourne, where my lifelong hatred of hospitals began.

When I turned up at the theatre one afternoon, I was told that an actor friend, Robert Berry, couldn't make the matinee because he had been attacked with a crowbar and badly beaten up. I went to visit him in hospital, but was so horrified by the state of him that I fainted, hit my head on a trolley and had to be revived. I didn't cope well with the experience at all.

A few weeks later, after the show had moved to Sydney, we were at the Taxi Club, where we always went after work, and I was just starting my first pint when someone started talking about

Robert's injuries. All the memories came flooding back and I was out cold again! That time, I hit my head on a silver ashtray that ran the length of the bar, and was knocked unconscious. When I came to, the bouncers accused me of being drunk and threw me down the stairs and out of the club.

Fortunately, my friend Lesley was there and she took me to the hospital to get my head wound seen to. I still get the feeling I'm going to pass out whenever I am visiting a medical centre of any description.

Lesley and I were great friends, but we had a secret casual fling going on as well. She was so much fun to be around, and had a laugh that would make hyenas recoil in horror. I loved her laughter and still do. We have always tried to keep in touch, reminiscing about the past and the absolutely mad times we shared.

We once talked about having a child together, but dismissed it due to the fact that I wasn't ready to settle down in that sort of way. I couldn't imagine how I could possibly support the idea either financially or emotionally.

It was while I was in *Me and My Girl* that I became the victim of a fantastic prank. I went to a dinner party at a mate's house and we had a lovely meal, a few glasses of wine, loads of laughs, and then I left and went home: a normal night as far as I was concerned. Two weeks later, a photo appeared on my dressing-room mirror, in full view of the cast. It was a picture of me, completely stark bollock naked, lying on a sofa. It was ghastly.

'I don't remember that,' was my first thought. Apparently, after the main course at this dinner party, I'd got up from the table, sat on the couch, and fallen fast asleep. While I was snoozing, the other guests undressed me, laid me out, took photos and clothed me again. I woke up and had dessert and thought I'd just nodded off for a few seconds.

I'd had no idea what had really happened until the incriminating photo arrived.

As my twenty-first birthday loomed, in 1986, I decided to show Ballarat a really good time. I hired a bus to take all my Sydney and Melbourne friends to a fancy-dress party at our house on Ditchfield Road. The cast of *Me and My Girl* and *La Cage aux Folles* piled on to the bus in Melbourne for the two-hour journey, and we drank fluffy ducks (advocaat, vodka and lemonade) all the way there. Magatha has always complained that he in fact walked the distance to Ballarat: with no seat for him on the bus, he was put in charge of mixing the drinks and spent the entire journey handing out cocktails, pacing up and down the aisle. I don't think he'll ever forgive me.

I had opted for a country-and-western theme, but everyone got a bit confused. Half the family, including my Uncle George and Auntie Shirley and most of the Lancaster clan, came in Victorian dress from Sovereign Hill, wearing bizarre top hats and great long skirts. I had been imagining checked shirts and jeans!

As it was January, which is summer in Australia, it was a beautiful, hot, sunny day. Dad put hay bales around the tennis court and even constructed an outside toilet out of more bales. The family put flags everywhere and had a huge barbecue going. They had gone to so much trouble.

The party was packed with people and Ballarat had never seen the like. There were folk from all walks of life. Ronne Arnold, who at the time was probably the only black American in the country besides Marcia Hines, was there, so everyone was gawping at him. There was a real transsexual called Corinne, who had boobs, but hadn't had the chop. She's so gorgeous, you'd never know she used to be a bloke. We drank shedloads of champagne and things got quite silly. At one point, I looked up and Ronne Arnold was giving my dad a piggyback around the paddock, then they both collapsed in a heap in the long grass and screamed with laughter.

The people of Ballarat weren't used to these outrageous theatrical types, but everyone got into the swing of things. It was insane.

At the time, I was sharing a flat with a friend whom we affectionately called Chelsea Bun. He owned a pink Volkswagen. He was a nurse by day and a drag queen by night, and he was hilarious to live with. Together, we did a *Dreamgirls* routine at the bash, which went down a storm with everyone.

It was one of the best parties I've ever had and people still talk about it to this day. It was magnificent.

In the evening, we went to a nightclub and I left all my twenty-first-birthday presents on the bus, in the luggage compartment. I remembered just in time, and as the bus drove off, it was pursued by a gaggle of bizarrely dressed queens on foot. Luckily, we managed to catch up with it and get all the gifts back.

Not long after my birthday, I made one of my perhaps more questionable artistic decisions by agreeing to appear in an advertisement. Yes, I was Australia's original Kentucky Fried Chicken nugget boy – now there's a title!

The ad was for drive-in KFC stores. I'd auditioned with a load of mates. The producers just wanted someone mad who could leap about a bit and do the splits: enter yours truly. The strange thing was that I couldn't even drive – but I got the lead male role anyway. Megan Shapcott was the leading lady. I'd known her for a while through the business – we used to call her Strapcock for a laugh – but this was the first time we'd been the 'stars' together in such a big push.

I had to sit in this Volkswagen convertible and act as though I was driving, and the production crew wheeled me in as I pretended to steer. Then I jumped out of the car and sang something like: 'I said, "Nah, nah, nah, nah, nah, Kentucky nuggets. With or without sauce? I'm asking you: when you taste Kentucky nuggets, what do you do?" You go, "Nah, nah …"' Then Megan and I had to feed each other nuggets while we danced.

We began filming at six in the morning. It can get swelteringly hot in Australia, which is why they start shoots so early there. This day was no exception. I break sweat just doing a *plié*, so I was surrounded by make-up artists who were all trying to cool me down. I was also constantly eating Kentucky Fried Chicken. I had to dance my way around the set, looking lovely with all these nuggets. The amount of fried chicken we ate that day was truly disgusting.

In 1987, I moved to Sydney and took a part in a show called *Olympus on My Mind*, which was an absolute disaster. It was on at the Footbridge Theatre. I was playing a tap-dancing poof in a pink toga and roman sandals, which doubled up as tap shoes.

On the Thursday night before we opened, we had a special gay preview and all these drag queens turned up. There was a massive storm howling around the venue as we were getting ready in the wings. Five minutes before curtain up, the whole roof caved in.

All the water that had been building up outside cascaded down on to these drag queens and everyone was running about panicking. No one was seriously hurt, thankfully, but what a sight for sore eyes. I peeped out through the curtain and the whole audience was saturated and shrieking. I've never seen so many screaming queens.

Needless to say, on that occasion, the show didn't go on. Perhaps it was an omen. When it did open, on 30 October 1987, it only lasted two weeks because it was so terrible.

I loved Sydney and that whole era. I was surrounded by opulent, beautiful people and was doing fabulous things – partying, waterskiing, taking wonderful trips. There are huge public gardens in the city where they have open-air concerts, so we would take a BBQ chook and some champagne and go to the opera in the park.

I was carefree and it seemed I was going to be young forever. Now I'm old. At least, compared to the dancers I work with, I'm ancient.

One night, my friend Gerard Symonds and I went out for dinner dressed as women. Gerard and I had met in *West Side Story* and become close mates. He was roughly the same height as me, so we were the two 6-foot-plus boys who matched each other and were often cast in shows together. Even in the West End of London, we were always after the same jobs and frequently followed each other into roles.

It was our mutual pal John Eva's fortieth birthday party. I always called John 'Mag's mum', as he and Magatha were very close. Mag's mum looked after us both, handing out advice in troubled times and teaching us a sense of responsibility, like the day I smashed a Waterford crystal brandy glass he owned and he made me write a A$80 ($37) cheque for its replacement. I adored him and we still keep in touch today.

That evening, Gerard donned a white tunic dress, with a black belt and cinched-in waist, and I put on my only frock, the green one that Lavish always wore. It took us hours to get ready, because we stuck on false nails, plucked our eyebrows, had very close shaves, applied the make-up and then carefully fixed our wigs. Walking up Oxford Street in Sydney, we got quite a few wolf whistles, so we must have looked good. (Either that or it was abuse. We chose to see the positive side!)

We found a table in this lovely Italian restaurant and Gerard, stupidly, ordered a spag bol. He was a bit nervous about being in drag in public and we were both smoking as we sat waiting for our food. Gerard was telling me a story with a cigarette in his hand and forgot he was wearing inch-long synthetic nails. His fag burnt down to his fake talon and, suddenly, it caught fire. He started waving his hands around wildly and yelping. I was shrieking with laughter because he looked so hysterical and panic-stricken.

He managed to extinguish the small blaze – and then he spilt spaghetti bolognese all the way down his white frock. We went to the ladies' loo so he could take off the dress and wash it, but of course he had to walk back out in wet clothes. Gerard's a little bit taller than me and didn't make, how shall I say, the prettiest woman, so the sight of him that night was truly unforgettable. I have never laughed so much in my life.

After dinner, we went to our old haunt the Taxi Club, which had poker machines, low lighting and a very smoky atmosphere. Loads of trannies used to go there and get picked up by straight guys. It gained its name for the simple reason that quite a few taxi drivers were regulars.

In truth, it was the sort of bar where your shoes stuck to the floor, but it was open until 7 a.m., which suited us night owls. A lot of theatre people used it because it served food and drink so late. The club delicacy was a 'lamb burger', which comprised slices of lamb, mint sauce and mashed potato in a burger bun. They were delicious, actually, and very cheap. Gerard and I sat there in drag, sipping our gin and tonics, while several guys sidled over and tried to pick us up.

By the time I got home, I was busting for the toilet. I had three pairs of tights on, and a dance support to hold everything in place, so to go to the loo while I was out was a logistical nightmare. Instead, I waited until I got home – which was a mistake. I put the key in the door and promptly pissed myself. There I stood in my frock, on the doorstep, wetting myself, only to have my landlord and housemate, Charles, open the door and see the whole thing. Honestly, what that tired green dress hasn't been through could be written on a postage stamp.

On another occasion, in Brisbane, I lost my whole thumbnail when I was in drag one night. I got home and started ripping off my false talons, and forgot that I'd superglued the thumb one on. I pulled so hard, I wrenched my entire nail off.

It didn't grow back for about six months and even then only half a nail grew. I went to my doctor and said, 'You need to do something about this. I need a prosthetic nail. I can't go through life without a thumbnail.'

The doctor looked at me and then, patiently, explained, 'We don't do prosthetic nails. Just try leaving it for another six months and see what happens.'

Of course, it grew back.

It was around this time that certain experiences with my old flatmate Cecily put me off driving for life. Every time we went out in the car together, it seemed that there was a dramatic event. On one occasion, we had a head-on crash. We were the innocent party: the other car, a Mini, turned over before our eyes. Its driver was completely at fault. Luckily, there were no serious injuries, only a bit of whiplash. The girl who climbed out of the vehicle in front, which was on its roof, was remarkably unscathed. Our bonnet was up to our faces and her car was upside down, with wheels spinning and smoke everywhere, but we were all OK.

The most horrific incident was when our car fatally hit someone in Port Melbourne. We were on our way to meet my boyfriend Mark Gogoll and a few other chums for dinner. The night had closed in and it was a wet and dark evening. We came away from the house and pulled up at a set of traffic lights. After we crossed the intersection, this guy, who was absolutely hammered and carrying six tinnies under his arm, walked straight out in front of our car. We didn't even see him. There was nothing Cecily could have done. His head came through my side of the windscreen, he flipped over the top of the car (ten feet, according to an eyewitness at the trial that later followed) and we immediately pulled up a little further down the road in total shock.

Cecily called out from behind the steering wheel, 'What the hell was that?'

I replied, 'I think it was a person,' and looked back to see if I could spot anything.

We walked to the scene and saw this poor fellow lying face down in the middle of the road. It was just awful. Ces was a complete mess. Crowds of people began to gather around the body.

I was subpoenaed to appear in court. Cecily was so upset that she couldn't take the stand. I had to tell the whole story, which was quite nerve-racking. The court came to the conclusion that his blood alcohol level was four times above any safe limit and he had just stumbled into the car – what was amazing was that he could walk at all.

Tragically, he had lived just across the road from where the fatal accident had happened. His family had been waiting on the other side of the street and seen him walk out into the oncoming traffic. You can imagine how distraught they were as I was describing the collision in court. I said, 'It was like a brick through the windscreen,' and they were shouting, 'That's my father. You killed my father.' It was horrible.

Curiously, Ces has never, before or after these two events with me, had any other car accidents. After the incidents, I decided not to get my driving licence. I tried to learn when I first came to the UK and I got L-plates, but I was just too nervous behind the wheel. I don't want to be responsible for the death or injury of anyone. That's what bothers me about driving, and since those two accidents I've been a bit funny about it.

The court case came up as I was performing in one of my favourite shows of all time. *Sugar Babies* is a revue-style musical comedy, a tribute to the old burlesque era. I was in the barbershop quartet, which sang, tap-danced and acted in the comedy skits. I also understudied the MC, who was compère for the evening, played the straight man and sang a few songs to link the acts.

During the run, I was laid off work with suspected glandular fever. I'd been dieting again and had lost loads of weight, which lowered my immune system. My glands were really swollen and as one of the boys in the production had already been diagnosed with the illness, I was signed off from performing until I learned the outcome of my blood tests, in order to protect the rest of the cast. Fortunately, the results came back negative; I was just severely run down.

Then I hit another problem. While I was laid up, I ate and ate and did no exercise. Suddenly, I'd ballooned in size.

A helpful friend suggested that I attempt the Scarsdale Medical Diet, which is a high-protein, fat-free regime. I tried it, and it was really effective. I ended up living my whole dance life on that diet.

I would have half a grapefruit in the morning, lunch was tuna with vegetables, and dinner would be a chicken breast with broccoli or green beans. I lost loads of body fat under the regime. You are only meant to stay on it for two weeks, but I was on it constantly, which was terrible in retrospect. You could have two boiled eggs a week, and five olives as your treats. Of course, I was dancing every night as well, so I slimmed down very quickly.

The Scarsdale proved a godsend. Thereafter, at any point throughout my dancing career when I got worried about my weight, I'd turn to it for salvation.

I've always been an all-or-nothing guy. Often, when I wasn't eating, I would suffer from attacks of dizziness. Even on the Scarsdale, which doesn't allow any sugar, I would get giddy spells. You are allowed fruit twice a week for lunch, on Tuesdays and Saturdays, so if my blood sugar level dropped on those days, I'd whack a banana in my gob, but what my body was really craving was carbohydrates, because I was working out so much.

The weight issue really has plagued me for my entire life. It's horrific. At my heaviest, I have been 106 kg (16 stone 10 lb). The lightest was 72 kg (11 stone 5 lb).

I tried to keep my dance weight at 75 kg (11 stone 11 lb), but I remember, on one occasion, standing on the scales and watching the needle go to 83 kg (13 stone 11 lb). I nearly had a heart attack. I couldn't believe how heavy I was. I'd gone up to a 34-inch waist and I thought that was an absolute disgrace. I really beat myself up about it.

The worst thing was that it didn't take anything to make my weight start to soar.

Dancing is wonderful exercise and it seems strange that my weight could yo-yo even in the middle of an intense show. But it did. Even dancing my arse off every night, I could pile on the pounds. It drove me insane and I worried about it every single day.

Just after *Sugar Babies*, I was cast in a show called *Starkers*, in which I had to strip completely naked. After landing the role, I went home and took off my clothes in front of the mirror. I scrutinized every inch of my body. I still wasn't happy with what I saw. The diet had worked and I was thinner, but I looked way too puny.

So, I started going to the gym; I knew I had to build my muscle tone. That's when I began to achieve my healthiest weight. I was eating an enormous amount of food, to maintain the bulk, but it was the right kind. I would eat a whole chicken for dinner, snack on nuts, and eat some dairy products too. By the time the show opened, I was at the peak of physical fitness and happy with my body for the first time.

As a young dancer, whenever I was unsure about my future, or wanted to make a decision, I would read tarot cards. I enjoyed it. I did a sort of DIY apprenticeship for about two years and learned how to meditate on them, so I would use them as a guidance tool mostly. Occasionally, however, they have been known to throw up a prediction that comes true.

In 1987, I was living alone in a tiny one-bed apartment in Rushcutters Bay, Sydney, dancing in *Sugar Babies*. It was a particularly quiet night and no one from the production was going out for drinks, so I made my way home directly after the show.

I was wide awake, as I always am after a performance, and needed time to wind down. Generally, I have a glass of wine and eat some food before watching telly or reading, but this particular night, I thought I would do some work on my tarot reading, the studying of which took up a fair amount of time, as you have to get to know the cards and learn what each one means to you. I decided to give myself a reading.

As soon as I began, cards appeared that had never come up before. A lot of them were major arcana cards, which was not good. Everything was leading to a death or loss in the family. I couldn't make head nor tail of it, as I didn't think any of my relatives were seriously ill.

Lo and behold, only two days later, my nanna Constance passed away at the age of eighty. I didn't tell anyone about the cards' prophecy, as at that point it may have freaked them out and, of course, it's easy to say after the fact. I use the tarot not as a way to tell the future, but to understand the past and present.

I still love doing readings with other people and I find they open up and discuss things that they perhaps wouldn't normally talk about. It interests me – not because I'm Mystic Meg and like crystal balls and wearing big hoop earrings, but because I really enjoy talking to people about their lives and learning how they feel about things.

In fact, it's benefited me enormously as a director and choreographer because I can help the performers to connect with their characters and the episodes they experience. You have to appreciate what makes people's brains work in order to direct. The more life knowledge you have, the more you can understand certain extreme situations, be they a rape scene or the motives behind a murder.

Of course, more often than not, plots are about happier things, such as falling in love, but you still have to understand the way people act when they first meet, and how silly they get, or why a person says one thing, but really means another.

I have always picked up on atmosphere easily. If I walk into a room, I can instantly tell who is sleeping with whom, who has had an argument and who is unhappy. I can tune into the aura surrounding them and generally I'm right. It's nothing mystical – more a power of observation. I learned as a young actor to observe everything you possibly can and absorb it, so I tend to people-watch and then I come up with a whole story of what I think has happened. It's part of being creative; you paint a picture in your head and tell a tale. The tarot is a fantastic tool in understanding why people do what they do and discovering what might be around the corner, because you can change your future, which I love. You are responsible for your own happiness, so you don't have to wallow in self-pity.

My attitude is that when you're down on the wheel of fortune, there's only one way to go and that's up.

Life is about making a series of decisions and, for me, the tarot cards are a way of forcing yourself to take time out, reflect on the dilemma and make a choice – by yourself. At some point, we all come to a fork in the road and don't know which way to go, and the majority of people will ring a friend or partner and talk it over, which means that they are persuaded by someone else. But that other person might want something from you in the life path they're recommending, so I listen to myself, and my inner voice, and that's what the cards have taught me. I take advice from people, and listen to them, but the decision is my own.

The tarot is a quiet way of evaluating, and asking yourself questions. It doesn't tell you which way to go – *you* have to decide – but it can tell you, 'If you take the left fork, it will lead you here. The right will lead you here. What do you want?' Hopefully, after a reading, you discover what it is that you aspire to and as soon as you know that, you just have to decide how to get it.

When I first started out in show business, tarot really helped me to choose my path. It opened up my mind to the limitless possibilities of what I could be in life.

The one thing I never did predict was that I'd end up on a national television programme judging a ballroom competition!

'Come to Paris,' said Magatha, for the second time. He was dancing at the world-famous Lido and had been trying to persuade me to join him. I'd just finished *Starkers* and had decided to try my hand at straight acting. I couldn't do that if I was cavorting in Paris every night.

'There's a contract going here. You should come,' implored Magatha again, but I wasn't interested.

A few days later, I was walking up to King's Cross in Sydney and I suddenly thought to myself, 'I could be strolling along the Champs-Elysées and speaking French right now.'

The third time he rang, I said, 'Yes.'

I bought a tape to help me to learn French and signed an eight-month contract with the Lido. Thanks to Magatha's recommendation of me to the creative director, I didn't even have to audition. The night before I left Sydney, in June 1988, Mark and I threw a party in the apartment we shared and my friend Robert Berry gave me a spectacular Eiffel Tower cake, with Lido-like feathers sticking out of the top.

Getting off the plane at Charles de Gaulle International Airport, I was horribly jet-lagged, but very excited. I'd been overseas before, of course, with Mr X, but I'd never been to a foreign-speaking country, so it was quite bizarre. It felt strange that I couldn't just walk into a shop and ask for something.

Although I'd listened to my tape, I couldn't understand

anything or speak French very well. The lessons had been full of words and phrases like '*Le douanier*', which means 'customs official', and '*Je n'ai pas un passeport.*' How often does anyone need to say, 'I don't have a passport'? As time went by, I learned pidgin French at the Lido, but when I arrived, I couldn't talk to anyone or request a single thing.

I felt very isolated. In Paris, in the eighties, the people weren't very English-friendly and hardly anyone spoke the language. It was quite a challenge for me to get by. The hardest thing was having your own apartment because, if something went wrong, you had to sort it all out in French. It's not easy having a conversation about plumbing in a language you hardly know!

My flat was absolutely tiny. It comprised one room with a bed and a kitchenette, which had two little rings on a hob for cooking, and there was a separate bathroom. It was in the 15th Arrondissement, which isn't too far from the Eiffel Tower. It was the only place I could afford. Most of my other friends, including Magatha, were in the 9th, so I really wanted to live there, but I didn't think it was worth trying to find new accommodation for just eight months. I'd inherited the apartment anyway, in a manner of speaking. Flats for the Lido cast got passed on: when one person left, another moved in.

Despite the size of my Paris home, I really enjoyed living by myself. As there was no TV and little to do, I wrote a lot more and sent countless letters to everyone at home. You'd be forgiven for thinking that this letter writing was my sole way of expressing myself in English while I was away, but in fact the rest of the cast were largely American and Australian and we only ever spoke in English, except when we were communicating with the dressers. That's why it was difficult to learn French; there was just one native girl in the entire company.

During rehearsals, Magatha threw a party at his place. I drank way too much – a whole bottle of cheap cooking brandy, so my good friend later informed me. The next day, I was doing a number where I had to run on stage carrying a palm tree, climb up to the top and then sing – or mime – 'Happy Holiday'. I reached the top of the tree and thought, 'Oh my God, I've got to go and lie down.'

I staggered back to my dressing room and was groaning, 'It must be food poisoning. I have never been this ill in my entire life.'

It was alcohol poisoning, sadly. I was so incapacitated that I had to be sent home. What a great start to my Lido career – luckily, the opening night went without a hitch.

While the incident didn't stop me from partying, I never made myself that sick again – although I did have a long, boozy lunch once that almost led to disaster. It had been my intention to have a bit of a kip before the show, but, inevitably, we all kept drinking. Then I went to work. In between the dances, we had to run up a flight of stairs, swap outfits and run straight back down again. I was so slaughtered that I couldn't do the costume changes; one of the other dancers, whom we called Olive, had to dress me.

My stage attire usually consisted of a G-string and a few feathers, with a blue fish on my head for additional extravagance. In other routines, I dressed as an Egyptian and pranced behind a real camel, which would poo all over the stage. The Lido doesn't use camels any more, they have a horse instead, but we performed alongside llamas and camels. You know you've made it when you're dancing with a camel, wearing a fake palm leaf and a fez. That was the high point of my career – dodging camel dung! How tragic!

In the past, I'd usually tried to conceal my diets from my friends and family, but in Paris, there was little point because I was constantly on the Scarsdale. With my unforgiving G-string costume, there was nowhere to hide. My body was on show the whole time, so my obsession with body fat became even more intense. There wasn't a day I didn't get out of bed and go straight to the mirror to make sure that I hadn't put on any weight overnight.

My time in that city was a curious existence, which I dubbed 'Lido Land' because it was not at all like the real world. You slept during the day and worked at night, finishing the show at about two in the morning and then going out for a meal afterwards. So dinner was at 3 a.m., you went to bed at 5 a.m. and started your day at two in the afternoon. The only people you were with, all the time, were other members of the company, except on your days off – because the show had to go up seven days a week, you couldn't take time off at the same time as anybody else. The nature of the schedule was so peculiar, however, that you never had the opportunity to make friends outside of the Lido. Therefore, your days off were always spent alone. On the days I wasn't performing, I would go to a museum or wander round the city. It was a very weird way of life.

During the run, I fell for a guy called Paul, who was nicknamed Pooh. He was gorgeous – oh, but he was a calamity on stage. He was always sliding off the stage on to people's tables, or injuring himself, or falling down the stairs or involved in some other catastrophe. In one performance, he fell backwards into the waterfall.

Needless to say, he's no longer a dancer and in fact has had a varied career. Nowadays he manages a Homebase store in Wales.

When I met Paul, I was still in a relationship with Mark; I was supposed to be going back to him in Australia when my contract was up at the Lido. Given the potency of my attraction to Paul, though, I sensed it was over for good with Mark. Somewhat deplorably, I was too confused and cowardly to tell him. Instead, I finished my fling with Pooh just before Mark came over for a visit. I decided I should give our relationship another chance.

We went on holiday to Italy. It was October 1988, and I'd been away for four months, so I was looking forward to spending time with him. However, seeing him again just made me realize that I had no choice but to move on. I knew I had to break it off.

It was awful trying to choose the right moment. I finally plucked up the courage and said, 'Look, I think I want to stay in Europe, because I really like it here.' I knew it wasn't fair to cheat or lie and I felt dreadful about it, but I couldn't tell him about Paul. It was a lovely day and we were sitting around a fountain in a beautiful square in Florence. I can't think of a more romantic place to dump someone.

Our relationship had been a very strong one. We'd been together for nearly three years and we really did love one another. He was a wonderful support to me as well, but, at that time, I simply couldn't be with him. I needed to grow up. I wanted to live an alternative life to the one that I'd had in Australia. I couldn't go back to that same existence; I wanted to push myself forward, in a different direction.

Afterwards, I felt too guilty to hook up with Pooh again, but it didn't take me long to fall in love with someone else. Mr America, as I shall call him, was another guy I danced with at the Lido. I was totally besotted. I thought he was too, so I moved in with him. We lived in a minuscule flat, with the tiniest bath you've ever seen, but I was very happy there.

Mr America spoke Spanish – consequently, he loved weekends away in Spain. He took me to Barcelona and Madrid, where I was inducted into the cultural tradition of bullfighting. The first time I saw the kill, I felt physically sick – but then, a strange thing happens, and you get used to it. The next thing you know, you're shouting for the matadors to finish off the job, which is horrible.

The two of us were attacked ourselves one night in Paris. We were part of a group that had just finished work at the Lido, and were waiting for a taxi with Magatha and Olive on the Champs-Elysées. A big car pulled up at the traffic lights and someone shouted something at us. Magatha said something back in French, which I didn't understand. Suddenly, seven Arab men got out of the car and laid into us all. Thankfully, Olive had managed to run off. Mr America was fighting with one of the men (that sounds ridiculously superhero-esque with his pseudonym, doesn't it?) and another was coming at me, while I was just standing there like a lemon, holding everyone's bags. I looked round for Magatha ... only to see him on the floor, being kicked in the gutter.

The next thing I knew, Mr America's shirt had been completely ripped off him and he was grappling with his attacker. The guy who was headed in my direction was just about to hit me when a security man, carrying a gun, turned up from out of the blue.

Unbelievably, all this happened before the lights changed and, as the guard came over to break it up, the lights turned to green and our assailants piled into their car and sped off.

The security man asked us if we were all right and then went on his way. Magatha got the worst of it and had been badly bashed up, but not seriously hurt, thank goodness. We were all so shaken by the incident that we decided to go for a drink, so the three of us ended up in a nightclub and I lit up a fag. I had arrived in Paris as a non-smoker, having given up for over a year, but that horrendous night shattered my nerves and sent me straight back to the weed.

Sadly, I didn't stop at the one, and for the rest of my time in France I smoked daily. The natives, of course, smoked all the time, so it was difficult to stay off the cigarettes anyway. Every *tabac* was fume-filled and although I could handle it for a while, that episode tipped me over the edge.

After I started smoking again in Paris, I continued on and off ever after, though I've tried to give up on numerous occasions since. I read Allen Carr's book and stopped for about two-and-a-half years, then I had one at a party, after a few drinks, which was stupid. I most recently gave up in October 2007 – yet again. So far, so good.

On 9 January 1989, I received news from Australia that proved even more distressing than the physical assault we'd suffered. The drink, I learned, had almost driven Dad to murder.

I was thousands of miles away from home and had to hear about the violence second hand. As I was on the other side of the world when it all kicked off, I've asked Sue to tell you in her own words about what happened on that awful day:

I was six months pregnant with my first daughter Isabelle when my husband David and I took a holiday back home to Ballarat from Sweden. We had been in Sweden for a year and the company allowed us a trip home in the middle of our contract to catch up with family and friends. Our visit was almost over.

The day before we left, a family gathering was planned as it happened to be my father's birthday and our first wedding anniversary combined. As a special treat, David and I bought ourselves an antique bed, but any other romantic ideas we may have had diminished as the day's events unfolded.

My father has been an alcoholic from as far back as I can remember and I fully expected the situation to be the same as ever, but this time things were different. Dad had spent the days leading up to his birthday getting drunker than usual and even more inappropriate in his behaviour.

He would rage about the house in violent outbursts, yelling and screaming at anyone in earshot. He had a glazed look in his eyes as if nothing and nobody were being registered. I had hated him in the past, but he had never terrified me. This time, I was petrified. He was aggressive and unpredictable and seemed to be focused on abusing and hurting Mum. Trent and Mel were young and still living at home; I feared for their safety as well as Mum's. I knew Dad had a gun in the house and I was worried that he might take it out and use it.

Although I was booked to return to Sweden the very next day – and my pregnancy was so far along that I had to go back sooner rather than later or I wouldn't be allowed to fly – I couldn't leave without knowing that Mum, Mel and Trent would be OK. On the morning of 9 January, after Dad had had a particularly drunken night, I convinced Mum to visit the police station and talk to a policewoman about his behaviour and find out how they could protect themselves. The conversation was a difficult one because we had never before let another person, let alone an external authority, into the secret of the abuse in our lives. It made the situation real for the first time.

The policewoman talked about restraining orders. She also asked us if there were any firearms in the house. When we replied that there were, she told us that, as soon as we returned home, it was vital that we separate the bullets from the guns.

Mum, defensive at the implicit suggestion, interjected, 'There is no way he would ever do that! He would never bring out the gun. He isn't that bad.'

We had taken separate cars to the police station. Mum decided to drive straight home to get on with her preparations for Dad's birthday, while I shopped for a few things to pack before the journey back to Sweden. I told Mum that as soon as she got home, she must do the 'gun thing'. She said, 'OK,' but there was no urgency in her tone. I truly don't think she believed there was any risk.

I finished my shopping and pulled into Ditchfield Road. There was a crowd of people in the street, standing outside the front of the house. I parked the car and could see Mum standing next to our neighbour, Julie.

'What's going on?' I asked.

Mum told me that Dad was on another rampage. He had thrown a perfectly cooked roast dinner out of the kitchen window into the garden. They were all scared and didn't know what to do. I asked Mum if she had done what the police had told us to and she said that she hadn't had time.

As we spoke, a family friend, Corinne, ran up the driveway, screaming, 'He's got a gun!'

The whole street cleared and scrambled in all directions. Luckily, my sixteen-year-old sister Melanie was at a friend's place down the road, safe and sound, but my eleven-year-old brother Trent was with us. I had no idea where my husband David was.

People were running in all directions. Mum, Trent and I headed for Julie's house across the road. We ran through her back door, down the hallway and into the bathroom. It's interesting what goes through your mind at a time like that, but all I could think was: 'I don't want us to be splattered over the tiled walls of this bathroom. There is nowhere to go. Nowhere to escape.'

I took the lead and directed everyone to spread out around the house. We were under beds, in cupboards, beneath desks. I threw Mum and Trent under the beds in someone's bedroom and I got under one in there too. I just lay there and listened. Mum was hysterical at this point, screaming, 'Susan, your baby, you might lose the baby.' I assured her that I felt tough and healthy and would be fine.

Then some of Julie's boys ran into the house. They yelled out that they had heard gunfire – and that David had been shot.

Strangely, nothing they said made me panic. I didn't feel it – so I firmly believed it hadn't happened.

After lying there briefly, I decided to call the police. I crawled out from under the bed and, on my hands and knees, picked up the wall-mounted phone in Julie's kitchen, keeping a firm eye on the window that Dad would have to walk past if he were to come into the house. I didn't know where he was, so I kept low.

At that point, one of the boys told me that David was OK after all and had led Dad away from Julie's house. That was a huge relief. I made the call to the police. Emergency 000. I told them that a man was in the neighbourhood with a gun. They said they would send a team as soon as possible.

I went back to my hideout under the bed. Mum was still overwrought. Trent joined Julie's sons in their quest to find out what was happening and promised to bring back reports. I felt strong and didn't feel any threat to the baby. I told Mum she had to keep quiet or he might hear her and kill us all.

It seemed to take forever for the police to arrive. Apparently, the SWAT teams had had to meet at the top of the hill and put on their bulletproof vests. When I heard sirens, I finally ventured out from under the bed. Peering through the window, I saw Dad wearing his daggy old pyjamas – and a pink windcheater with 'Sugar Babies' emblazoned across it (a show in which Craig had once performed). He was getting into the back of the police van. David was there too, thankfully unhurt. Nobody had been physically injured, but it could so easily have ended in tragedy.

David told me later that, as he was aware the guns were in the house, he was keeping a close eye on Dad. That morning, after Dad's outburst over the roast dinner, he saw him collect the guns from their storage place and take them to the garage. He told Corinne to warn us that Dad had the guns; this is when we all ran for our lives. What Dad's intentions were, no one knows. My father has told me that he had an alcoholic blackout on that day and has no recollection of the incident. Apparently, such blackouts can happen after a person has consumed a certain amount of alcohol; although they are conscious at the time, they have no memory of what has occurred.

During the drama, David had checked to see if we were all safe, and then gone back to find out what Dad was doing. While my father wasn't looking, David grabbed the shotgun from the garage and ran down the garden with it. He didn't realize that Dad also had a .22 rifle, which he lifted, aimed and fired over David's head.

David said he thought he was safe at such a distance, but

has since found out that a shot fired at that range could have hit him if discharged in his direction.

That time in my father's life was one of extreme instability. He was an accident waiting to happen. Nobody means to go out of their way to terrify the people they love, but it was clear on that day that whatever his intentions were, a raging alcoholic experiencing a blackout should be nowhere near a gun.

After Dad's arrest, he was taken to the police station and put in a holding cell. Mum and I followed and sat in the waiting room, where we could hear him yelling and being abusive. We didn't go in. I felt he needed to dry out and get the alcohol out of his system. Plus he sounded very unpleasant and we didn't need to expose ourselves to that again.

When Mum heard his voice, she shuddered violently and then turned to face me, looking at me with what seemed like hate in her eyes – almost accusingly. I felt at the time that she blamed me for making the phone call to the police and reporting the incident, thereby bringing it all out in a very public way.

There was nothing more we could do, so I went to the hospital and had a check-up, just to make sure my baby was OK. I felt all right and I knew she would be too.

The police rang later that night and told me that Dad would be released from jail unless charges were laid, and it was up to one of us to say that we feared for our lives in order that he should be kept in. I was frightened for my family and thought it was an opportunity for Dad to dry out at last and work out his problems, so I took on that responsibility and gave the go-ahead for my father to stay in the lock-up.

David and I postponed our flight to Sweden for a week, so that we could set Mum and the kids up in a Salvation Army accommodation centre for women, where they would stay until it was safe to go back home. Leaving them in that place while I returned to my life overseas was such a difficult thing to do.

Before we set off, I visited Dad once in prison. He was sober, but very edgy. I gave him some toiletries and clothes and a book about healthy living. Well, it was worth a try. He seemed grateful, but didn't remember anything. Leaving my father behind bars, scared and alone, to face the consequences of his excessive drinking wasn't easy, but at that time I thought it necessary.

Dad stayed there for seven days and was then transferred to a rehabilitation clinic. He later told me that the time he spent in jail is something that will remain in his memory forever. The lock-up – or 'can', as Dad called it – really was a foul, deplorable place. He was on medication for several service-related disabilities at the time and the impact of being confined, without access to an alcoholic drink, aggravated his medical and mental conditions, and brought on chronic claustrophobia. Those conditions have led to his being classified as a totally and permanently incapacitated veteran, so they were a significant affliction.

He mixed with some very colourful inmates there. Apparently, one told him all about the local drugs situation ('interesting'). Another always splattered his rubbery breakfast eggs on the ceiling of the cell – and not his own cell, either.

Dad read the book I'd given him, surprisingly. He said it was a great help. Its topics included hypnosis, and Dad became a dab hand, with the other prisoners even requesting he employ his recently acquired hypnotic skills on them. Everyone there wanted to remove themselves – however briefly – from the terrible place they were in.

There is no doubt that Dad has suffered in some ways for his vices. He always says that the three months of his life after 9 January 1989 were hell and he never wants to live through anything like that again.

*I believe he loves his family very much, although he has a
rather twisted way of showing it. His children interact with
him to this day, albeit from a distance, and I think all of us
realize that, although he is still living and breathing and has
his freedom, he lives in his own private hell.*

Stranded in Paris, with this news dribbling through in ever more
alarming updates, I felt totally cut off. All the information I got
was from our family friend, Corinne. No one would let me speak
to Mum because they didn't want anyone to know where she was,
in case it got back to Dad. My family in the safe house were only
allowed to communicate with certain people; I was classed as a
'friend' of my father's, so I had no idea how they were coping.

To make matters worse, my Parisian apartment didn't have a
telephone and there were no mobiles back then, so I had to rely
on public phones to find out what was happening.

The local Ballarat newspaper reported the incident under the
headline 'Shotgun Phil', so the whole town knew about the
dreadful lie we'd been living all our lives. I didn't bear any of the
brunt of it – neither the public scandal nor the private torment of
the family falling apart – because I wasn't in the country; it
certainly didn't make me want to go back. I longed to believe that
I'd escaped at last.

It's always a nasty moment now when 9 January comes round,
because it's no longer just Dad's birthday and Sue's anniversary;
forever more it's also 'Shotgun Phil' day.

On a positive note, the short spell in jail did Dad some good,
at least temporarily, because he stopped drinking for three years
after that and became a member of Alcoholics Anonymous. He
was even chair of AA meetings in Victoria, Australia, and also in
London, Ireland and Paris. He visited Sue when she lived in
France and she has really fond memories of our sober dad. They
even went to an AA meeting together. Sue stood up and said, 'My
name is Sue, and I am the daughter of an alcoholic.' In front of

everyone, she explained how Dad's drinking had affected her and how proud she was that he had stopped. She told me later that she wasn't bothered if the others were listening or not. All she cared about was whether Dad was.

Mum dropped the charges. By the time Dad was released from jail, she and the kids had moved to the shelter that Sue had organized; they wouldn't be coming back. Mum and Dad had separated before, but Dad would just take off and go grape-picking for three or four weeks and, on his return, she always took him back. Not this time. The episode was the final straw for Mum, and they never reunited.

After three dry years, Dad went back on the booze and never got off it again. It's ironic in many ways that he helped so many other alcoholics give up the drink when he was involved with the AA, but he just couldn't help himself. At least he wasn't abusing us or Mum any more.

These days, he approaches life 'one day at a time'. In addition to alcoholism, he's got skin cancer – from spending twenty years on-board ships without using any sort of sun cream – which keeps coming up all over his ears, his face and his arms. He gets it cut out, but it's left him quite disfigured.

I still visit him when I go back to Australia. He lives a reclusive life on a fish farm on the outskirts of Ballarat. He's in a big old place by himself with his 'friends': the yabbies (crayfish) and the trout. The family have learned to tolerate him. If we go there, we know he's going to get completely legless and that's what he wants to do. His attitude is 'take it or leave it'.

'If I have offended some, I apologize,' he told me as I was writing this book. He doesn't put on airs and graces, and he has no social skills whatsoever when he's drunk. That's my dad.

After 'Shotgun Phil', things weren't the same in Paris. I knew the time had come for me to move on from the Lido. So, I was thrilled to be taken on as the principal vocalist at the celebrated Moulin Rouge, in a show called *Formidable* – a role I saw as my chance to showcase my singing voice. Although the production was mimed, the company recorded the whole score and then lip-synched to that, so at least I would be faking to my own voice. I trained for three months and then went into a studio and laid down the tracks, in French.

The other principal singer was Debbie de Coudreaux, who was away when I recorded my lines. On her return, it seemed she didn't like the sound of our duet. The next thing I knew, my voice had been sacked from that song. The producers told me I could have my voice for all the other numbers, but not for the duet. They wanted to get a French session singer to do it instead. I offered to re-record it, saying, 'If Debbie's not happy, I'll do it again.'

Then I knocked on her dressing-room door and politely enquired, 'Are you unhappy with these vocals? If you like, perhaps we could re-record them.'

'No,' she replied, with her back turned to me. 'I'm very happy with mine!'

Again, I offered to redo the song and she looked at me in the mirror – not even straight at my face – and then raised her hand to dismiss me. She had been the one to complain and had got my voice demoted, so I was furious. I took my opening-night flowers and everything in my dressing room, and, on principle, walked out.

The next day, I refused to let them use my voice at all. They had to get Roland Leonar to record the whole show before that evening's performance.

After I threw in the towel, it was a pretty grim time, but that decision probably saved my life. If I hadn't walked out, I might still be on playback to this day, because Paris is enticing and it was a tempting contract with fantastic money. But would I have been happy? Most certainly not. Miming to my own voice, year after year, two shows a night, six nights a week, would get very dull indeed. It would have been professional suicide.

Nevertheless, at the time, things were difficult. I soon learned that principles don't pay the rent. Having stormed out of *Formidable*, I didn't have a valid *carte de séjour*, which is a resident's permit, as my Lido paperwork had long ago expired. I was told I had five days to get out of Paris. The Moulin gave me 10,000 francs (£1,000) to leave with, as a pay-off, so I had that to live on. I also had a flexible plane ticket, which was open-ended for a year. I decided to follow my original plan, which had been to do eight months at the Lido and then travel around Europe.

With such short notice before I had to leave France, I was forced to think quickly about where to go next. My sister Susan was still living in Sweden, where her husband David was based, so I decided to go and stay with them. Luckily, she was at home when I showed up – unlike I had been when they'd popped over to Paris for a visit a few months earlier.

I was so ditzy that I'd screwed up their trip dates so, when they arrived, I wasn't there to meet them from the train. To make matters worse, I'd gone out – and they had no idea where to find me. It was before the days of mobiles, so they had no choice but to wait. I didn't get home until four in the morning, when I found two very unhappy people sitting on my doorstep. I felt terrible and Sue's never let me live it down.

She did, though, let me stay with her when I turned up with all my worldly belongings in the wake of the Moulin saga. It was such a relief to see her after everything that had happened in our family. She and I raked over the events of 9 January at length, and generally put the world to rights. I also met my niece Izzi for the very first time. She was adorable; I felt ever so broody.

From Sue and David's house, I rang a guy called Clifford, whom I'd met in Paris, because he was the only person I knew who was living in London. I asked him if he knew of anywhere I could stay and said, rather hopefully, 'You did mention I could come to your place.'

Unfortunately, Clifford was in a squat at the time and he

replied, 'The squat's full, but I know a girl called Jane you could stay with.'

She later phoned to offer me a room and I thought she sounded really posh. Actually, she was Welsh, but I couldn't tell the difference.

Little did I know then that I had just spoken to my future wife.

CHAPTER 9 *London Lights*

When I first set foot in London, I planned to stay for a couple of months. If anyone had told me then that I'd still be here after twenty years, I would never have believed them.

Ever since my trip with Mr X, it had always been my intention to go back to visit London. I'd always had a soft spot for the UK and it helped that it was English-speaking, which was a huge relief to me after so long in Paris. There, my lack of French had been a real hindrance.

London was like home, only a lot busier. I loved the racially diverse nature of the city, which reminded me of Sydney, and I relished the pace of it. The downside was that it was very, very expensive and I only had £1,000. Though I'd been struck by the UK's affordability during my last stay, things had been different when Mr X was picking up the tab. It wasn't just cassette tapes I was paying for now. Once I'd shelled out a month's rent and a month in advance, my money was pretty much gone, so I resolved to leave when the rent was due again.

One look at *The Stage* newspaper was enough to change my mind. I couldn't believe my eyes. There were so many auditions compared to Australia, where you would hang around for six months waiting for one to arrive. There, most performers had to have another job because there were only two large-scale musicals a year so, if you missed out on those, you had to have something else to fall back on. In London, you could maintain a profession working in the theatre, which I thought was incredible. That's when I knew I would have to stay.

The decision meant an end to my relationship with Mr America – although it soon became clear he'd reached that point well before me. I'd wanted to continue the affair when I left Paris, even though I knew it would be difficult, loving one another long distance. We'd said our goodbyes, but as far as I was concerned we were still a couple.

The next time I saw him, however, it was apparent that he was already sleeping with other people. He flew over to London to visit me – and left me with a nasty surprise. I had to fly back to Paris to see a doctor with him, which wasn't the most pleasant way to break up with someone.

So Mr America stayed in France while I began a new life in London. I've since employed him as a dancer on a couple of occasions, and we're still really good friends, but I was heartbroken at the time.

Of course, the best cure for heartbreak is to achieve dazzling success. I threw myself headlong into the process of establishing my UK career. Visiting London all those years before had been so inspiring that I had my sights firmly set on the West End. I knew I wanted to work in the theatre and that I wanted to be someone. This was another piece of the puzzle that I had to decipher.

In the meantime, I was realistic enough to know that I had to get a job. I'd never waited on tables before, but I went to work in a restaurant called China Joe's in the Trocadero Centre, Piccadilly Circus. It had just opened so they were offering two weeks' training as a tray-and-trestle waiter. It was useful experience, although I had to work for nothing while I learned the trade.

At night, I worked the tables. During the day, I wandered around the West End, looking at all these amazing shows. It was truly a land of opportunity for an unknown actor, singer and dancer.

As the new boy in town, I didn't have an agent, so I tried to organize my own auditions. I heard on the grapevine that there were try-outs at the Prince Edward Theatre for *Anything Goes*, the musical based on Cole Porter's wonderful songs. I marched down to the theatre and handed in a CV and photo at the stage door. The doorman kindly passed them on ... and I was invited inside to audition.

When I'd finished, they asked me to learn the songs and come back. Unbelievably, I got down to the finals for one of the leading roles. I remember thinking, 'I'm *so* staying in this country!' I'd just waltzed in and managed to get a shot at stardom.

Unfortunately, the part went to a good-looking young actor called John Barrowman. I wonder where he is now?

Although I was disappointed at missing out on the role, the audition secured me an agent, which was a real breakthrough. I was asked to go to an agency called Talent Artists, where I met Jane Wynn Owen. While I sat in her office, being interviewed, a phone call came through from Hubbard Casting to say they were looking for a young Australian to play the lead role in a soap, so she said, 'I have just the chap.' She sent me off to Hubbard Casting and I ended up having five sessions with them.

Strangely, the character was a performer in *Cats*. It was perfect for me because I had to dance for the audition as well as act.

The soap was to be filmed in Germany, and though I got the job at this end, when Hubbard sent the tape of my screen test to the Germans, they said they wanted someone who looked 'more Australian'. They were looking for a blond, Aussie surfer type, not a bloke with my dark-haired, Latino appearance.

After the excitement of supposedly bagging the role, it was a horrible disappointment, though as it turned out, the soap was never made. Luckily, Jane was impressed enough to take me on and she became my first agent.

Actually, that was the second time I almost became a soap star. Back in Australia, I had landed a role in *Home and Away* that I never got to play. I'd just finished *Starkers*, in which I'd performed my first real acting role, with no singing, and had enjoyed it so much that I'd decided acting was the way to go. So, I started auditioning for things like *Neighbours* and *Home and Away*.

Finally, after loads of try-outs, I was offered an eight-week walk-on part in Summer Bay, just as I was going overseas. I had every intention of coming home from Paris to film it, but in the end I stayed and completed the contract at the Lido.

Appearing in a soap could have altered my life irrevocably – and not for the better in my opinion. My career path has been a slow, steady rise, with each job preparing me for the next one and becoming progressively more interesting.

Mind you, if I'd been an Aussie soap star, I might have been a contestant on *Strictly Come Dancing* or *Dancing with the Stars*, rather than one of the judges!

I waited on tables for only a month before I secured a part in the UK tour of *The Danny La Rue Show*. I was familiar with the production, of course, having completed that six-month stint with Danny in Australia and New Zealand several years before. Since then, I'd put on lots of muscle weight because I'd worked out for the Lido show; my self-consciousness about performing in a G-string every night had meant I'd gone to the gym religiously. I'd also grown up a lot – I hadn't really been much more than a boy on the previous tour. As soon as Danny saw me, he said, 'Oh Craig, I remember you from Australia and New Zealand. You've put on a bit of muscle.' Then he said, 'You don't need to audition, love. You've got the job.'

Clutching my first UK contract in my sweaty little hand, I made my way to the offices of Equity, the actors' union, to register Craig Horwood as a fully-fledged member of the show-business community. This was a moment I'd been waiting for my whole career.

Imagine my horror when I was told that I couldn't use my own name. There was another Craig Horwood already on their books and the rules of Equity are like *Highlander*: there can be only one. After the faff of becoming Trent Horwood the hairdresser and Craig Stevens the fitness instructor, it transpired that I couldn't be Craig Horwood the performer after all. Having protected my name for so long and so assiduously, I was mightily pissed off, but there was nothing I could do about it.

I had to decide, quickly, how I would be known in the trade. I considered using Revel Lancaster instead, employing my mother's maiden name as it sounded starry (or so I thought). But in the end, 'Craig Revel Horwood' got the slot. I was a bit worried that it might be too long, but in fact it turned out to be better and much more interesting than any made-up name.

The UK tour of *The Danny La Rue Show* was a shock to me. When you go on the road in Australia, the hotels are supplied, the transport is sorted and you are totally looked after (notwithstanding those occasions when you find yourself washing off your make-up in a horse trough). In the UK, they take you to the centre of each city in a bus, and then you have to go and find your own accommodation in some lowly guest house. I spent many an afternoon walking around looking for a bed for the night.

To this day, that still happens here, which is awful. Chorus dancers are not paid much to start with, so it's hard on them to have to find cheap digs everywhere they go.

Touring always throws up some interesting experiences, though, wherever you are. One of the landladies I stayed with in Australia, for example, was a total drunk who kept trying to kiss me. She was about eighty, and she used to put on her make-up like Bette Davis in *What Ever Happened to Baby Jane?* She was permanently slaughtered and one night she attacked me, desperately trying to snog my face off. She ended up chasing me around the room, jumping over furniture like a woman half her age. I was staying with her for a fortnight, so it made for a rather hairy two weeks!

It was somewhat poetic that Danny was the first to offer me a job when I got to London. He and I always got on very well. As

I've mentioned, it was he who originally named me Lavish. He gave me that title because I often used to borrow his personal hairdryer, which he thought was funny. I was never nervous of him at all, possibly because of the stage-fright incident on the Australian tour and the way he handled it. It's amazing that he ever hired me again, but he was very understanding and probably got me over it, to be honest, because he was able to help me out of the situation by making a joke. He was very quick and witty, and had enviable ad-libbing skills.

We had a riot on tour. That whole company loved their drink. We would have gin and tonics lined up in the wings and there was always champagne on the tour bus. Danny had the front of the bus and at eleven o'clock in the morning, the champagne cork used to pop. We were all sitting at the back and we'd hear the telltale sound and say, 'Oh, he's started!' But he was nice with it. I'd suddenly hear him shout, 'Lavish, come and look at the scenery with me.' So I'd go up to join him and he'd explain the British countryside to me.

With all that booze, he did put on a bit of weight. One night, his Dolly Parton costume gave up the ghost and ripped from top to bottom. As one of the boys in the chorus, I stood behind him for most of the show while he took centre stage. The whole of the back of the outfit was open; they couldn't zip it up. We carried on regardless, but it was quite a sight to behold, as we struggled to keep a straight face mid performance.

In theatre, it never rains but it pours. As soon as I started working on *The Danny La Rue Show*, I was offered a part in the UK tour of *Cats*, for which I'd auditioned before I'd landed Danny's gig. It was a once-in-a-lifetime opportunity for me and I simply had to do it. So, as it turned out, I toured with Danny for only one month.

He was not pleased about me cutting short my contract. It really upset the applecart. With barely any notice, it's difficult to find a 6-foot-2 performer who can sing, dance, act and do all the things that the show required, and keep the standard high. It also had to be someone who fitted the costume. You're not easily replaceable in a production like that.

In the end, I found someone myself, taught them the routines in my living room, and then paid their first week's wages, just so I could get out and take the next step in my career.

Despite his disappointment, Danny understood what a fantastic break it was. I was booked in the swing position, meaning that I was understudy for everyone. It was a huge challenge because I had to learn eleven different parts, but I was ready to take on the world at that point. As a bonus, of course, it was *Cats*, which was one of the first professional shows I'd ever seen. I'd thought since then that it was a phenomenal musical. I couldn't wait to get going.

The tour opened at Blackpool's Winter Gardens Theatre in May 1989 and, after six months there, transferred to Edinburgh and to Dublin. I was earning £220 a week, before tax and agent's fees. The salary you receive when you're starting out really is horrendous. By the time you've paid for rent, electricity, travel and other essentials, there's not a lot left. For that, I was doing eight shows a week and working my arse off.

Blackpool was the first place where I'd had to put money in a meter for electricity, which I thought was the weirdest thing I'd ever seen. The digs were terrible, but that's all we could afford on our low pay. Sometimes finding 50p for the meter was tough enough. But I was doing something I loved and I have always respected that, whatever financial recompense I've received.

During the tour, I very nearly succumbed to that old demon stage fright. I felt the familiar panic and went blank, but when I tried to speak, the words came out. I was playing Munkustrap one night, who starts the show by climbing out of a boot, moving in a feline way to centre stage and singing T. S. Eliot's wonderful line: 'Are you blind when you're born?' In this one particular performance, midway through the first act, I was climbing up to the top of the boot and I knew I had to deliver the famous 'twelve lines' in 'The Invitation to the Jellicle Ball', so I took a deep breath in … and I had nothing in my head. The chords that introduced my part finished. I opened my mouth – and, luckily, the words materialized. They came from muscle memory. I couldn't think of the lines at all. I was praying, 'Please don't let this happen to me again,' and thank God, it didn't.

A new job inevitably brought new romance. I fell madly in love with Mr Hull, an acrobatic dancer who was about half my size, and we enjoyed a luscious liaison. In Dublin, we were all staying at a place called Donnybrook Manor, which was a bizarre estate of rental homes in the middle of nowhere. They put us into two-bedroom apartments and I was sharing with Mr Hull and a girl, Nads, who coincidentally had been on the Learjet modelling gig with me when I was seventeen.

After the run ended, we all got on the plane back to London. I'd assumed that Mr Hull and I were going to set up home and live happily ever after. At the airport, we collected our bags and I said, 'Are you coming with me?'

'No,' said Mr Hull. 'I'm going with Michelle. I'll call you tonight.'

That was the last I saw of him for six months.

I kept calling him without success, I tried to contact his parents and I rang everyone I could think of, but he had simply disappeared off the face of the earth. I was devastated and actually quite worried, because I thought something awful might have happened to him.

Six months later, I randomly bumped into him outside a theatre in London.

'What happened?' I asked.

'Nothing happened,' he shrugged.

I discovered, much later, that he'd been in America with another boyfriend, but I was totally ignorant of this when I was trying to track him down.

He clearly had no idea how much the relationship had meant to me, and didn't seem to think he'd done anything to warrant an explanation. We went for a pint, but I never really got to the bottom of it.

Though romantically the *Cats* tour proved a bit of a damp squib, professionally it was a huge success, which put me in good stead with the iconic Cameron Mackintosh, the show's producer. That was the beginning of my long, yet not always harmonious, relationship with the West End's most powerful mogul.

While I was still in Dublin, an audition came up for *Les Misérables* in London, so I flew back to take a shot at it. My whole life I'd wanted to be in *Les Mis*. I hadn't been able to land a part in Australia, despite a brave attempt. Mind you, they wouldn't give me a job in *Cats* in Australia either. My old friend Gerard Symonds and I were both flown down from Sydney to Melbourne to audition, in direct competition with one another; he got the job and I didn't.

The director of the London production of *Les Mis*, Ken Caswell, called me back so many times that I was supremely confident the plum part of Enjolras, leader of the revolutionary students, was mine. Unfortunately, when the *Cats* tour finished, I discovered that I hadn't been successful.

Instead, the producers offered me the part of Admetus in the London production of *Cats*. It was only a dancing role and I wanted to sing as well, which was what I'd been doing for the last five weeks in Ireland as Munkustrap. So I said, 'No, I'm not interested in that.' My logic was that they would then maybe offer me *Les Mis*.

What a cocky so-and-so! They did nothing of the sort.

It had been a bold move – but then again, I knew what I wanted. I always knew what was right for me. Consequently, I was never scared of taking risks.

Luckily, the producers came up with another offer, which was *Miss Saigon* – my very first West End show. Although I'd had my sights set on *Les Mis*, the opportunity to join the cast of *Miss Saigon* was a gift. The show was in its first year, starring Jonathan Pryce and Lea Salonga, and it was huge. Everyone wanted to be in it, so it was actually better than joining a company that had been running for as long as *Les Mis*. I came into it through a sheer stroke of luck.

Jimmy Johnson, who is now quite famous in the theatre, had been cast as a singer and acrobatic dancer. When he left, they couldn't fill his part with just one person. There was no one else who could be both a tenor vocalist and an acrobat. So, they employed Louis Spence, who is now a judge on *Cirque De Celebrité*, to do the acrobatics and they hired me to sing and dance as a G.I.

Miss Saigon was seven months into its run when I became a member of the company in 1990. I'd seen the show when it opened and had totally fallen in love with it: I couldn't believe my luck.

I didn't have long to wait to prove myself. After two days of rehearsals, they were short of dancers in the big number at the end, which was the only part I'd learned by then. The dance captain, Tash O'Connor, had a hurried discussion with the associate choreographer, Maggie Goodwin, and said to me, 'You've learned that number, haven't you?' Then he slung me on stage. Fortunately, I was a quick study and could pick up routines in a very brief period of time. After being a swing dancer in *Cats*, the *Miss Saigon* 'American Dream' number was a doddle.

Standing in the wings of the Theatre Royal Drury Lane, about to perform on a West End stage for the first time, is a moment I will never forget. I stopped for a second to catch my breath. It was so big, it was amazing, but I could see the audience already enjoying the show, so I had no time to be nervous. All that was going through my head were the counts – 5, 6, 7, 8 …

Sadly, I can't remember the actual performance. I was too busy counting to know what was going on around me. Usually, I would have had more on my mind while I was dancing, but if you don't know a routine terribly well, you have to concentrate on the count or you will slip up. After you have performed it a few times, your body goes into muscle memory. When I was in *Crazy for You*, later on in my career, I could come off stage at the end and not even know I'd done the show. My body would sing and dance at all the right times, out of repetition, but my mind could be entirely elsewhere. It's rather dangerous and, at that point, it's advisable to change jobs.

At the end of my first performance in *Miss Saigon*, there were no fireworks or fanfares, just a quiet drink with the rest of the cast in the theatre bar. After all, they'd been doing the same thing every night for over half a year already.

Bizarrely enough, my wish to portray Munkustrap in the West End production of *Cats* was granted eventually. The show was on at the New London Theatre in Drury Lane; the Theatre Royal, where *Miss Saigon* was playing, backs on to Drury Lane. One evening, they'd run out of Munkustraps because they were all injured or sick, so the producer called me up and asked if I would go over the road and be a 'cat' for the night. It had been six months since I'd done it and it's a very wordy part, but I went through it in my head and I thought I could remember it all.

Of course, I had forgotten that *Cats* in London was in the round (where the audience sits on all sides of the stage). I'd never done it that way before. On tour, it was a proscenium arch show, meaning the audience faces the stage. That first night in London, I was completely disorientated. I did a speedy run-through before the performance, but then I just had to go on, without any further preparation. I didn't even meet the major cast members beforehand, so the first time I encountered Ria Jones, who was playing Grizabella, I was hissing at her on stage. Afterwards, I didn't know who anyone was because I'd only seen them in their cat make-up.

The stage was on a moving revolve. As usual, Munkustrap was

supposed to be popping out of the boot for his big entrance, but I had no idea where the boot was. I was running around backstage, saying to any 'cat' I could find, 'Where's the boot? Where's the boot? Where *is* the fucking boot?' I had to crawl into it to be able to pop out of it.

I finally found it at the very last minute, only to discover that it was a lot smaller than the one we'd used on tour. As I came out of it, I scraped the skin off my back and then had to jump out, walk forward and sing the opening line of the show. Luckily, I didn't feel a thing as I was on a major adrenalin rush, trying to zone back into the role I'd performed six months earlier. It was exhilarating not knowing anyone and just winging it.

The rest of the cast couldn't believe I'd simply walked in and done it. They thought it was amazing because it was my first experience in the round. In London, Munkustrap doesn't dance in 'The Jellicle Ball', which is the seventeen-minute high-energy finale of act one. Instead, he remains stationary on a rubber tyre at the back of the stage. However, on tour he's included in the choreography, so I just did what I had always done. The dancers were all whispering to each other mid routine: 'Munkustrap's come off the tyre. What's going on?' It was hilarious, but I was like a cat on acid that night. I was so wired. I was thoroughly exhausted after the performance, from sheer nerves.

For a whole month, I was doing four shows a week in *Miss Saigon* and four in *Cats*. There can't be many people who have been in two West End productions at once.

Most nights after the show, the *Miss Saigon* cast ended up in PJ's Bar and Grill, which is opposite the Theatre Royal Drury Lane. It's a restaurant, but we would put the chairs and tables round the outside of the room and then get up and dance. Ruthie Henshall was often my partner in crime on those nights. She was in the chorus with me and danced opposite me in the 'Dreamland' sequence – *Miss Saigon*'s opening ensemble routine, which is a drug-, drink- and sex-fuelled scene set in a very smoky bar, in which all the girls play prostitutes in bikinis. Ruthie and I used to get up to so much mischief together, on stage and off.

We were with a crowd in PJ's one night when I commanded, 'Come on, darling. White Cat Lift.'

That's a move from *Cats*, where you lift the girl with straight arms and she does the splits at the top, upside down. So we abandoned our chairs, I bunged Ruthie up there and she did the splits – only to reveal that she wasn't wearing any knickers, or so the present company told me. I could see nothing as her dress was well and truly over my face. There I was whirling her about, and she was doing the splits with her dress round her waist and no underwear. Everyone was screaming.

It was always an eventful evening in there. On one occasion, a lady from *The Woman in Black*, which was playing at the Fortune Theatre round the corner, stood up on the bar and started swinging from the chandelier into the centre of the room. She loved a drink and she was great fun.

That company was insatiable, partly because it was the first year of a new show. Additionally, they were all a bit pissed off because they'd anticipated massive roles, but *Miss Saigon* is really a group piece. Everyone thought it would be like *Les Mis*, in which nearly all the performers get some really nice individual bits to do, but *Miss Saigon* has five leads and the rest is chorus. The cast were a talented bunch, but quite frustrated.

We were fortunate that the show wasn't our only performance outlet. The cast were often asked to participate in various events for charity and publicity. One such task was to appear on *TV-am,* a breakfast programme that was popular in the eighties and early nineties.

Four of us were asked to take part in a live exercise class alongside the programme's fitness expert, Lizzie Webb. We were commandeered to do it in our costumes, which for the lads meant our army get-up. It was my very first TV appearance in the UK: doing a Jane Fonda-style workout live at 7 a.m. in my jungle greens, complete with army boots, dog tags, a pistol and a holster!

Lizzie led the routine and we followed her instruction to the music of the *Miss Saigon* song 'Solo Saxophone'. We were trying not to laugh as we did this very serious exercise plan, yet – as professionals – we were also really nervous in case we went wrong. Lizzie was great. Funny as it may seem, it actually looked really good when we saw it back. It certainly goes down as one of the more bizarre experiences I've had, and I remember it fondly.

Recently, Lizzie came across the video of that particular episode and, because she'd seen me on *SCD*, she sent it to me, along with a note saying: 'Remember this?' Oh, it made me howl with laughter.

As well as marking my debut on the West End stage, and on UK TV, *Miss Saigon* allowed me to fulfil another lifelong ambition – meeting Joan Collins.

Joan was playing in *Private Lives* at the Aldwych Theatre at that time. Keith Burns, who had the role of Thuy in *Miss Saigon*, arranged for her to switch on our company's 'Christmas lights'. Before she arrived, we adorned our dressing rooms with festive decorations and had a competition to decide whose was the best. Of course, all the queens in the dancers' dressing room won. It was a fantastic display, inspired by the opulent theme 'excess'.

As Joan came up the stairs – followed by fifty of her closest friends – the trumpeter from the band, who was standing at the other end of the corridor, struck up the theme from *Dynasty*. It was brilliant.

She came in and flicked the switch, and we all cheered with glee. We couldn't believe it. For me, it had always been a dream to meet her, and I wasn't alone in my aspiration. The amount of people who were squeezed into that corridor on the third floor would put a rush-hour Tube to shame. The eighties had just ended and *Dynasty* was finished, but she still had this massive profile and had recently launched her own perfume.

I even got to speak to her. I said, 'I'm one of your biggest fans.' (Original, I know.) It was true: I had modelled Lavish on the *Dynasty* look and everything Joan was about. That night, all I could think was, 'Oh my God! I've made it! I met Joan Collins!'

I managed to get hold of a round cardboard advertising sign promoting her new fragrance, which she signed for me. She wrote: 'To the boys in 20 [that was our dressing-room number at the Theatre Royal Drury Lane], much love, Joan Collins xxx.' I still have it at home. If you look very closely at the pictures in this book, you can just see it hanging up in the background of the photo of me at the Heartbreak Hotel.

Thus far, our paths have not crossed again, but I'm sure if death doesn't beat me to it, they will. Thinking about it, Joan would make a magnificent *Strictly Come Dancing* contestant. Over to you, Ms Collins ...

CHAPTER 10 *Miss Saigon and Mrs Horwood*

Life took a bizarre twist once I started *Miss Saigon*. I found myself falling for my flatmate, Jane. We'd been getting closer and closer since I first arrived in London, and now that my job was based in the big smoke rather than in random towns across the country, I was spending much more time with her. Gradually, our intimacy developed into a proper relationship.

Jane had in fact thought I was gay when we first met. That was because our mutual friend Clifford had told her, 'There's some drag queen coming over from Paris,' as he'd only ever seen me in my Lavish get-up at Halloween. So she was expecting a garish queen to turn up on her doorstep, but she got me instead. I did have matching floral luggage – God only knows why – but that was the extent of it.

Shortly after I moved in with Jane, we had a fantastic holiday together on Lundy Island, just off the coast of north Devon. She and Cliff and a few others had hired the Lundy lighthouse from the Landmark Trust and they happened to have a spare ticket. I'd only just arrived in the country, and had no money at all, but I couldn't resist.

Lundy Island was beautiful and I loved it. It was supposed to be a puffin sanctuary, but we didn't see one bloody puffin all the time we were there. Just loads of seals.

The lighthouse is a gorgeous old building and the island is

tiny, so everything was within walking distance. There was nothing much there except for a few cottages and a public house with a little store attached, but we had a crazy time, partly because one of our group had brought some dope with them. We sprinkled it on to bread-and-butter pudding and totally overdid it. We were all off our faces at the local pub, and I started tripping out. I was awash with waves of paranoia, thinking that everybody was staring at me and talking about me. It was awful.

Another night, we threw a party at the top of the lighthouse and invited all the inhabitants of the island. We had Madonna and the Gipsy Kings blaring out and, from somewhere, a whip was produced. One female friend was topless and being whipped, and then Clifford was whipping himself. I'm not sure the islanders had ever been to a party like that before.

We spent two weeks there and the break really solidified my burgeoning friendship with Jane. The downside was that I hammered my Australian credit card and got into horrible debt – again.

At the beginning of 1990, Jane and I became an item. We resided in a one-bedroom flat in Crouch End, which was very romantic – a bit like Robert Redford and Jane Fonda in *Barefoot in the Park*. She had a great social network, as did I, so we lived life to the full and maximized every moment of it. We had so much fun together. I loved her zany qualities, her appreciation for the arts, her outgoing nature, her ability to converse with anybody, her strength, her passion – even her Welsh accent.

Jane adored having a tan, so one day, as a surprise, I splashed out on a sunbed. We used to indulge in these luxurious tanning sessions – we'd sit there, playing footsie and drinking wine, while we soaked up the rays. The bed used slow-release bulbs, so it was impossible to burn. We lived in that thing, which seems terrible now, knowing as much as we do about skin cancer, but it was just so relaxing.

Eventually, I decided I was in love with Jane and, in a rash moment, I asked her to marry me. The proposal was not thought through at all; there was no getting down on one knee. I blurted it out one evening after dinner at our local Greek restaurant. To my surprise, she said yes.

Soon afterwards, we went together to the Wood Green register office to enquire about the wedding. We had a long discussion about the music and the other arrangements and then the registrar asked, 'When do you want to get married?'

We answered simultaneously. Only I said, 'Spring,' and Jane said, 'Summer.' She won, of course. We tied the knot on 20 August 1990.

The wedding was lovely, but very low-key. We didn't want a big fuss. My mum wasn't there, sadly, because my dad had chosen to come, as he tied in the trip with seeing some of his old friends from his navy years. He was accompanied by my sister Sue, her husband David, and their young daughter Izzi. A few close friends rounded out the numbers.

Dad wasn't drinking at the time, so we were getting on well. He was to be the barman at the reception, which I'm sure was a testing time for him, not to mention the rest of the family. We were all worried that he might start drinking again, but to his credit he stayed dry for the whole event.

I was so nervous when it came to the big day. I had been fine up until then – in fact, organizing the whole thing had brought Jane and I even closer together – but when it came to taking my vows, I was shaking like a leaf. I was trembling too much to get the ring out. Trying to place it on Jane's hand was another battle, as both our fingers had swollen up due to the hot weather and nerves, so the wedding bands were not exactly gliding on as one would have liked. I went into a bit of a panic at that point.

Finally, after a struggle and what seemed an eternity, Jane's ring went on. Then, as mine was being placed on my finger, she had to grab my whole hand to stop it from wobbling. I have never been more grateful to hear the words 'You may now kiss the bride' in my life.

After the ceremony, we held the reception in Hampstead at the New End Theatre, of which Jane was administrator at the time. It's an old mortuary, which sounds deeply inappropriate for a wedding reception, but it's a beautiful little venue that looks a bit church-like, so it was the ideal setting for us. Hampstead was also the very first place we went out together for a drink. We both loved the area as it was so picturesque. It was perfect.

Perfection appeared contagious at that stage in my life. No sooner had Jane and I tied the knot, I bagged a promotion at work that was to change the course of my entire career. Joining the company of *Miss Saigon* halfway through the first year proved an unexpected stroke of luck. Not long after I came in, there was a full cast change, so some of those who had been employed from opening night left. As I was staying on, I was offered the position of dance captain, which I took and relished for two years. Later, I was also asked to be the swing, meaning my performance role changed every night. Variety really is the spice of life, so that kept everything interesting.

As dance captain, my job was to look after the whole company, deal with last-minute changes and help new recruits to learn the steps. I loved it because it kept my brain as well as my body busy. If people were sick, or anything changed, it was my task to go round the cast and tell them about the differences in the show, and generally maintain the production. The dance captain also had responsibility for informing the stage management how many props were needed, where and at what time, and which ones should be removed if they were not being used in a particular performance. It involved thinking about the entire theatrical behemoth, not just your own tiny part in the show, so I became much more aware of the bigger picture behind the scenes.

Another duty was to give notes on people, telling them what they were doing right and wrong; the role taught me how to deliver criticism of the constructive kind. Believe it or not, being a dance captain honed my people skills and made me aware of the importance of diplomacy in delivering feedback. I'm not sure the *Strictly* contestants quite appreciate that particular string to my bow!

My first task in the job was to teach the incoming company the choreography. The day before their technical run-through, all the new dancers were watching the live show to see the routines they would soon be doing themselves.

We were set to perform the 'American Dream' number, for which I wore a really flash, blue, 1970s-style suit with sequins. I said to the attentive gang ahead of time, 'Whatever you do, don't look at anyone else on stage except for me. I'm the only one doing it the right way.'

I was always one of the first company members out on stage, so I was easy to spot. All the men played johns in that routine – clients of the prostitutes in the show. I was with the first johns, who were usually the best dancers. After us came the second johns, who danced almost as well, and then the third johns, who were the singers. The person who couldn't dance at all (the Chris Parker of the production) went into the limousine that flew in during a dream sequence and operated that.

That evening, I was gasbagging on the telephone upstairs in the dressing room when I suddenly heard the music for 'American Dream' start up.

'Oh my God! I'm so late,' I thought, as I ran downstairs. I threw myself out on to the stage and went straight into the routine.

I had misjudged my cue. Jonathan Pryce was on stage singing and I had jumped out from the wings and started dancing my socks off – at completely the wrong time. I'd told the whole company to watch me and then got it totally wrong. Poor Jonathan must have wondered what the hell was going on.

Jonathan is lovely to work with and hugely talented, but he can be a bit bossy in my opinion. He used to get on the tannoy backstage and give us all notes. I worked with Jonathan again on a Christmas album, which was good fun, and he took part in *Hey, Mr Producer!* the 1998 tribute to Cameron Mackintosh's work, in which I was also involved. Claire Moore, who played Ellen in *Miss Saigon*, was wonderful too. She always had a glass of Chardonnay before the performance 'to lubricate the throat', she'd say.

In 1991, I was dancing in *Miss Saigon* when we did a charity performance for the Entertainment Artistes Benevolent Fund, which Queen Elizabeth The Queen Mother attended. Afterwards, we assembled in an orderly fashion to meet her. As the receiving line took place immediately after the show, we were all still wearing our costumes and some of the girls were in their hookers' attire, so it was quite a surreal moment.

We met her on the stage itself, which had a six-foot rake. This meant it was on an extreme slope so that the audience could see the whole performance. The actors and dancers are essentially working on a hill, but we quickly get used to it. The poor Queen Mum had to walk horizontally across it. The rake changes the gravitational centre in your body, so you tend to start moving downhill; the receiving line was going further down the slope with each hand she was shaking. But, bless her, she coped really well and she was very sweet.

She was so small that she had to crane her neck a bit to talk to me. She said, 'I really enjoyed the show. Thank you.'

It was lovely to meet her, and I was so glad the moment was captured on film – it's a photo I've kept to this day.

Another treasured memento, for very different reasons, is a picture of three generations of *Miss Saigon*'s dance captains: Tash O'Connor (who moved up to resident director when I took over the job), me and my friend Gerard Casey. Sadly, I am the only one of the three who is still alive.

Tash was HIV positive when he went back to his hometown in New Zealand and died. Though he'd been formally diagnosed, no one knew he was ill. He would drink himself into oblivion every night on Jack Daniels and coke. He'd prop up the bar all evening and then come backstage, hammered. We all loved him. He was such a party animal, really great fun and hugely talented.

Gerard died at thirty-five from an unknown cause. It was dreadful, probably one of the biggest shocks of my life because we were very close mates.

His death came out of the blue. I'd seen him only three days before in Amsterdam, where he was performing in *Die Fledermaus* and I was working on *Titanic: The Musical*. Gerard was due to come to our run-through on the Saturday, but was suddenly taken ill and rushed back to London. A couple of days later, I got a phone call, saying that he'd died. I could not believe it.

The funeral was so sad. I couldn't stop crying the whole day. I thought I would be fine, but as soon as I saw the coffin, I thought, 'Oh my God, Gerard's in there. It's real,' and it all kicked in.

Whenever I look at that photo, it makes me immensely sad to think of two incredible talents taken from us at such a young age. It also makes me grateful that I'm still here.

Time passed on *Miss Saigon*. The moment came when Jonathan Pryce decided to move on, so he had a leaving bash. The redcoats from the theatre, as usual, served the drinks. They are the guys who do front-of-house meet-and-greets and look after royals and dignitaries in the champagne rooms.

As I chatted to various members of the cast, one of the redcoats came up beside me and accidentally spilt champagne over my shirt. 'I'm so sorry,' spluttered the flustered server. Any irritation I might have felt disappeared when I turned round to look at him, only to see the most gorgeous guy I had set eyes on in quite a long while. That was the first time I met Lloyd.

At that stage, things were magical between my wife and me, but my feelings towards men had not entirely jumped ship. Nevertheless, I brushed them off and didn't think about Lloyd until several months later, after my relationship with Jane had hit the rocks in spectacular fashion.

Despite the perfect wedding, the marriage, as it turned out, was not quite so flawless. It didn't last, mainly because our sex life diminished somewhat and I suppose that led to the inevitable scenario – Jane slept with someone else.

I discovered the affair just before our two-year anniversary. We had a friend whom we called Lightning, on account of his not being very quick off the mark, and I found out that they were sleeping together. I moved out and he moved in.

We are friends now, Jane and I, but it wasn't very amicable at the time. It got really stressful and silly. She even chucked my fridge down the stairs. I'd asked for my fridge back and I got it – on the pavement. It was horrible and we didn't talk for a long while. It all seems so petty now, looking back, but at the time I was very hurt. Thoughts raced through my mind as to who was at fault and why: I blamed myself, I blamed Lightning, I blamed Jane … Frankly, it was just a big mistake. I thought I could have everything – the wife, the kids and the boys – but I was immature and needed this lesson to grow up and be true to myself.

The divorce, of course, was very difficult to cope with. You see your future just torn up and dropped in the gutter. It was all so technical as well, with paperwork flying backwards and forwards, and it drove us to distraction. We both wanted an easy annulment, but there is no such a thing, that I had to learn.

Jane's relationship with Lightning came to an end after a few years and she was devastated. That's when we became mates again and knew truly how much we adored each other. Now we can go out for lunch and talk about life honestly. I love her deeply as a friend, now and forever, and wish her all the happiness in the world. She has since remarried and has a beautiful son with her second husband.

After my split from Jane, my path again crossed Lloyd's. This time, I was free to explore my feelings for the handsome redcoat. I couldn't wait to see what happened next.

CHAPTER 11 *Jacaranda and the Heartbreak Hotel*

L loyd, it transpired, was not just a pretty face. As well as working at the theatre, both on front of house and as a backstage fireman, he was studying to be a lawyer. All the girls and several of the boys in the company had spotted this eligible bachelor and were saying things like, 'Who's that cute guy on off prompt? Who's the fireman? Someone needs to go and ask him out.'

Gerard Casey decided that it would be me, even though I was convinced that Lloyd was married or had a girlfriend. For some reason, I assumed he was straight, despite our instant chemistry over the spilt champagne.

Towards the end of the performance that night, in a break before the 'American Dream' number, I plucked up the courage to attempt Gerard's dare. My objective in the task was to get Lloyd to come out drinking with us after the show.

As Lloyd was at law school, my opening gambit was to ask advice on getting a divorce! Then I said, 'Do you want to come out with us tonight?' as a general invitation. It was my dear friend Tracey Odell's birthday and we were all going over to PJ's Bar and Grill – but I had double-booked myself, as I always do, and had also promised another pal, Ali Kane, who was a dresser on the show and the best mate of Gerard, that I would go to a party at her house.

I was successful in my ploy, and persuaded Lloyd to come to the grill with me. Still thinking he was straight, I said to Tracey, 'I've brought you a birthday present, darling – this cute guy from backstage.' She was single at the time, so I thought it would be a nice gift for her. We still laugh about that. I brought her a birthday present ... and ended up keeping him for myself! Lloyd and I celebrated Tracey's birthday, then went to Ali's party where, to my surprise, we shared a sneaky kiss in the kitchen.

After that, we were always together. It was a marriage made in heaven. We both adored cooking, good food and good wine. We had similar tastes in art and design. We longed for beach holidays and appreciated spectacular views. We stuck up for each other and offered support when either one of us was broke, stressed or down. I had never been so happy.

Eventually, we moved into our own place, a very expensive studio apartment in Russell Square, which was really handy for *Miss Saigon.* The rent was £650 a month, which isn't extortionate for London now, but back then, it was a fortune. My take-home salary was around £180 a week, and with Lloyd still at law school, it wasn't easy.

It was a tiny flat, too, with a Murphy bed – one of those beds that folds out from the wall – and a kitchen that was literally the size of a cupboard. The stairwell cupboard in my current house has the same dimensions. The sink was so low that I had to stand with my legs in second position just to do the washing-up.

It did have a lovely big bathroom, though, and it was located in a place called Endsleigh Court, which had huge revolving doors and a very swish entrance, so it felt like we were living in a hotel. The studio flats came off the landings and it was fabulous living there – but finding the money to pay the rent every month was a constant challenge.

I was £800 overdrawn and in such economic dire straits that my bank manager would only give me money if I made an encashment call once a week, when he would give me an advance of £50. Out of that, I had to pay £12 for a travelcard and the other £38 had to last me the entire week. We couldn't afford to go out because I was paying back the terrible debt that I'd run up, which seemed enormous. Since then, I've been £125,000 overdrawn through various business ventures, but at the time, £800 felt like millions.

In those days, you had a personal contact at the bank, so you could talk to them if you had money problems. Mr Cooper, who was my liaison, was really nice to me because I got him free tickets to *Miss Saigon*. He looked after me after that.

There was a time when all we could afford to eat were sausages. We bought some of those horribly cheap packs, sixteen for 99p, and lived on sausage and mash for a whole month. To vary it, I would try to make a pie with them, but it was still just horrendous. We also made cottage pie with really cheap mince, which used to swim in fat. Actually, that was very tasty – but the calories!

Those culinary escapades put me off mince and sausages for a long time, as we always had to buy the awful economy variety, which are mostly fat and offal. They put all sorts in cheap sausages. Of course, when Britain was in the grip of its mad-cow disease scare, Lloyd and I would say to each other, 'If anyone is going to get it from bargain-basement meat, it'll be us.'

Oddly enough, sausage and mash is still one of my favourite meals: great comfort food.

Although we were still broke, in the winter of 1992 Lloyd and I took some time off and went on a trip to Australia for six weeks, which was wonderful. We travelled to Ballarat, so that Lloyd could meet my family, and we went to Sovereign Hill and Lake Wendouree, where we fed the swans. We visited Sydney and saw some old friends, and just generally explored the country.

Returning from that marvellous holiday meant coming down to earth with a huge bump. We'd spent so much while we were away that there was no way we could afford the rent at Endsleigh Court any more. Added to which, we came back to hundreds of bills, final reminders and demands – we could hardly open the door for brown envelopes. The landlord said he was going to kick us out and wanted the money straight away, so I had to take a wad of cash to him in person.

About to become homeless, we rang a couple of friends in despair. Happily, they agreed that we could move in with them in Belsize Park. There were four of us sharing a three-bedroom flat for £50 a week each, which was much more like it.

Unfortunately, this solution lasted only six months because we were, unintentionally, the neighbours from hell.

The property was a first-floor conversion in Park Hill Road. It was stunning. We shared with a friend we called Lady Kath, who was a dresser at *Miss Saigon*, and Nigel Shilton, a stage manager, so we all worked at night. We would come home and put on our washing at some ungodly hour in the morning and the whole place would shudder when it got to the spin cycle. The people downstairs were renovating and they didn't have a proper ceiling, so the noise in their apartment was awful. Even if we just walked across the floor, they grumbled. They would bang on the ceiling with brooms and we had people screaming into our video entryphone. We'd come home from work and cook a full meal and chat, which is normal for those of us employed in the theatre, but the people downstairs hated it. The complaints got so bad that we had to move out.

This time, we found a fantastic house in Pratt Street, Camden. It was a six-bedroom house, though, and we needed more people if we were going to be able to afford it. So we rang Clifford, who had been my first contact in London, and who had since become a very close friend, and asked him if he wanted to move in with me, Lloyd, Lady Kath and another friend, Cayte Williams, who is now a journalist. Nigel decided to get his own place.

The house was huge and always full of the most eclectic bunch of weirdos. Clifford – whom we nicknamed Clifftops because of his towering wavy hair that must have added, at the very least, an extra 10 inches to his already impressive 6-foot-4 frame – named it the

Heartbreak Hotel. He even painted a sign to place outside, which is still there today.

Of course, once he'd put the sign up, people thought it was a brothel. We did have a red light inside as well, which I guess did nothing to refute the suggestion. By chance, there was a lady next door who was definitely selling her body, so when people saw the 'Heartbreak' sign, they assumed that our house was hers. We had guys knocking on the door at all hours of the night.

The neighbourhood also boasted an old vagrant lady, whom we nicknamed Cilla because she used to sit on our windowsill and chat to us through the casements.

We were like a family. There was Clifftops, Cayte, Lady Kath, Lloyd and myself, and there was always one room whose occupants were transient, with people moving in and out. We kept the final bedroom as a communal space and general living area. It was like student accommodation, only a lot more glamorous. We painted murals all over the walls and frequently changed the decor. It was a bit run-down, but instead of dusting, we'd paint.

That approach to cleanliness didn't solve everything, obviously. One morning, we found three dead mice at the bottom of the Dualit toaster. They were totally mummified and we had no idea how long they'd been there.

On one occasion, we painted the whole of the downstairs red and the entire upstairs blue, with white sheeting forming big fluffy clouds, and then threw a Heaven and Hell party. There were people arriving in coffins, burning crucifixes and dressed as the Ku Klux Klan. It was an insane party, but just one of the many wild times we had there.

One Christmas, we decorated the upstairs like a medieval hall and hosted another shindig. At the end of the night, Cayte came walking down the stairs, carrying a flaming candelabrum. Suddenly, one side of her hair went up in smoke. I was shouting, 'Cayte, Cayte, your hair's on fire!' but she had no idea because she was so drunk.

That house was pure chaos. Jasper Conran, Ruby Venezuela and all the other queens from Madame Jo Jo's (a Soho club with a drag cabaret) were regular visitors. We crammed so many people into the place that the ceiling would bow under the weight. I was waiting for an entire party of sixty people to fall through the floor.

One of the original Heartbreakers was Michael de Souta, whom Clifftops always called 'Michael de Squatter' – one, because he was on the dole, and two, because he acted more like a squatter than a flatmate; we'd only ever see him when he left his room for a cup of tea. He would hole himself up in the box room on the third floor and sit and write hundreds of songs. Every morning, like clockwork, he'd announce he'd written another one the night before.

He was a lovely man, but he always moaned bitterly about our late-night BBQs. We would have barbecues out the back all the time. The garden had a huge built-in barbie and we would break up and burn various bits of furniture that were falling apart. Michael said on one occasion, 'The whole house stinks of smoke,' and it did, but his complaint simply became one of our catchphrases every time we sparked up the BBQ.

It was at the Heartbreak that Clifftops and I invented 'flick the switch' parties. They were basically normal social gatherings … where we attempted to get everybody naked and into the bath at once. We'd say to each other, 'Have you flicked the switch?' which meant, 'Have you put the immersion heater on?' The first thing we would do when we arrived at a house party was to look for the switch, then, after a few drinks had been consumed, we'd fill up the bath and persuade everyone to climb in it.

We had quite a success rate. Very rarely did anyone chicken out. It's surprising how many people actually do it. It starts with two or three of you in the bath and, after a while, everyone just joins in. We had about six bath parties and they were hilarious.

On one occasion, there were six or seven of us in the bath

and we ran out of booze. Everyone was saying to me, 'Come on, Lav, get us a drink.' So I said I would, if they all performed a certain act on me. They were so desperate for beer that they did – and the awful thing was that when I got to the fridge, there was none left.

When I went back and told them there wasn't a drop of alcohol in the house, oh, how they screamed at me!

We always hosted over-the-top, theatrical parties. The Heartbreak had a real carnival atmosphere. Our street despised us because the music was always blaring until six in the morning and weird things often happened there, but we adored the whole adventure.

After two-and-a-half years on *Miss Saigon*, as dance captain and performer, it was time for a new adventure on the professional front. I joined a show playing at the Prince Edward Theatre called *Crazy for You*, which starred Ruthie Henshall. It was terrific to be working with her again.

Crazy was a magnificent musical, with loads of snazzy Gershwin numbers, which I loved because they inspired wall-to-wall dancing. It opened to fabulous reviews in March 1993.

The one drawback about it was the awful Russian costume I had to wear. It included a pair of horrendous maroon tights, which featured in a serious wardrobe malfunction that beset me one night.

For someone who has always been paranoid about my arse being flabby, having to execute a tap routine on corrugated iron with my back to the audience was a regular nightmare. Imagine my horror at this performance when, as soon as I began the sequence, my tights split. My bottom was hanging out in front of the entire theatre. I was mortified. Then I came off stage and some kind soul took a photograph of it – thank you, Edwina Cox.

Towards the end of the run, Ruthie and I were offered the Australian production and I thought, 'Here's a ticket home. That will be handy.' I'd signed only a one-year contract for *Crazy for You* in London because I didn't want to do a long stint again in a single show, having just come out of a lengthy run in *Miss Saigon*. As much as *Saigon* was a challenge, I don't agree with staying in shows for prolonged periods because I think you stop learning.

So Ruthie and I said 'yes' to Australia and our London jobs were assigned to other performers. Strangely enough, my role went to Gerard Symonds, one of my best mates from Oz, who had also taken my place in *Miss Saigon* when I moved to *Crazy for You*. Gerard stepped into my shoes and then, to my horror, the Aussie production fell through. I remember coming into Ruthie's dressing room and saying, 'Ruthie, darling, have you heard?' She said, 'No, heard what?' And I had to drop the bombshell: 'The Australian show's not going on. We're totally jobless.'

Both Gerard and Helen Way, Ruthie's replacement, had already been contracted, so there was no way she could go back to the leading role and it was impossible for me to get my dance captain post back. We were completely out of work.

Miss Saigon offered me my old job, but I turned it down because I didn't want to go backwards in life. Consequently, I ended up having three months off. It was a terrible worry because I had taken a major salary cut for *Crazy for You* anyway. I'd been back to chorus wages – £350 or £400 a week – so I didn't have much spare cash to fall back on. I had to find work, and quickly.

Somewhat bizarrely, I turned to my childhood passion for creativity and became an artist. Believe it or not, I had a very successful art exhibition. Perhaps I shouldn't have been surprised at that outcome given my previous form as winner of the Ballarat colouring competition!

I became involved with a company called Artbite, through the efforts and contacts of the *Crazy for You* company manager Nick Bromley – who was acting as my art agent and who encouraged me to pursue my talents in the field – and my friend Suzi Rapoport, with whom I shared a floor at the exhibition. Suzi is a dear friend of mine, and an amazing poet. We met through Clifftops, and she was always at the Heartbreak parties. I will be forever in her debt for introducing me to the world of London art.

Suzi has always been a great support throughout my years in England, and not just when I was down on my luck. She has a heart of gold. She's the type of person you can have a fun time with and she brightens the day if you're feeling low. It really was an honour to do the exhibition with her.

Artbite wanted a water theme to coincide with the Henley Regatta, so my whole collection was inspired by the River Thames. I did two months' work and sold the lot in one day of exhibition. Thankfully, I made enough money to pay my rent for the time that I wasn't employed in the theatre.

At this point, I said to myself, 'This is the opportunity to change your life completely. This is when you start saying "no" to chorus and just go for leading roles.' If the leads didn't come, I reasoned, I'd choose another profession. I knew the only way I could pursue this approach would be with a major acting course under my belt, so I signed up at the Actors Centre, a training academy in the centre of London.

Soon afterwards, the gold phone rang in the Heartbreak Hotel. We all had our own personal phones in the bedrooms, but this was our communal work phone. When we did up the house, we spray-painted it gold and gave it a jewel-encrusted handset. We never answered it, though, because that was also the number we gave to our banks – and none of us were going to like anything they had to say! As soon as it rang, the whole Heartbreak would freeze in panic.

This time, however, I picked it up. It was fortunate that I did because it was Susan Stroman, the choreographer of *Crazy for You* on Broadway, calling from New York. In her stateside drawl, she purred, 'Hey Craig, how ya doing? Are ya working?'

I told her I'd just put on an art exhibition that had gone very well, but she simply asked in response, 'Do ya remember all the steps from *Crazy for You?*'

I said I certainly did. She asked me if I had the show written down and notated, which, as the former West End dance captain, I did.

Then Mike Ockrent, who was the director of the show, came on the line. Mike is an award-winning director with Broadway and West End successes such as *Me and My Girl*, which earned several Tony Awards, to his name, so I was a bit dazzled to be speaking to him one-to-one. 'You don't, by any chance, have all the direction written down as well, do you?' he queried.

'Well, yes, I do,' I said enthusiastically. 'I've taken down the whole show – every scene, every entrance and exit.'

'Great,' he replied. 'We'd like you to put the show on in South Africa because we're too busy to take it there. Can you get to New York by Monday?'

It was Saturday morning, so I had one day to organize myself, but I wasn't going to pass on an opportunity like this. I was in the Big Apple bright and early on Monday morning and went straight into rehearsals with the Broadway company. From there, I joined the touring troupe in Baltimore, to study the off-Broadway American version of the show, and became equal dance captain with Stacey Todd Holt. I learned the New York production and the touring adaptation so that, combined with my West End experience, I had all three variants up my sleeve. With that broad knowledge, I could take the show to South Africa and stage it with a whole new cast.

Before South Africa, the American company and I played in Berlin for three months over the summer of 1994. It was oppressively hot, but I was really fit at that time, so I felt good about myself. I took a tap class every day with the cast. I have to confess that I'd thought myself a bit of a charlatan when I'd been in the show in the West End, as my tapping wasn't up to scratch; I'd had the mind of a dance captain, but not the feet. I had to put in very long hours and work really hard to learn another discipline that late in life. I was twenty-nine – no small age for a dancer, a fact of which I was becoming ever more aware.

Of course, it wasn't the first time I'd tapped in my career, but it had never been a strength of mine. In *Sugar Babies*, back in Australia almost a decade before, I'd even been told that if my tap-dancing didn't improve, I'd be out. So I would go into the studio at 8 a.m. every morning before the main rehearsal and tap for two hours, which was exhausting.

There's always some compromise in casting musicals; I was employed in that musical because I was a tenor. The boys in *Sugar Babies* have to sing in close harmony in a barbershop quartet, and I happened to fit in with the voices. Unfortunately, I wasn't a strong tapper. It was a nightmare because I really thought I was going to be sacked. It made me feel that I was a terrible dancer, but then again, I'd never had any formal training in tap, past the bare minimum at Tony Bartuccio's, so I couldn't really help my inadequacy. It didn't come as easily to me as other forms of dance, though. I used to get frustrated with it and not practise enough. But with tap, you simply have to go that extra mile. I wanted to enjoy it, so I decided to use those months in Berlin to train myself.

I was in the right company because Americans really can tap. They are phenomenal – like they were born with tap shoes on their feet. The best have had the steps passed down from generation to generation and it's always fast, like Ann Miller. Her tap was like a machine gun going off. I wanted to tap-dance like that and I wouldn't be happy until I did. So, instead of hiding and pretending I could do it, I exposed myself to the group and really started to improve. I gained confidence and conquered my fear, so I was all set to go to South Africa and say, 'This is how we want it,' and give a flawless demonstration.

South Africa was brilliant. It gave me the experience of mounting a show and, although it was someone else's choreography,

I had to use communication skills I didn't know I had to teach the routines. It's a difficult musical with a lot of steps, so it was a real challenge.

We were staying in Pretoria, which is the dullest part, but I still loved the country. Cape Town, where we later transferred, is absolutely beautiful. Even in Pretoria, there are jacaranda trees everywhere and, in October, every street is decked in the most amazing mauve blossom. It is a stunning sight.

We were there from October to December. I was staying in a gorgeous hotel, with a big swimming pool on the roof. Every morning, I'd get up really early and go for a swim, then sunbathe between 7.30 and 8.30, before going to work at 9 a.m. to prep for the rehearsals. I'd dance all day long, then in the evening I'd go out for huge, delicious dinners with Lisa Kent, who was associate director. We had wonderful weather, good company and loads of fun. I was living the life of Riley and loving every minute.

I hadn't earned money for months, except for the proceeds of my art exhibition, so suddenly I felt incredibly wealthy. I had £10,000 paid straight into my bank account, which was a hell of a lot of money to me.

In 1994, of course, South Africa was going through major – and painful – political change. Apartheid had come to an end and Nelson Mandela had been elected President in the first free election, but there was still a lot of violence, particularly in Johannesburg. In Pretoria, where the majority of the population were of Dutch descent, it was fine, while Cape Town was more like a holiday resort.

When we visited Johannesburg, however, there was a definite threatening undercurrent. We just didn't feel safe in certain areas. There were news reports of racial violence every day and the white South Africans were still learning how to cope with the new order. Some took it in their stride, but others, those of the old school, kept on treating their maids like slaves. I guess you can't expect people's mindsets to change overnight.

Two years after *Crazy for You* finished, I went back to South Africa to scout for talent on behalf of producer Cameron Mackintosh, when we were trying to put together an all-black company of *Les Misérables*. I also went out to see if it would be worth setting up a Cammac School there, to train people in musical theatre, because at that point South Africa was importing musicals. Disappointingly, at the time we couldn't find enough people to warrant it.

Theatre is much bigger there now. A lot of tours go through, but they are also originating their own shows, like *Umoja*, which is a musical based on traditional African dance.

In all, I was away for seven months with *Crazy*. It was the first time, since meeting Lloyd, that I'd been abroad that long. Because he came to Berlin to visit, our longest spell apart was actually three months, just while I was in South Africa, but it was still a difficult experience. He complained that I wasn't phoning enough, but there were no mobiles then so I had to call from the hotel, which cost a fortune.

After I came back, I was working in the West End again, which made us stronger than ever. Or so I thought.

CHAPTER 12

Hey, Mr Producer!

C*razy for You* was my first taste of being on the other side of the fence and calling the shots. I knew I had found my vocation.

I thought to myself, 'This is exactly what I want to do. I'm absolutely loving it.'

The South African production was a huge success. As a result, Cameron Mackintosh offered me the position of resident director on *Miss Saigon*, so I went back for a year. I took over from Matt Ryan, when he went out to stage the show in Australia. He taught me a lot and showed me how to deal with companies in that role, which was brilliantly helpful. He's really creative and I took my lead from him in making the job my own.

Before starting on *Miss Saigon*, there was a gap of a month or so. To pay the bills, I took on some shifts working as a waiter at The Engineer in Primrose Hill. I was helping my friend Tamsin Olivier, Laurence Olivier's daughter, to kick-start her restaurant. Lloyd was the manager, which he fitted in around his law studies, and Clifford was also working there. I mucked in for a month and I really enjoyed it. It didn't have the pressure of performing, but, oddly enough, I used to get nervous before a shift. My old fear of making mistakes in a restaurant environment came back to haunt me.

One evening, I looked at the reservations and saw that a Mr Hytner had booked a table for four. I thought, 'Please don't let it be Nicholas Hytner.' He had been the director on *Miss Saigon* when I was dancing there and now I was waiting on tables. I couldn't bear the embarrassment.

Sure enough, of course, Nicholas Hytner rocked up at the door.

'Oh, hello Nick,' I said, breezily. 'How are you? Let me show you to your table.'

'Are you working here?' he asked, somewhat surprised.

'Yes,' I said. 'As a matter of fact, I am. But I'm leaving in a week to become resident director of *Miss Saigon*.'

Thank goodness I had landed that job before he came in. I was still on the back foot, but at least I could throw that into the conversation.

Actually, it was lovely working in the restaurant. It was all very showbiz. Tamsin's mum, Joan Plowright, and Maggie Smith used to pop in, while Kylie Minogue had dinner there. Adam Ant was always visiting, drinking his alcohol-free beer, and it was loads of fun. If you've got to earn money, after all, you have to have a job, and I'm not proud. I could end up there again, you never know.

After my stint on *Miss Saigon*, I became involved with a show called *Martin Guerre*, which was to put me on the map as a choreographer. That musical really got me noticed in the business, even though I was working under a colleague's name and umbrella, that of Bob Avian. It's quite common for a choreographer to have a couple of assistants, and Maggie Goodwin and I were his. I generally work without one now, but I have had excellent assistants in the past.

Bob won the Olivier Award for Best Choreography for *Martin Guerre* in 1997. Maggie and I went to collect it at the official ceremony on his behalf because he was in America at the time. As a team, we worked well together. Maggie and I came up with some of the choreography in the production, through workshopping it together in breaks. Lots of that material made it into the actual show, so we were both thrilled.

I guess my instinct for choreography began developing when

I used to devise my own routines for Lavish on the drag circuit. I always adored making stuff up, but it's difficult to be objective when you're the only one dancing your material. I believe you need a second eye on it to be able to judge its merit.

What I discovered on *Martin Guerre* was that I felt very passionate about particular moves and understood why they would work to help to tell a story. I became almost obsessive about certain rhythms and beats within the score, and felt proud that what I was doing felt like it was working in context. Of course, it was a combined effort from all of us in the company that brought the narrative to life and made it work; one could never in my mind be so bold as to take sole credit, as it is collaborations that make it all work.

Martin Guerre starred Iain Glen as the lead in the first year and Hal Fowler, who is married to Kim Wilde, the following year. The director was Declan Donnellan, co-founder of the Cheek by Jowl theatre company, and he was superb.

Ken Caswell was associate director, so he and I were finally working together, after he turned me down for *Les Mis* all those years before – and ruined my life! (I'm being theatrical, of course, he didn't really; I just like to tell him he did.)

Despite the artistic brilliance of those involved in the production, it was a tense time. Declan is a master director – I love how he operates, to the extent that I have based my own working style on his methods; they have been an essential tool for me in many directorial tight spots – but this was a difficult situation. To be brutally honest, there were too many creative temperaments and it became pretty explosive.

There was Bob Avian, Maggie, Cameron Mackintosh – who always has strong opinions – and me. Then there were the writers, Claude-Michel Schönberg and Alain Boublil, who had previously written *Miss Saigon* and *Les Misérables*. This was the third of their trilogy, so there was a lot of pressure on them to build on their genius, and outdo their former achievements. Add to the mix

Declan, Nick Ormerod – Declan's partner and co-founder of Cheek by Jowl – who was working as the designer, Ken Caswell and Marcus Bray, who was Declan's notary, and that's a lot of people with input. Perhaps inevitably, there was a real threat that too many cooks might spoil the broth.

It was a tough task. Things were changing daily and everyone was confused. It was a very stressful *four-month* rehearsal period, which is unheard of. Ultimately, it was a critical disaster.

We opened on 10 July 1996 and the press hated it. Tony Purnell, in the *Mirror*, wrote: 'At its foot-stomping best, it appears to have snapped up offcuts from *Riverdance*. At its worst, it's a crashing bore and had me praying for the final curtain.'

The *Guardian* commented, 'People are prophesying the end of the big musical. Frankly, *Martin Guerre*, by Boublil and Schönberg, is more likely to hasten than to delay its end. For all the qualities that one looks for in the musical – wit, passion, a heady ecstasy – are conspicuously absent from this lugubrious, heavy-going spectacle.'

The choreography was the one aspect that was praised in most of the reviews, which endorsed Bob's later triumph at the Olivier Awards.

As the producer, Cameron had already spent £3.5 million on the show, so he wasn't prepared to let it fail. He decided to throw another £500,000 at it, and they rewrote, redirected and then closed for a week so that the cast could re-rehearse. Then they put it on again. It was a higher standard and a much better show. Consequently, it received a much warmer reception, but it still lasted only two years and never made it to Broadway.

Shirley MacLaine came to see the original production during its West End run. As the resident choreographer, I would entertain the VIPs in a special room in the theatre, so I was looking after her that night. At the interval, Shirley wanted a gin and tonic, but she was also desperate for some Twiglets. I dispatched one of the front-of-house staff to go out and buy her some. We guzzled two gin and tonics and a bowl of Twiglets, and consumed it all sat in the stairwell because Shirley didn't want to go into the VIP room. She said she was happy on the stairs, so we just sat there talking about the show.

She was really interested in the subtext and said to me, 'Craig, I was wondering, is this a gay story? The two lead guys, the imposter and the real Martin, go to war together – are they having a relationship?'

I said, 'They're not meant to, but I suppose it could look that way.'

It was wonderful listening to her points of view, especially after reading her books, which I'd loved.

I kept the glass that she drank her gin and tonic out of and took it triumphantly back to the Heartbreak Hotel as a memento of our evening. Unfortunately, some 'helpful' person there washed it, which was rather devastating.

Cameron Mackintosh is legendary for his wild parties. One of the best he ever threw was the *Martin Guerre* do, which was in fact better than the show itself and probably cost more to put on. He took over Bedford Square in London and erected a huge marquee. There were big hogs on spits and we savoured a rustic medieval banquet, washed down with massive goblets of wine. He even laid on medieval games.

I dyed my hair blue for the bash because, for some bizarre reason, I wanted it to match the blue shirt I'd bought for opening night. The first colour wasn't intense enough, so I sprayed more blue into it just before I left the house. Unfortunately, it was a swelteringly hot night. As I started perspiring, my sweat mixed with the dye and then ran in indigo streaks down my face. Not a good look.

Cameron loves throwing Christmas parties at his house in north London, too. Every year, he gets his office and production staff to put on a panto. He sets up a stage and a giant marquee and you have a day to rehearse the pantomime. One year, Ken

Caswell and I were ugly sisters; Howard Harrison, who is one of the leading lighting men in the West End, played Spurterella; and Cameron took the role of the king. At the end of each party, he fills the entire marquee with foam, or it ends in a mud wrestle or a food fight. At a Cameron shindig, you expect to come out looking a mess.

For Cameron's fiftieth birthday bash, Lavish came back from the dead, dressed as Wonder Woman, to jump out of his cake. She'd been resurrected for my thirty-first birthday, when I'd thrown a superhero party. Someone from the Mackintosh office saw my costume there and asked me to pop out of the cake. So I got all tarted up in my Wonder Woman garb and gave Cameron the surprise of his life. I was the only one dressed up so I felt a bit of a prat, but he loved it. He laughed his socks off.

It was a tight little team at the Cammac office and we all got on really well. It was a mad and eclectic crowd. All the staff were fabulous characters, but none more so than Cameron himself. He loves to party, he adores the outrageous and he's an extreme personality. He's also remarkably generous, as I was about to discover for myself.

In 1997, the time finally came for me to move out of the Heartbreak Hotel. In truth, I'd got sick of sharing the house. There were just too many people living there. Transferring into direction and choreography had meant that my salary had improved, so I'd managed to pay off my debts, start saving, set up a pension and even make some investments. It suddenly occurred to me that I didn't need to live with loads of other people. I thought it would be nice if Lloyd and I had our own place.

Serendipitously, the house next door was for sale. The property was only £160,000 and it was a six-bedroom house in Camden. The two of us couldn't afford it alone, so Clifftops, Lloyd and I all went to apply for a mortgage. We thought we could club together on the home loan, but the bank turned us down. Clifftops was a waiter; Lloyd was still studying law and was working at The Engineer too. The majority of their money came in tips. On paper, it looked like they earned little more than £5,000 a year. The bank wasn't willing to risk it.

I decided that I would have to go to the Halifax and see how much I could get by myself. They said they would lend me £120,000. I received a certificate to confirm it and then I went shopping. For months, I just looked around. Although I told Lloyd about it, I didn't mention what I was planning to anyone else at the Heartbreak. I didn't want to fragment the family.

One day, Lloyd and I went for a stroll and came across an adorable little house around the corner that was for sale. We enquired about the price and were told it was £149,000. Naturally, we tried to get it for £120,000. The estate agent said that the value had already gone up £50,000 since the property had gone on the market, and that the vendors wouldn't accept less than the asking price.

There was nothing else for it. I put on my most engaging smile and went to ask Cameron Mackintosh for a loan.

He was amazing. Cameron is really into property and owns a lovely Nash house near the area I wanted to move to in north London. I said to him, 'I've found this exquisite place, darling, and I would like to have a financial meeting.' He agreed. We talked about the weather for a few minutes and then I got straight to the point.

'I've seen this gorgeous Grade II listed house,' I said. 'It's £150,000 and I'm £30,000 short. I was wondering if I could borrow £40,000?'

Naturally, ever the extravagant one, I'd calculated that I needed ten grand extra for furnishings.

I told him I'd pay him back, with interest at the going rate, and that I'd worked out a payment plan over five years. He looked at the estate agent's details for the house and commented, 'Yes, it's a beautiful property.' I waited with bated breath. Unbelievably, at the end of the meeting he announced, 'We'll go down to see my accountant now and the money will be in your account tomorrow.'

I said, 'Thanks, darling,' and the deal was done. The next day, forty grand landed in my account, and the house was ours.

As it turned out, Cameron didn't make any money out of my 'financial plan' because I'd worked it out at 5 per cent, which he informed me was less than the base rate, which at the time was 6 per cent. But he accepted my proposition nonetheless. I can't thank him enough because I couldn't have done it without him. His generosity gave me independence, got me out of the Heartbreak Hotel and provided me with an investment. I don't think Cameron would have done it for just anyone, but by then I was firmly established as a member of the Cammac clan. Sometimes, I guess, you have to be bold and ask for help.

When we told the gang that Lloyd and I would be moving out, the reaction from Clifftops was not great. Not only was he losing his friends to the property ladder, but he would also have to find another couple for the Heartbreak to make the rent as cheap as it was when Lloyd and I were there. The paperwork and practicalities were a real stress, but our friendship endured all the same. Clifftops eventually got some other people in and has managed the property ever since. It's thankfully still the same old Heartbreak; it's just the cast that keeps on changing.

When Lloyd and I first moved into our new house, it felt really small, as we were used to a sprawling four-storey pile. Nevertheless, because it was our own, I fell in love with it. It was gorgeous: loads of light came streaming down the stairway into the entrance hallway; a wall of ivy cascaded down the garden wall; a big magnolia tree bloomed boldly in the middle of the verdant lawn; beautiful arched windows adorned the bedroom at the front of the house ... and it was all located on a tree-lined street that was dotted with traditional gas lamps. It couldn't have been more perfect. The property needed a lot of work done to it, however, as it didn't have gas central heating or any kitchen or bathroom to speak of. My extra £10,000 went within days.

Mel, my sister, was in England at the time. She came over to experience life in London and we got her a job as a waitress at The Engineer, the restaurant owned by Tamsin Olivier, where Lloyd was manager and Clifftops also worked. We made our dining room into a bedroom for Mel, while Lloyd and I lived upstairs.

Mel fell in love with London – and also with *Martin Guerre*. I would come home and she would have the CD player blaring at major decibels. She'd be singing along to all the tunes; I swear she knew that score better than the writers. She was so much fun to live with. It was an amazing opportunity to get to know my little sister, after I'd left home when she was only ten. She was well and truly all grown up now, and a total unit (an Australian expression for someone who comes with the whole package!).

Lloyd and I thought it would also be a good idea to rent out a room to touring actors in order to raise some extra cash, given that money was so tight when we first moved in and began our extensive renovations. Two Americans, who were performing in *Damn Yankees* in the West End, took us up on the offer and stayed until we got settled financially.

So, although I had desperately wanted to get away from sharing, I ended up in a two-bedroom house with four other people and one tiny bathroom! But when you own it, it feels completely different. Actually, it was good fun all being together, and the lodgers helped with the payments on Cameron's loan.

There wasn't a huge garden, but there was a wonderful roof terrace, on which we were always having barbecues in the summer. Barbecues remind me of home, so I put a whole row of eucalyptus trees up there, to complete the effect. My dad was the barbecue king and I think I inherited my passion for them from him. He loved having barbies and put hours of preparation into them. They're very Australian anyway, but he made them into an art form. When we'd go and visit relatives, he'd show up with 30 kilos of raw meat and a trailer full of booze – cans of Melbourne Bitter and 20 litres of Coolabah (which was wine in a cask, otherwise known as 'goon juice').

One Fourth of July, soon after we moved in, my dear American friend and colleague Heather Douglas, whom I'd met and befriended on the USA/Berlin tour of *Crazy for You*, persuaded me to have a barbecue on the roof terrace. Carried away with the celebratory spirit, Lloyd unintentionally blew everyone up. He put a firework – a rocket – into a pot plant and dug it all the way in, then lit it. The roof terrace was full of our friends and the whole thing exploded over everybody. There were holes in people's clothing and one of my friends received quite a bad burn. I escaped, totally unscathed, because I was standing at the opposite end, but everyone else ran towards the door and that was the direction in which it went off. It was awful. Luckily, there were no serious injuries, but it goes to show you how dangerous those things can be.

Lloyd and fire were not a good combination in general. He set my outfit alight once. Admittedly, I was wearing a shell suit, which is not cool, but in my defence I'd been rehearsing all day and it was the nineties. We were having some drinks upstairs on the roof terrace. Lloyd had purchased some new gel fuel that produced the effect of candlelight and, while it was lit, he tried to add more in. It splattered all over me and I was aflame. I couldn't put myself out. The gel kept burning and the shell suit was going up quickly. It was a nightmare. I screamed and screamed and Lloyd just stood there killing himself laughing. I managed to put myself out without any injury, but he was no use at all.

My career as a choreographer in my own right started in a urinal in 1997. I became involved with *West End Bares*, a benefit for AIDS charity West End Cares, which was looking for people to contribute a number. The idea of the event was that individuals from all the West End productions came together and performed various original sequences. Each one had to be about baring something – in layman's terms, stripping.

I was still working on *Martin Guerre*, and a touring production of *West Side Story*, at the time. I was asked to put something together for non-dancers, using weird and wonderful people whom you would least expect to see on a stage, let alone stripping; like the staff in Cameron's office. I collected together an eclectic group of lads who were willing to expose themselves and came up with a reverse strip.

After looking through my albums for inspiration, I decided the music should be Rickie Lee Jones's song, 'Easy Money'. I started with all the boys stark bollock naked. The curtains opened and there was a row of naked men with their backs to the audience, peeing in a urinal, and pumping their hips at the same time. This was just before *The Full Monty* was released in August 1997. Then, individually, you saw their characters come to life as they started getting dressed. They all wore construction workers' clothes, but the underwear beneath gave away their fetishes. For example, Bob West, who was a Cammac exec and a company manager on *Cats* when I was in it, donned pink frilly knickers, others slipped on stockings and suspenders, and so on. It brought the house down.

In the audience, unbeknownst to me, sat a girl called Rebecca Quigley. She worked for production company Pola Jones and she wanted to know who had come up with the choreography for the number because she thought it was hilarious. It wouldn't be the last I heard of Rebecca, though our paths didn't cross again for some time.

In 1998, Lloyd and I set up a little business empire – entirely by accident. I was working on *West Side Story* in Plymouth and lodging with a couple called John and Anne Henning, who were on the theatre digs list and have become almost like family. They were furniture importers and, while I was there, they received a container full of outdoor goods from Indonesia. They were desperate to get rid of the stock because they didn't have enough room for it in their warehouse.

'What are London prices like?' they asked me one day.

'Well, they sell furniture in Camden, near my house,' I told them. 'If you want, I'll go down and have a look for you.'

I visited their warehouse to take photos of the goods, so that I could match up the items with what was on sale in London and compare prices. Seeing me engrossed in the work, the Hennings suggested that I set up a shop of my own, which on reflection seemed a rather nice idea, especially given my artistic flair. I mentioned it to Lloyd, thinking that it was a venture we could perhaps try together. He was applying for law jobs and still working as a manager at The Engineer then. What with all that and my contract on *West Side Story*, we decided in the end that we were too busy to take on such a time-consuming challenge.

However, I left the photos of the goods on our coffee table and a few days later, a friend of ours, Janine Ruby Fay, happened to pop round and started flicking through them. They showcased really elegant outdoor furniture, which was very trendy at the time. After scanning the pictures, Janine said in her broad Australian accent, 'Jeez, I absolutely love this stuff. Where can I get some?'

I told her that I could get it for her at cost price from the Hennings and she travelled down to the warehouse to look around. While she was there, John and Anne again mentioned the idea of opening a London shop and Janine got very excited about the suggestion. She rang me and said, 'Craig, do you want to do this shop with me?'

As before, I liked the idea in principle, so I said, 'I'll help you to run it, but you'll have to look after the shop on a day-to-day basis because I have my theatre career.'

After all that, at the very last minute, Janine had to pull out of the whole business. Lloyd came into the picture again as a possible replacement and so we ended up taking it forward together. The only way of getting the money for the first investment was for both of us to pool our resources. We negotiated a lease for ten years on a shop in Chelsea, which was terrifying. I remember saying, 'Lloyd, we have to pay the rent on this place for ten years! If it doesn't work, it will be a nightmare.'

I'd only bought the house the year before, so I was slightly concerned about the situation; and then even more so because, just as the enterprise was looking solid, Lloyd was offered a job in Woolwich. He had finished his law degree and had tried for a year to get a position, but without success. You have to do two years of articles and he had completed a year with a firm in the City, but then they didn't take him on. So when he was offered a job as an article clerk in a criminal law firm in Woolwich, he had to give serious thought to the new offer.

He sat there one night, saying, 'Law or shop? Law or shop?'

I said, 'Let me ask you this, Lloyd. You have trained for seven years to be a lawyer; we've been through your schooling, all the bad stuff, you've worked really hard to pay for it all and you have learned it all. What do you know about wood? What do you know about sales and marketing? Nothing!'

He went to see a psychic, who opened his door and said, 'You're not meant to work in an office if that's why you're here.'

'Shop' it was. Oh my God! We signed on the dotted line and opened our baby. We called it Revelloyd. I bought ten books on wood and furniture and we were in business.

Fortunately, the shop performed well – so well, in fact, that in 2000 we closed the Chelsea store and launched two branches in Upper Street, Islington. An opportunity also came up to invest in a restaurant – the Duke of York, in St John's Wood – which we seized with enthusiasm. Unexpectedly, Lloyd and I were becoming quite the entrepreneurs. We were building up a rampant and wide-ranging empire.

In 1998, my theatrical workload became dominated by *Hey, Mr Producer!* a one-off event that celebrated Cameron Mackintosh's life work to date. The list of stars who participated read like a who's who of show business: Dame Judi Dench, Dame Julie Andrews, Michael Ball, Jonathan Pryce, Hugh Jackman and

Stephen Sondheim, to name but a few. It was a fantastic experience, but for me it was somewhat tainted. Cameron and I had always seen eye to eye in the past, but on this production, we didn't agree on every aspect of the show, which was rather unsettling.

When you work with Cameron, he says, 'What about this, dear?' Then you go away and come up with a concept, take it back to him, and he rips it to shreds and reconstructs it. It's your job, afterwards, to pick up all the pieces, put them together and make it coherent.

Cameron is very talented and has a very good eye, always seeing things that others might not. That's why he is so successful. He doesn't always listen – but then, what producer ever seems to? I'm sure us 'creative types' are all of a similar opinion, always thinking about 'the art, darling,' without much consideration for where the money's coming from or how much is at stake if the show fails. I respect Cameron very highly indeed, as he would lay his last penny on a production if he believed it had legs.

It was Cameron and Julia McKenzie who came up with the idea of the showcase. I was attached to choreograph from day one, sitting through all the meetings and helping them pull it together. Cameron then brought in Bob Avian to oversee the work, though, which was a huge disappointment to me. Bob was credited as 'Staged By', while I was named under 'Additional Musical Staging'.

Despite the discouraging credit, I had a large amount of responsibility, with the bulk of the rehearsals falling under my remit, and all sorts of issues left for me to resolve.

For the event, Dame Judi Dench was performing a Sondheim section with Broadway actress Bernadette Peters and Lea Salonga, the original star of *Miss Saigon*. They were perched beautifully on stools and one by one they were going to sing their individual bits and then take their own stool off the stage. One afternoon, Dame Judi was on stage mid rehearsal and I was talking to her through my 'god mike', which is a microphone that enables me to direct from the auditorium without having to shout over the orchestra pit.

Above: Sue and me with Fluffy the cat.

Above: Dull, dull, dull: even as a baby, it took a lot to impress me.

Above: Me at thirteen, with the giant Easter egg I won in the colouring competition.

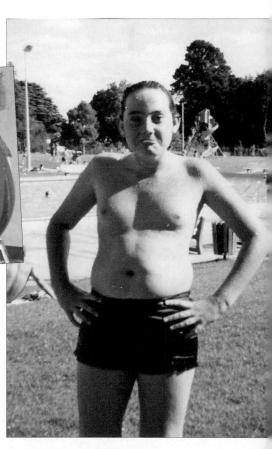

Right: At the swimming pool in Ballarat. Growing up, I was bullied mercilessly about my weight.

Left: The Horwoods en masse: *(from left to right, back row)* Diane, me, Melanie, Susan, *(front row)* Dad, Trent, Mum.

Below: With Angela at the debutante ball, where I discovered I could dance.

Below: In training for *Celebrity Masterchef*, winning the Sunbeam Junior Chef of the Year competition with my very own Jellied Prawn Cocktail.

Right: My 1985 audition photo for *La Cage aux Folles*.

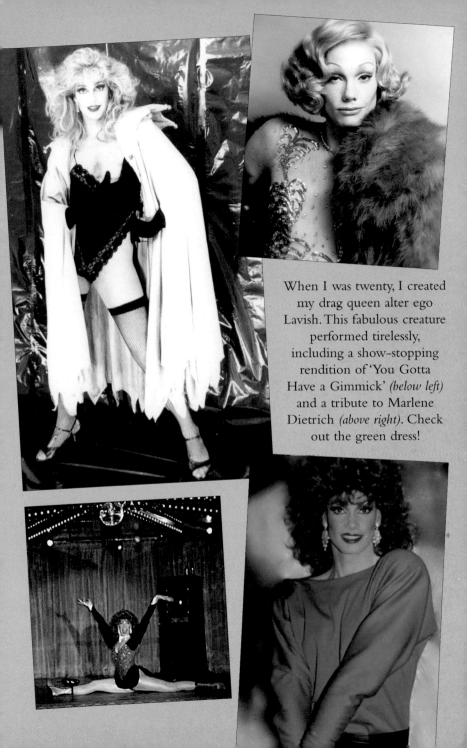

When I was twenty, I created my drag queen alter ego Lavish. This fabulous creature performed tirelessly, including a show-stopping rendition of 'You Gotta Have a Gimmick' *(below left)* and a tribute to Marlene Dietrich *(above right)*. Check out the green dress!

Left: Happy birthday to me! At my twenty-first birthday bash in Ballarat.

Right: With the fabulous leaving cake I received when I left Sydney for the Lido de Paris.

Above: My first TV appearance in the UK: a *TV-am* workout with Lizzie Webb.

Right: Meeting the Queen Mother with the cast of *Miss Saigon*.

Above: On my wedding day with *(from l to r)* Dad, Sue, my bride Jane, brother-in-law David and niece Izzi.

Above: With Lloyd, in happier times.

Above: Just another day at the Heartbreak Hotel.

Left: In New Zealand, overcoming my fear of heights – by skydiving from 15,000 feet!

Above: Maggie Goodwin and me toasting our success after collecting the Olivier Award for Best Choreography for *Martin Guerre*, on behalf of Bob Avian.

Above: With Sir Cameron Mackintosh and Dame Shirley Bassey at *Hey, Mr Producer!*

Below: Strictly a success: with my fellow *SCD* judges, and presenter Bruce Forsyth, at the Christmas special in 2004.

No more Mr Nasty: relaxing backstage with *SCD* contestants *(clockwise from above left)* Claire King, Penny Lancaster-Stewart, Jodie Kidd (and my beloved other half, Grant), Carol Smillie and Emma Bunton.

Left: On a wild night out with friend and *Comic Relief Does Fame Academy* winner Tara Palmer-Tomkinson.

Left: December 2008 saw me having frequent meetings with the Duchess of Cornwall. Here Grant and I chat to her at Clarence House.

Below: Friends at last: with Julian Clary on the *Strictly* tour in 2009.

Above: Grant and I celebrating the West End transfer of my critically acclaimed production of *Sunset Boulevard.*

Left: 'Oh no, you don't!': Playing the Wicked Queen in *Snow White* is my panto debut.

'Dame Judi, could you please just take that stool off at the end?' I requested politely.

Suddenly, Cameron came rushing up to me in a panic and whispered, 'Craig, what are you doing? You can't ask Dame Judi Dench to drag a stool off stage!'

'But Cameron, everyone is taking off their own stool. She doesn't have a problem with it,' I replied.

He was having none of it, so I had to mastermind a way to get Dame Judi downstage and off, while someone else had to carry her stool as well as their own.

Dame Judi is absolutely adorable and would do whatever was asked of her. It was only Cameron who was worried about a member of theatrical royalty hauling this big old stool off the stage. I suppose that's a lesson one learns on the way: respect royalty.

When Dame Judi performs 'Send in the Clowns', it's stunning. Standing ovation material. She is not the most talented of singers, in as much as she doesn't have the voice technically, but she understands that singing is about telling a story. You don't have to have the pipes, all the time.

In auditions, I have had scores of famous actresses come in and sing a song badly, but they tell the story so well that I am left gobsmacked.

Hey, Mr Producer! was a Royal Gala performance, so the Queen and Prince Philip were going to be there. Dame Julie Andrews, who was the show's compère, was really concerned about their presence. She came up to me beforehand and asked, 'How do I address the Queen? Should I call her Your Majesty?'

Of course, I didn't have a clue.

'You're asking the wrong person,' I told her. 'I'm Australian. I don't know anything about Royal protocol.' Nonetheless, I assured her that I would find someone to help, and that I did.

Julie was terribly concerned about her voice at the time too. She was backstage tapping her chest and broadening her diaphragm, trying to maintain the level of vocals that her audience expect of her. It must be so difficult when you're that big a star and your voice is that famous. She'd had problems with it in the past, and had to stop singing, so she was totally paranoid about it, which wasn't surprising.

Julie is so wonderful. She's polite, and very kind and generous backstage. Not a hint of the diva at all. Like many of those who are really famous, they no longer have anything to prove, so they take direction really well.

Bernadette Peters was the same. She's fantastic to work with. I was actually quite nervous about meeting her. We rendezvoused at the Theatre Royal Drury Lane and rehearsed the whole number in the front-of-house bar. I choreographed 'You Gotta Have a Gimmick' with her, Julia McKenzie and my old friend Ruthie Henshall. It was just brilliant because they are all divas, but each one in a very different way. Julia is out there – all bold and Broadway – while Bernadette is a smaller version, laid-back and funny, and Ruthie has that edgy, feisty, youthful quality about her.

It was tricky for Ruthie because she was still up-and-coming at that time, yet she'd been put on this pedestal with these two huge stars. In addition, Ruthie was starring in *Les Misérables* and shows like that can affect your voice. If you're singing soprano, your chest belt range goes, so she was having some small vocal problems as we rehearsed. Also, she was on a very tough schedule, rehearsing from nine in the morning for one production and then going to rehearse another musical in the afternoon, *and* putting on a show in the evening.

I think she found it quite a struggle, especially as she felt she had to prove herself on this single performance. Not only was it in front of the Queen, but it was being filmed, so it was going out worldwide and it was for, and about, the biggest theatre producer in the world. Ruthie cracked a little bit under the pressure, just for a split second in the rehearsals, but like the trooper she is, she came up with the goods in the end. And then she wasn't just good; she was out of this world.

I brought my mother over to the UK for *Hey, Mr Producer!* I knew it was going to be special. Mum was excited that she'd get to meet Julie Andrews, but she wanted to meet Hugh Jackman as well. Hugh wasn't a mega movie star back then; he was appearing in *Oklahoma!* at the National Theatre. He is one of the nicest, most generous guys you will ever meet. He is so loving and down to earth. My mum had her photo taken with him and his wife. That snap is now blown up and displayed prominently in her house in Ballarat – except she's cut Hugh's wife out of the picture.

It was shortly after *Hey, Mr Producer!* that Hugh's career really took off. I went to see him in *The Boy from Oz* on Broadway in 2003, and he was absolutely fantastic.

My mum wasn't the only one meeting idols that night. I met the Queen, but even more importantly, I met Dame Shirley Bassey. In 1983, when I was on tour with *The Black and White Minstrel Show*, Shirley Bassey was all I ever played. I had a new ghetto blaster back then, so I used to put that on in my hotel room and listen to her formidable voice blaring out in stereo. Magatha would come along the corridor and bang on my door, shouting, 'Craig, turn that bloody thing down!'

For a former drag queen such as myself, meeting Dame Shirley was a true life experience. She looked amazingly young and she had a vibrant personality, sparkly and vivacious.

In contrast, the Queen seemed very subdued and looked, the whole time, like she had something else on her mind. It must be so difficult, though, when you're meeting loads and loads of people, to come up with something new to say each time. Cameron told her that I had pieced the show together, so she said she thought I'd done an absolutely wonderful job. I kept waiting for her to say: 'Off with his head!'

The success of *Hey, Mr Producer!* was bittersweet. It was a tremendous event, but it marked the beginning of the end for my working relationship with Cameron.

From 1998, I spent a great deal of my time in Europe. My old colleague Ken Caswell started putting on productions in Amsterdam and other European cities, and he asked me to do some choreography with him. I appreciated the opportunity to gain experience overseas, which would hopefully ensure that I wouldn't make an idiot of myself in the UK when I came to take up my first West End choreography brief in my own name.

In Holland, I choreographed *Fiddler on the Roof*, then *Titanic: The Musical*, and I also directed and choreographed Dutch productions of *Sweet Charity* and *Copacabana*. I was doing one show a year there and it felt like my second home. I adore Amsterdam and I love the Dutch because they are a friendly, amiable nation. The gigs did involve me being away from Lloyd, but he would come over for a week, and was always there for the opening night. We were never apart for longer than a fortnight.

When in Rome, as they say, you do as the Romans do, so I admit I have been known to try the hash cookies and space cake in Amsterdam. The problem is, you don't get very much work done. Crossing the road, meanwhile, is downright hazardous. If a bike doesn't run you over, a tram will. They come at you from every direction, which isn't at all safe if you're high.

Harder drugs, however, have never been my thing. As with cocaine, I wouldn't want to repeat my experience on Ecstasy. I couldn't control it; if I'm drinking, I'm all right, on the whole, but I really don't like losing control.

I took my first – and only – Ecstasy tablet one New Year's Eve. I was at a gay club in Brighton, with Lloyd and his mum. Everyone else on Ecstasy gets up and dances, but I just ended up sitting down, in a corner, staring into space all night. I can remember everything that happened, and I wasn't much fun on it. It's ironic that it makes everyone else think they can dance, yet it stopped me from boogieing altogether.

It's funny what you recall. Lloyd's mum had a backpack on and she was dancing with a gay bloke with no shirt, who was wearing flashing fairy wings and was lit up like a Christmas tree. It was a peculiar night. I've had much better evenings on a glass or two of champagne.

The gigs in Europe provided invaluable experience. The ongoing tour of *West Side Story*, in which I took the role of associate director/choreographer for two-and-a-half years in the late nineties, was also significant. All my other jobs, such as *Martin Guerre, Hey, Mr Producer!* and *Fiddler* slotted in around *West Side* – I had a lot of balls in the air. The tour was organized by production group Pola Jones and went backwards and forwards across the UK, including two runs in the West End.

The company were completely mad. The story of the show, for those that don't know it, is a Romeo-and-Juliet-style romance between members of two rival street gangs, the Sharks and the Jets. The characters are fired-up juvenile delinquents, who go against anything that is socially responsible.

Unfortunately, some of the cast ended up taking their characters to heart, to the point that they were getting into fights outside work, with knives, the lot. They would go out to clubs, get into brawls and would come into work the next day with black eyes.

Backstage was a nightmare too and the number of bust-ups was unbelievable. There was a Liverpudlian girl who went round bashing up all the boys, all the time. She would grab the lads by the scruff of the neck and really lay into them. It was bizarre.

I took her to one side to have a word with her and she responded, 'That's what we do up north. We don't talk, we hit.'

'Hang on, darling,' was my stunned reply. 'If we were in an office and you disagreed with a secretary, for example, you wouldn't just go up and punch her in the face, would you?'

'Yeah, yeah, that's what we'd do,' she said.

Oh dear! This kind of method acting I could do without. She was simply uncontrollable.

The tour ran for four years in total, on and off, although I didn't stay for the full run. Stacey Haynes, who has since become a TV judge herself on *Strictly Dance Fever*, took over from me and she had to deal with the rabble from then on.

In fairness, the company were very young, straight out of school, and had been chosen precisely because of their feistiness. They'd landed these fantastic roles and they felt like they owned the world. That, coupled with their lack of experience of backstage etiquette, was an explosive combination.

To some extent, we caused their hostility too. They were playing rival gangs and their sense of loathing towards each other was encouraged, for dramatic realism, in the improvisations we did in rehearsals.

Arthur Laurents, who wrote it, told me that when they first did *West Side Story* in the States, they put all the Jets in dressing rooms on one side of the stage and the Sharks in rooms on the other side. Then they kept them separate the whole time. That way, they ensured the fight scenes were full of tension and drama, but my lot took that to extremes.

I felt like an old man, with all these seventeen- and eighteen-year-olds in the company, and they really tried my patience.

Nonetheless, it was a fantastic production and I was directing and choreographing with Arthur, which was inspirational. I was also working closely with Alan Johnson, who puts on *West Side*

Story all over the world and has notated the entire show, every single step and scene, lighting cues, design: a massive undertaking. It's called 'the bible' and enables others to restage the musical in exactly the way it was intended by the original creators. Arthur and Alan are both legends of the theatre so they really taught me a lot, which prepared me for my next challenge – *Spend Spend Spend*.

The fact that I was offered the gig was all due to Rebecca Quigley from Pola Jones, who had seen and noted my choreographic efforts in *West End Bares* back in 1997. *Spend Spend Spend* had premiered at the West Yorkshire Playhouse in 1998 and been a big hit there, but in 1999 it was coming to the West End and the producers wanted to introduce more comedy elements. They aspired to find a choreographer who could inject a bit more humour into the show. Enter yours truly.

Rebecca found out who I was and had a word with Andre Ptaszynski, the producer of *Spend*, and he asked me to come in for an interview. We talked about the *West End Bares* number, and everything else I'd achieved, and he gave me the job. It was my first big break and I am really grateful to them both for that. With hindsight, it was amazing of him to offer it to me, not to mention brave to take such a risk with a virtually unknown and unproved choreographer on a new musical.

The show was based on the life of Viv Nicholson, the 1961 pools winner who promised to 'spend, spend, spend' and did just that, eventually ending up penniless.

It was a fantastic period in my life. Perhaps some of Viv's *joie de vivre* infected the whole company because we partied very hard. It was one of those companies where loads of us went out, every single night, and we wouldn't get home until six in the morning. Then we'd all be in rehearsal by ten.

We were based in Plymouth, and spent a lot of time at the Hoe, a large, open, public space that commands magnificent views of Plymouth Sound, Drake's Island, and across the River Hamoaze to Mount Edgcumbe in Cornwall. We'd party there all night and come up with some mad ideas for the show. It was as though nothing else mattered in life.

Barbara Dickson, who starred in *Spend*, has the most incredible, haunting voice. It was great to see her back on stage and I was thrilled that she won Best Actress for the role at the Olivier Awards that year. Of course, Barbara wasn't involved in all the late-night shenanigans. She is quite clean-living, not one to go out and let her hair down. She's like the mother I'd love to have – if I didn't already have a wonderful mother myself – and she's a pleasure to work with. There are no dramas or tantrums. So many theatre actors have huge chips on their shoulders and the amount of work that goes into unravelling their personal lives to get to the acting beneath is huge. There's none of that with Barbara. She's a joy and, in fact, the whole company were. We all clicked. On any production, there is usually at least one member who is prone to hissy fits, or there are a few moments of diva-style outburst, when someone throws in the towel and minces off. On *Spend Spend Spend*, we were completely drama free.

The young Viv was played by a fabulous girl called Rachel Leskovac, who was straight out of the Liverpool Institute of Performing Arts. Steve Houghton of *London's Burning* and *Bugs* fame, meanwhile, really came into his own. He's had a successful West End career since then.

We were under the direction of the talented Jeremy Sams. He allowed me to be at my most expressive with choreography. This was the first time I'd choreographed a whole show and I was quite apprehensive, but it went very well. There was just one number, 'Doing the Dance of Love', on which I kept getting stumped, but Jeremy helped me out with that one. He told me to think of it as ballroom and I thought, 'That's a great idea.' It really worked.

Then came Saturday 11 September 1999 – opening night in Plymouth. Suddenly, I was really nervous. Panic set in as I realized that this was my first big gig and everyone would be judging my work. Thankfully, it was a huge success and on 12 October that year, we transferred to the Piccadilly Theatre in the West End.

Every opening night is the same for me, but this particular show had a lot riding on it as it was my first ever West End debut as a fully fledged choreographer. In my mind, this would either make or break me.

As a general rule, I zone out on first nights and go very quiet, reeling from the shock that all our work is actually going in front of an audience and theatre critics, who can be extremely harsh in judgement.

Yes, I know, I can hear you saying to yourselves, 'That's rich coming from you!' and I agree, but vicious criticism can close a show in a week, putting hundreds of people out of work.

Your life in the theatre and future employment do sometimes depend on good reviews. Bollocks to the people who claim never to read them; you simply can't avoid them or other people's reaction to them. There will always be a 'friend' who will just adore coming up to you in a public place and announcing how bad that review was in last week's *Guardian*. Reviews tend to worry me.

On the night, I also fret about the cast and if they'll remember all the notes I gave them; I'm concerned about the crew and whether that troublesome piece of scenery, which never actually went right in the tech or the dress rehearsal, is going to make it into position at the correct time; I worry that the lighting board will crash halfway through the performance; I brood that the laughs aren't going to be where they were intended; I panic about whether I've been brave enough with the material I have been given to work with by the writers; I agonize that I have let down the cast, crew, other creatives, producers and the audience; I stew over whether I have made all the right choices for the company and given them steps they can be proud of each night; I'm anxious about whether I have told the story clearly enough and whether everyone will understand it and be moved or excited by it.

As you can imagine, I sit through the show in a cold, nervous sweat, living every moment with the cast and crew, and it's exhausting. Some moments of high tension, some of agitated anticipation, some of pure relief and some of elation. It's a roller-coaster ride of emotion and sometimes feels like a form of medieval torture. In fact, that could be more pleasurable – at least you would know what was going to happen next. The theatre is such a horribly public domain in which to crash and burn. Is it any wonder that one hurries to the bar before the performance for a stiff one, before losing complete control of the evening and having to sit in a dark space and leaving it to the gods?

At the end of the evening, I brace myself for the 2,000 opinions I'll hear at the after-party, where very few colleagues actually tell you the truth in any case. It makes me wonder sometimes why the hell I do it to myself, but it's a passion I have for real drama and dance in the theatre that spurs me on. If, by some strange fluke, it's all right on the night and pulls together to make a unique theatrical experience that will stay in the hearts and minds of the audience, then it's all been worth it.

On this occasion, I had a couple of calming drinks at the bar before the show, with a few friends and my mum, whom I'd flown over from Ballarat at the very last minute to see it. Then, in a state of anxiety, we took our seats. Flicking through the programme, I discovered that they had misspelled my name by muddling up the 'w' and 'r' of 'Horwood' and also given me the wrong biography, printing that of the set and costume designer, Lez Brotherston, twice. The blurb read: 'Choreography by Craig Revel Howrood.' Then: 'Lez began his design training at …' My biog was nowhere to be seen.

The amount of ribbing I got for that misprint after the show was outrageous. 'Oh look! It's Craig Revel How-rood! HOW RUDE!' They were all saying it, elongating the 'roooooooooood' to the point of nonsense. Little did I know what I'd become known for by the nation five years later!

It was hilarious, though, and set a tone for the evening that could only be one of joy and insanity. The audience and the critics went mad for it. It got better reactions than I could possibly have asked for or even imagined.

The opening-night party was spectacular, as we all arrived in pink Chevrolets – but the reviews the following morning were even better. Maeve Walsh, in the *Independent on Sunday*, called it 'the best of British', while Charles Spencer, writing on the Monday in the *Daily Telegraph*, commented: 'Popular entertainment at its best, devoid of the cynical contrivance of so many musicals and blessed with heart, humour and irresistible humanity.'

In February, my joy was complete when I was nominated for an Olivier Award for Best Choreography. In fact, the show was nominated for seven awards altogether, as well as winning both the *Evening Standard* Award and the Critics' Circle Award for Best Musical.

It wasn't my first Olivier Awards ceremony, of course, as Maggie Goodwin and I had collected the 1997 award for *Martin Guerre* in Bob Avian's absence. But it's an entirely different story when it's your own name that's announced alongside some of the leading legends in choreography. Other nominees were Peter Darling for *Candide*, Garth Fagan for *The Lion King* and Stephen Mear for *Soul Train*.

Sadly, I didn't win the award, which went to Garth, but to be nominated for a show that was, effectively, my West End debut as a choreographer was breathtaking.

To be honest, I never thought for one moment that I was really in with a chance, considering the esteemed figures that I was up against and the success of their work. At least, not until the split second before, when you can't help thinking to yourself, 'What if they do call out my name? What shall I say? Whom should I thank?'

Naturally, I was disappointed when my name wasn't read out, but I felt so proud of myself and the *Spend* company, and of what we had all achieved, that it spurred me on and made me hungry for more. Andre Ptaszynski was on the board of the

Olivier panel and told me that it was a really close call, so I was truly chuffed.

The nomination also gave me the most enormous confidence boost – and, at last, some clout in the industry. Directors wanted to work with me on all sorts of projects and the year ahead was filling up really quickly.

After the big event of *Hey, Mr Producer!* in 1998, Cameron's showcase lived on in several different incarnations. Ken Caswell and I had just finished staging it on the cruise liners in 2000 when Cameron himself phoned to tell me about *The Witches of Eastwick*. It was a brand-new musical adapted from the book by John Updike and would star Ian McShane as the devilish Darryl Van Horne, who exerts his charismatic influence over three women and increases their magical powers.

It was an exciting project. I assumed when I got Cameron's call that I would be devising the choreography alone. Maybe that was presumptuous of me, but I really thought that after the phenomenal success of *Spend*, I had proved myself. Once again, however, Bob Avian was brought on board. I love working with Bob and have nothing against him, but I felt I needed credit if I was going to continue working and growing. I wanted to be named co-choreographer if I was expected to create steps.

As it turned out, when the contract came through, they were offering me only the title of associate choreographer, which would mean I had no ownership rights to the material and would be working under Bob's name.

It's a similar situation to the fashion industry, where a lot of people design frocks for a label, but just one person gets the credit. I wanted my own label. I wanted to be independent and I wanted to have my name anywhere, even in the back of the programme in small print, so that people knew that I had had a part in creating the steps. I could then move on as a choreographer, instead of always creating for Cameron under someone else's flag.

I nervously approached the producer and told him of my concern.

'Bobby is the choreographer and your position will be that of associate,' Cameron responded. 'I've never seen you do comedy. No, that won't be possible.'

'I have just choreographed *Spend Spend Spend*,' I replied. 'That is a comedy, Cameron, and I was nominated for an Olivier Award for it.'

I knew I was placing poor Cam in an awkward position and it really wasn't fair of me, but I was speaking with my heart rather than my head.

He replied, 'Yes, dear, *that* is a British musical comedy; *Witches* is an American musical comedy.'

I couldn't answer that, except to say, 'I'm really left with no choice, Cameron, but to say no. I can't accept associate. I can do the gig only if I'm credited as co-choreographer.'

There was no stamping or shouting, no big song and dance. It was all very calm and relaxed and actually quite sad. I went on to thank him for all the work he had given me, the support he had always offered, the fun and opportunities he had blessed me with, and then I had to walk away from the production and out of the office with my stomach in my mouth. I *so* wanted the job and I knew I'd be suited to it. It was right up my street, choreographically. It was a terrible risk to lay myself on the line like that, but I seriously thought that the situation would progress and I would eventually be given the co-choreographer credit.

In fact, the opposite occurred. At the time, I was terribly embarrassed because everyone in the business thought that I would be doing the gig, as by that stage I'd taken all of the auditions and created the routines for them. A month went by and I have to admit I was stewing over it, all the while thinking that the decision would be overturned.

The phone finally rang and it was the Cammac office, wanting to arrange a meeting between Cameron and me. We agreed a time and I went to see him, only to be kept for an hour in the waiting area. That really built up the tension, as I still had no clue what he wanted to tell me. I went into his office and he told me the news …

'I just wanted to let you know before the posters come out tomorrow that Stephen Mear has accepted the job and will be billed as co-choreographer with Bob Avian.'

Stephen Mear, who is my contemporary and a really good friend, is now quite famous within the theatre world for his input on *Mary Poppins* and, more recently, *The Little Mermaid* for Disney on Broadway. We've been up against one another for Olivier Awards. He's a brilliant choreographer, and Cameron's decision to employ him at the last minute, giving him the exact job title that I'd requested, was the hardest thing in the world to accept. I am eternally grateful Cam told me before I saw it on the posters.

'Thank you very much for letting me know, Cameron, it's been a pleasure to have worked with you,' I replied, and that was it.

I couldn't believe it. I left the office after eight years of working for Cameron, feeling totally at sea.

I'm not bitter about the outcome, though, as I see now it was the best thing for me. Cameron had told me that having Bob on the show was like handing over the baton, whereas I believed I was ready to run solo. Sometimes I think if you work in a big company like that, you can get stagnant, or others can't see all that you have to offer. In leaving Cammac, I was now completely free to explore my potential.

Cameron had taught me so much, but it was time to stand on my own two feet and take a different path, so actually he did me the biggest favour. I can only thank him for that.

It put me in the poorhouse for ages, I will admit. Yet as soon as the double doors of the Mackintosh empire closed on me, I was spurred on to other things. I knew that this was the beginning of what was going to be my final rise to independence – and the most creative and important work of my life.

CHAPTER 14 *Work and Play*

I f you are used to dishing out criticism, it's not easy to put yourself in a position to be judged, as I know more than most. When Christopher Tookey, the long-term film critic on the *Daily Mail*, wrote *Hard Times: The Musical*, he suffered the curse of the critic-turned-playwright. His fellow journalists couldn't wait to get the knives out.

The show was to go on in the summer of 2000 at Windsor, and then at the Haymarket Theatre in the West End. Another choreographer had been due to create the routines, but had walked out after some sort of altercation with Christopher, so they got me in at the last minute. It sounded like a fun project, and with *Witches* out of the picture, I thought, 'Why not?'

Brian Blessed was playing Mr Gradgrind. He'd occasionally throw tantrums when he was learning a song and wasn't getting the timing or pitch right, which often happens when you're attempting new material. In the middle of rehearsals, Brian would stop abruptly and you would hear his famous booming voice shouting, 'I climb mountains. I am not a singer!' before he stormed off in a frustrated rage; but of course he is a singer. His co-star Roy Hudd would persistently run after him saying, 'Come back, come back.'

One night after the run started, Brian was on stage performing his big solo, which is all very quiet. He was building to a dramatic finish and, as usual, rose from his chair on the key change.

191

Suddenly, he stopped singing and toppled backwards on to the floor, like a huge felled oak tree. The orchestra played on as he just lay there. I was in the audience and I thought he was dead. I was thinking, 'Oh my God. Brian Blessed has done a Tommy Cooper and gone down like a ton of bloody bricks.'

The stage manager instructed the curtain to close and it came down as it does after the end scene of *La Traviata*: very, very slowly. The audience must have thought it was an extremely odd conclusion to the show. All was quiet, then a bizarre applause crept in, the house lights came up gradually and the audience had no clue what on earth to do. People began to murmur and then an announcement was made into the house, saying that due to technical difficulties we would be taking a brief intermission.

I ran backstage and Brian was sitting in his dressing room, absolutely fine. He had fainted, but he came back on. The play ran over by about forty-five minutes because he kept referring to the incident throughout the rest of the performance and cracking jokes about it, like, 'I climbed Everest and go and faint on stage!' Every second line became a gag and it felt like the night would never end. Good on him for carrying on with the show, however. It was certainly a night for that particular audience to remember.

In 2001, Denmark and the director's chair came calling. Danish actor Stig Rossen and musical director Mikkel Rønnow had recently set up a new production company, the aim of which was to bring great stage musicals to Denmark. They asked me to direct their first two productions, *Chess* and *Copacabana*, which was a real honour.

I found *Chess* a galvanizing experience because it was the first time I could be absolutely creatively honest. There was no one on my back saying, 'Do this, do that.' I could just stage whatever was in my head.

The result, even if I do say so myself, was brilliant. The show starred Stig, who had previously played Jean Valjean in *Les*

Misérables and who has a sensational voice. It was a truly international cast: Emma Kershaw, an extraordinary British talent, was Florence, while Zubin Varla took on Frederick Trumper.

Coincidentally, the Australian actor Michael Cormick, who was a really old pal and ex-London flatmate of mine, played the part of the Arbiter. He was a blast from the past. Michael was famous back home for winning *Young Talent Time*, and being a singer with the Channel Nine dancers. I had a huge crush on him when I first started at Tony Bartuccio's in Prahran. I'll never forget him strolling into the changing rooms at the dance school and slipping into his blue tights right in front of me: he was hot and I was overwhelmed. In one of those funny twists of fate, he went on to have an eight-year relationship with one of my best friends, the theatre designer Christopher 'Master' Woods.

After Denmark, it was back to England to work on the opening ceremony of the 2002 Commonwealth Games in Manchester, where I teamed up with a certain colleague called Arlene Phillips. She was also choreographing *We Will Rock You*, which was a big risk, so I asked her how it was going. She replied dejectedly, 'It's not good news. The critics slated it. It might be coming off in two weeks.'

I said, 'Oh darling, I'm so sorry.'

That was in May 2002, but then the show had a stroke of luck that was to turn its fortunes around. It was the Queen's Golden Jubilee and, in June, there was a huge concert at Buckingham Palace to mark the occasion. The cast sang the rousing Queen number 'We Will Rock You' and they sold so many tickets after that performance that the musical exploded. I was so pleased for Arlene.

I had a success of my own on my hands when I took on the challenge of choreographing *My One and Only*, which played at the Chichester Festival Theatre and then transferred to the Piccadilly Theatre in the West End. I was thrilled to be nominated for an Olivier again in recognition of my achievements, especially because I'd had a bit of a falling out with the musical's stars when we'd moved venues. I never understood what happened. They were wonderful to work with when we did the show at the CFT and then something changed. Suddenly, we were clashing on everything.

I've learned that when you work as a choreographer and director (or even as a judge on *Strictly*), you run the risk of upsetting people with your comments – although I don't know that that was the problem in this case. What's bizarre is that actors and dancers often don't believe they are doing something wrong until they hear or see it for themselves. I've had to video dancers and play the tape back to them to prove that they're flailing their arms about, or to demonstrate some other fault. People simply don't like to hear criticism.

At the Oliviers that year, I was up against Susan Stroman for *Contact*, which was playing at the Queen's Theatre. That seemed remarkable to me. She was my mentor, someone I'd always considered a genius and whose work on *Crazy for You* had given me the confidence to think that maybe I could one day be a choreographer. The other nominees were Matthew Bourne and Company for *Play Without Words* at the Lyttelton, and Peter Darling for *Our House* at the Cambridge.

Even though I didn't win – Matthew Bourne triumphed on that occasion – I was exhilarated to be in such acclaimed company. All these choreographers were absolute legends and their work filled me with admiration. It was extraordinary to commiserate with the likes of Stro. She has been the most supportive colleague and, I hope she won't mind me saying, friend I have had. She has always made the effort to come and see all my shows and be honest about the work, and I adore her.

In 2002, Lloyd and I faced a crossroads. We needed to do some serious work on the restaurant, the Duke of York in St John's Wood, in which we were in partnership with Brendan Connolly. The toilets needed updating, the bar area required redecorating and the kitchen was gasping out for air conditioning. When we added up the costs, the total bill was going to be £150,000.

With our two shops, the house *and* the restaurant, we were already up to our eyeballs. Nevertheless, I believed it was a good idea to invest the money. We'd had the restaurant for about three years by then and it usually takes that amount of time for any new business to kick off.

Lloyd disagreed and said he didn't want to stump up the cash. In fairness, it wasn't my day-to-day responsibility and I didn't have to commit much time or thought to the venture. I pulled a few pints and waited on tables when it was extremely busy, but I had my packed theatrical career, so the businesses were Lloyd's concern. He decided we shouldn't shell out the money, so we didn't and we sold our share. Typically, three months later, after the renovations were made, the whole thing just took off. It's been a huge success.

Lloyd and I weren't all work and no play. We'd been together for a decade by then and had shared a host of wonderful experiences. One of our favourite pastimes was going on vacation; we specialized in motoring breaks. He would do the driving and I would navigate. We explored all around Wales, which I loved. I used to make mountains of sandwiches for our trips. I'm not joking – about two loaves' worth. We always scoffed the lot on the first morning as they were so tasty.

We'd stay at B&Bs and hotels all over the country. One in particular was gorgeous, the Swallow Falls Hotel at Betws-y-Coed. It remains in my memory, as the only room they had available for us was the honeymoon suite, with its king-size bed.

It was odd back then, as a gay couple, to ask for a double bed at reception; you'd tend to get some very strange looks or conveniently some places would no longer have any rooms available. So we got into the habit of asking for a twin room, as though we weren't in love at all. Consequently, as the kind hoteliers at the Swallow Falls offered us this amazing suite, they gave us their sincerest apologies that there were no twins available. We took the room, looking as if it was going to be a drag having to share a bed, and as soon as the door had shut behind us, we went wild. We were so excited. It was beautiful and the sound of the waterfall outside the window was exquisite.

On another holiday, later in our relationship, we drove all around Italy, which was stunning. It was one of those long hot summers that seemed to stretch before us, full of promise and temptation. We had more money at this point, so we stayed in really posh hotels with fabulous views and amenities.

I just loved driving around with Lloyd. He was so much fun to be with. We had loads in common and we could always see the funny side of bad situations – which came in handy at Christmas time, when there always seemed to be some disaster.

We would often spend the season with Lloyd's mum, Christine. Once, the three of us, along with our very close friend Amber Louise Ives-O'Brian, celebrated it at Christine's home in Brighton. The festivities began as they were meant to go on. We were running late for the train to Brighton, and already a little stressed from that, when upon our arrival at Victoria station, Tigger, Amber's dog, threw up all over the platform. We soon discovered, rifling through our bags filled with presents and wrapping paper and ribbons and smart Christmassy clothes, that we had nothing to clean it up with. Luckily, the guard came along and kindly did our dirty work, which was above and beyond the call of duty.

When we arrived at Christine's – Tigger still not well – Amber and I went straight into the kitchen to start preparing the dinner. Christine had done the shopping the previous day; a last-minute rampage around the supermarkets for the cut-price bargains, as was the family's way. Christine isn't much of a cook and will readily admit that. That year, she'd decided not to have a turkey, but had instead opted for a goose. It was a nice idea, but when we came to carve it at the table, it was all bone. There was barely any meat on the bird to plate up. We were howling with laughter over it.

There was many a Christmas to have a giggle at. It was my turn to host next. I planned a big fat turkey with all the trimmings, so as not to repeat the skinny goose travesty. It looked delicious. Everyone was waiting to tuck in after the Queen's speech; I went to carve the turkey breast ... and it was as dry as a nun's gusset. I was devastated.

I didn't mention it to anyone else, as I hoped that once the gravy was lavishly sloshed about the plate, no one would notice. I hate really runny gravy, so I'd made a really thick, viscous concoction. Amber's husband Mark went to pour it as I watched nervously from the head of the table. It stayed like a brick in the gravy boat, having set like concrete as I was carving the beast.

We all tried desperately to say nothing – but it was unavoidable. I could see with my own eyes that everyone was finding it hard to swallow. The food was literally sticking to the roofs of people's mouths.

Mark was the first to speak. He commented politely, 'I like my gravy a bit thinner than this, the spoon seems to be standing bolt upright in it.'

Then I asked if everyone's turkey was all right, as I was finding mine a bit dry.

After that, they all let rip on the dry insults. Christine was the only one who actually liked it. All fun and games.

That was what I loved about Christmas: the fact that we all got together and, by pure chance, created stories to dine out on for the year ahead. I hold those memories fondly. Amber and Mark had a baby a few years after that – and named him after me! That poor child: Monty Revel Ives-O'Brian is my godson, and I'm very proud of him. He's recently become a big brother to Digby Rolo Ives-O'Brian, who is also as cute as a button.

Family was important to Lloyd and me. I got on with my in-laws really well and became part of their gang. It was wonderful for me to have surrogate relatives in the UK to lean on, and to spend good and bad times with. Lloyd's sister Angela in particular soon became a close friend.

My family back in Oz emulated that welcoming feeling; they all loved Lloyd to bits. We would go on family holidays together, which was an enormous amount of fun. Angela and Christine used to come too. I remember one very hot summer afternoon, on one of our many trips to Australia, when we planned to go to a wildlife reserve in Ballarat. Christine came out of the house for the outing dressed in a tiny mini skirt, a tank top and the most outrageous sparkly sandals, which were purple with sky-high heels. I simply had to say something about how wearing those particular shoes to feed the kangaroos was somewhat inappropriate. We were going into the bush for goodness' sake – not to an opening-night red-carpet do! It was hilarious. We chuckled about that forever.

Australia was always mine and Lloyd's sanctuary. We often told each other that we would be together forever, no matter what happened. If the worst came to the worst with our careers, we agreed that we would go and make shell necklaces on the beach in Queensland.

But, on the contrary, we were going from strength to strength. In 2004, I returned to the Lido de Paris. This time, I was in charge and choreographing a show, *Bonheur*, which – I'm very proud to say – is still running today.

It was fantastic to go back, because I'd come full circle. As I went through the steps with the dancers, it was weird to think that my career in Europe had started on that very stage.

The experience was a challenge. I wasn't used to working with such tall dancers, for a start, who are generally few and far between in musical theatre. Plus, it was a huge spectacle. There were seventy dancers, only twelve of whom were boys, and the girls were all topless. That affects the choreography, as it means you can't include shimmies or 'titty-juggles' and you have to be careful about how far the dancers lean over and which side movements you employ. It was very different to my usual brief, and hard work. Yet it was also brilliant fun: wall-to-wall choreography and pure dance.

In the same year, I choreographed *Beautiful and Damned*, a musical based on the lives of F. Scott Fitzgerald and his wife, Zelda. We started the run out of London with previews at the Yvonne Arnaud Theatre in Guildford. John Barrowman played Fitzgerald for the Guildford season only. Also in the cast was Sarah Lark, who later found fame on *I'd Do Anything*, the BBC's search for an actress to play Nancy in *Oliver!* in the West End. She was amazing in *Beautiful and Damned*, and very helpful and creative.

One night, when I was going around giving out notes, I knocked on John Barrowman's dressing-room door and he yelled, 'Come in!'

When I opened the door, he was standing on the dressing-room table, bent over double, with his trousers round his ankles. He made me give his notes to his bare arse. It was hideous, but I adored him for it.

John is hilarious. He used to muck around on stage like you would not believe. As soon as he turned upstage, away from the audience, he would be pulling faces and trying to crack everyone up. He was always getting his willy out in rehearsals. You'd be in the middle of a dance number and you'd turn around to see John was flashing again. It was either that or his bottom. He is terrible. He's a naughty, naughty boy – but you can't help but love him.

He's great to work with if you are in the chorus, because he makes everyone laugh all the time. But if you're choreographing or directing, and you want to keep some decorum in the rehearsal room, he's a terror. He's professional, but he'll have everyone in stitches the minute you turn your back.

The only time I find John problematic is when he gets upset over something, for example, when he doesn't think a certain scene is working and feels that nobody is taking his points on board. When an actor doesn't trust a director, most people with talent will flare up. I can fully understand his frustration, but it takes quite a lot of effort to calm him down. Usually, however, he is right, so people should listen to him.

John is enormously gifted. I think once he started pushing for more control, his career really took off. Like any actor, he needs some guidance and help, and to be nurtured by his director. At Guildford, that was Phil Willmott.

Although I got on with Phil personally, we didn't see eye to eye on a professional level, so I became exasperated. There were lots of scenes in the production that I believed weren't gelling. Phil kept cutting the choreography, but to my mind, it wasn't just the steps that required an overhaul. The entire show needed to be sliced and diced and cut down to a decent length – it was three hours long and nobody wants to sit through theatre of that duration any more. In the end, I walked out. I just couldn't bear to work in a situation where the lines of communication weren't open.

After that, Phil and I had a chat and I said I would stay until opening night, but I wasn't interested in taking it to the West End. I would have to find something else to fill my time ...

CHAPTER 15 *Strictly Speaking*

Fate had a huge hand in my biggest break: becoming a judge on *Strictly Come Dancing*. In fact, the BBC had originally wanted just three judges and had already booked Len Goodman, Bruno Tonioli and Arlene Phillips. Then, at the last minute, they decided to add another one – and it happened to be me!

The call came during a hugely pressurized morning. I was working on *Beautiful and Damned*, and I was right in the middle of this major run-through with all the producers, so I couldn't have been more stressed out.

My agent, Gavin Barker, handed me his phone, as my mobile was switched off for the rehearsal, and asked, 'Can you go out and speak to the BBC, just for ten minutes?'

I agreed to a telephone interview and they asked me a series of questions like, 'What would you say if someone did this on the dance floor?' I knew nothing about the proposed show, so I was thinking, 'This is all rather odd.' At the end of the chat, they asked me if I would come in for a screen test. We found a morning in my schedule and I went to the BBC, but I had just an hour to spare. A week later, they called and said I had the job. It was only a few days before we went live on air on 15 May 2004.

Meeting the other judges for the first time was nerve-racking. I was introduced to them at rehearsal, in the green room, just before a production meeting. I knew Arlene already, of course, albeit from a distance. We had worked alongside one another on the

2002 Commonwealth Games, but the very first time I encountered her was when she'd choreographed me in the 1992 Royal Variety Performance, back when I was a dancer. It was easy to introduce myself and tell her that I'd worked for her a hundred years ago. She needed a bit of reminding about that, though, so perhaps it wasn't quite so memorable for her!

Arlene is from my world, but the more commercial end of it. We are both theatrical choreographers, but I tend to take on more arty-farty work, like Kurt Weill and Verdi operas, whereas Arlene executes sure-fire bets such as *Grease* and *Saturday Night Fever* brilliantly. Like me, she is used to being highly critical of herself. We are both very au fait with accepting feedback from reviewers. I think if you give out criticism, you'd better learn to take it. It's the nature of our jobs always to look for the missing element, the piece of the puzzle that will turn an average performance into a spectacular one. It's our bread and butter. After all, if we put anything substandard out there too often, we wouldn't work. Do three bad shows in a row and any choreographer is screwed; no one will employ you. You really are only as good as your last production.

When Arlene and I see a performance, we know what's wrong with it immediately, because that's what our eyes are trained to look for.

In contrast to my awareness of Arlene's work, I didn't know Bruno as a choreographer at all. I read a blurb about him before I went to the studio to meet him for the first time, so I knew he worked in film, TV and pop videos. That was obviously why our paths had never crossed.

My first impressions of him made me feel anxious, because he was completely over the top. I was worried that I didn't have that sort of over-exuberant character. I'm a lot drier, a lot calmer. I wasn't sure if I was supposed to match him – or even why I had been employed, because I was the last on the job. We judges never had any idea what our 'characters' were supposed to be. Though we must all have been cast for a reason, we weren't told why. We were recruited on the strength of our reactions to video footage, which is what they'd showed us in the screen test. On reflection, I guess that, as a director, I would have cast the series in exactly the same way.

Finally, I met Len, whom I thought was *really* scary, because he knows everything about ballroom; he's like a walking technical manual. I stood there with the three of them thinking, 'This is going to be awful. I'm going to be pulled up all the time.'

Of course, when we got going it was fine, because Len would talk about technique and we would comment on the performance. He wasn't called Head Judge on the first series. That title came later, when they introduced the dance-off, because someone had to have the casting vote and Len was the obvious choice.

As the first show approached, all four of us judges were nervous wrecks. I'd never done live TV before in this capacity, and the thought of having to critique these celebrities in front of millions of viewers was terrifying. The only celebrities I'd ever had dealings with were theatrical ones, like Dame Judi Dench and Dame Julie Andrews, and all in the comfort of a closed rehearsal room or theatre. Not in public.

None of us had a clue what we were doing in the beginning. We didn't know how it would pan out at all and, in fact, we all thought it would be an absolute disaster. I gave it three weeks, tops. We didn't think anyone was interested in ballroom dancing any more. Yet after that first programme, we came off and we were buzzing. We looked at each other and said, 'My God, that really worked.'

In TV, it's very difficult to predict how the masses will react to something. You have a studio audience, but they're warmed up and given direction on when to clap and laugh. You never know how the programme will affect the people sitting at home, until it goes on air. But we got a really good feeling about it all on show one and it took off, from that very first day. It was unbelievable.

It was fascinating to observe how the crowd in the studio reacted. The first words out of my mouth, live on the night *Strictly* first aired, were 'Dull, dull, dull!' which has become the comment for which many people best remember me. I was honestly surprised that people booed. Everything I had said was the truth – not what people wanted to hear or what I thought the Beeb wanted me to say. As far as I was concerned, it really *was* dull.

Unfortunately, that description happened to be directed at newsreader Natasha Kaplinsky, who went on to win the series, and her dance partner Brendan Cole. I did think she was boring to start with, but she grew on me.

In the original show, I sat where Bruno is now, next to Len, and Bruno sat at the other end, next to Arlene. The producers decided to swap us because Bruno generally gave good comments, whereas I tended to be harsh. The way the camera panned down the line meant that Bruno always spoke first, then Arlene, Len and finally me, which meant that we ended each routine with a big boo. So they put Bruno close to host Bruce Forsyth instead, so they could have a bit of banter, and stuck me – the vile social outcast – on the other end.

Watching *Strictly* take off was mind-boggling and quite scary, but only because I was giving away my anonymity. As a director and choreographer in the theatre, you are protected, because no one knows what your face looks like. People may know your name and those within the industry may know you well, but you're not accosted in the street. Even the most famous theatrical names, such as Nicholas Hytner and Sam Mendes, were totally anonymous in a crowd before they made movies.

After that first programme, my face was everywhere, which was really odd for me. I hadn't even considered that appearing on the series might make me famous. It was overnight celebrity and it felt very weird indeed, especially when I was branded the 'Mr Nasty' of the judging panel. The day after the broadcast, I walked out the door of my house and someone recognized me. I'd had no idea of the power of television, so it was surreal. It's easy to forget how much people talk about it – the show, us judges, the celebs and how they're all getting on.

I found it funny how many passers-by just said, 'There's that bloke off the telly.' It seemed to take five series before the public learned my name. Now, finally, I hear, 'It's Craig Revel Horwood.' It's a long name and people struggle to get the whole thing, so it took them a while. When you think how often the names are announced on the programme, though, before each and every scoring, it's strange that even ardent fans of *Strictly* were foxed by it.

In that first series, we didn't know how the show would affect us all. We were making it up as we went along. It was a brand-new concept and we were all finding our way: producers, directors, judges, celebs, dancers – in fact, everyone on the whole team.

In the beginning, it was all very chummy backstage, nowhere near as much tension as in the following series. I guess most celebs were thinking that it didn't really matter, it was a bit of a challenge and fun. Everyone entered into it for charity and nobody, back then, thought their career depended on it. It wasn't even seen as a career enhancer. Let's face it, all they were really going to win was a mirrorball on top of a plinth. Of course, that proved to be very small thinking.

The show, almost instantly, turned into a phenomenon. The series-one winner, Natasha Kaplinsky, became red-carpet fodder for the next four years. She was invited to every high-profile event in the UK – and she's a newsreader, for goodness' sake, not a Hollywood actress or supermodel. I thought that was a brilliant consequence of her success on *Strictly*, though, that it brought the news to the red carpet. Current affairs has always been known, in my mind at least, for its stiff, starchy approach, but Natasha glamorized it and made it fashionable. The presenters can't usually have emotional attachment or opinion on the material they deliver, so the viewers don't know what newsreaders are like behind their newsroom facade, but I think *Strictly* brought their personalities to the forefront a lot more, which was a positive thing as it has made the news accessible to all.

Natasha really didn't want to do the series right at the start, but as the weeks progressed, she got more and more into it. To begin with, she lacked confidence, but as soon as she realized she could move, she adored it. She fell in love with the dancing by the end because she was so good at it.

There were rumours, as you may recall, that it wasn't just the ballroom she had fallen for. A *Strictly* scandal erupted regarding her alleged relationship with her dance partner, Brendan Cole. Dancers and celebrities get very close during training and I'm sure that can occasionally lead to romance, but mostly they just become very good friends. The papers often get the wrong end of the stick. For example, in the same series, Martin Offiah and Erin Boag had a picnic together and were pictured laughing, so the media thought there was something between them. I didn't believe that, although they were close pals.

As judges we don't see any of what goes on backstage, so the first we know of any alleged relationships is when we read about them in the papers.

Natasha and I got on very well and used to chat in the bar after the live shows. I am one of the only judges to frequent the BBC bar following the programme. Len has his partner, Sue, so he usually has just the one drink before shooting off. Arlene has her family and likes to get straight back home after the show; she doesn't drink anyway so it would be a bit dull for her. Right from the start, Bruno and I were the ones who stayed and chatted to everyone. We soon got to know one another well and became great friends.

I like to talk to the celebrities afterwards to reassure them that anything I've said is not personal, because no one likes being judged, including myself. In fact, lots of the contestants come up to me in the bar to ask me to elaborate on my feedback. The judges generally have only ten or twenty seconds to comment on air. The contestants know I have a lot more to say, but I never get a chance to say it because of time constraints – and a lot of booing.

Being from the world of theatre, I'd anticipated that the television industry might be full of bravado and people being false. Conversely, I learned that there were actually a lot of people from the trade who were really into *Strictly Come Dancing*, unashamedly so. When I appeared on *Richard & Judy*, I'd thought that the eponymous presenters would probably put on the facade of being regular viewers, but it turned out that they are truthfully into it and desperately interested in everything. It's wonderful that the programme has captured the imagination of the nation.

Following the success of the first series in the summer of 2004, another was planned immediately for the peak autumn schedules. Series two ran from 23 October to 11 December 2004. I went into it with less confidence, strangely. I thought it would be difficult to repeat our success. The first season was unique, genuinely improvised because we didn't know what we were doing. We only really formulated it at the end of that series and though we knew we had something, we didn't quite know what.

I went into the new season with great trepidation, thinking, 'It's going to plummet and fall on its arse because the celebrities won't be as good and people will see it as a formula and nothing more.' I was also concerned that the judges would be branded and become caricatures of ourselves – and that I would become more well known and lose jobs in the theatre.

In fact, that's what happened. A lot of directors are apprehensive about working with me now because they think I'm going to be horrible to the company or too starry. The second series was the one that solidified that impression in everybody's hearts and minds. It was then, though, that we realized it wasn't just a one-off; it was a hit.

The grand Blackpool Tower Ballroom was the venue for the final of series two. We travelled up by train, then the whole lot of us were shoved into the same dressing room (with men and women separated for modesty, naturally). Bruno, Len and I had never been mixed with the celebs before so it was really weird, as it was the first time that we'd got changed together. We were all in our pants looking for make-up and hairbrushes, which was quite amusing, but scary for us judges.

Then, as usual, we weren't allowed to watch any of the rehearsals, so we were just stuck there. They have spies out in case we walk in on a routine. There's always a runner looking for us to make sure we aren't peeking, and everyone goes to great lengths to keep us from seeing anything too soon. Even in make-up, if the rehearsals come on the monitor in the room, they'll turn our chair away so we can't see. It makes us feel completely unwanted and unloved.

Backstage, the contestants are always rehearsing in the corridor, in a mad panic before they go on. We walk past and they suddenly stop dancing and move away, which is quite funny.

On that trip to Blackpool, we stayed in a hotel that was absolutely ghastly. It was really run-down and very 'end of the pier'. You wouldn't have put your dog in there. These days, when I'm on tour, I get to stay in decent hotels, but in the past, the accommodation has sometimes been far from perfect.

The Blackpool digs were dirty and poorly operated. Arlene even got bitten by bedbugs, which I found hilarious, but she was absolutely furious. She made us all look at her room and see if any of ours were any better. Naturally, they weren't. Arlene's always been the one to push for what she thinks we deserve. She's brilliant, in fact – a driven woman with a very strong mind who knows exactly what she wants and won't suffer fools lightly.

Needless to say, the hotel rooms have improved with the ratings.

At the final, Jill Halfpenny triumphed as the winner of season two. She really impressed me. Jill is from my world, the theatre: an actress who can sing and dance, and she applies herself to everything she does. Just after she swept the board on *Strictly*, she went into a stint in the West End production of *Chicago* as Roxie Hart and was a revelation in that. Her versatility is her strength; she can cross over from *EastEnders*, to Broadway and the West End, to ballroom dancing. Her jive will always live in my memory as something spectacular.

Series two marked the first time a contestant and I didn't see eye to eye; it wouldn't be the last.

By my own admission – and I hold my hands up here – I became personal in my comments to Julian Clary on Claudia Winkleman's spin-off show from *Strictly Come Dancing*, *It Takes Two*, the week after the final aired. One of the joys of *Strictly* is going on Claudia's programme; she makes me howl with laughter and she's really into the whole thing. She's sold on it, which I love.

On this occasion, I wasn't laughing. Everyone thought I was drunk, but I wasn't at all, I hadn't had a single drink. I was just upset about the things that Julian had been saying about me.

He'd been having digs at me for a while on the main show. He referred to me as 'the particularly ugly one on the end' and, in the semi-final, when I said, 'The jacket and the shoes did all the work for Julian,' he barked back, 'You've got too much foundation on.'

'That won't change the fact that that jive was terrible,' I retorted.

In the final, live from Blackpool, he called me a 'silly old queen'. I thought to myself, 'Yes, I probably am a silly queen – but I'm not old!'

Julian was on Claudia's show the following week. I was sitting at home, watching him on television. Claudia's producers had asked me to do a phone-in interview. I knew it was going to be about Julian and how I was taking these personal jibes.

So, live on air, I told the nation that I wasn't responding to them very well at all and said, 'Here are a few personal comments about Julian.' Then I reeled off a whole list of things that I thought were hampering his dancing. I was like a lunatic, raving about his insecurities and his career. Claudia looked a little shocked, but, ever the professional, turned to her guest and asked, 'Well, what do you think about that, Julian?'

He sat there patting Valerie, his dog, and then, with a very quick wit, replied, 'Oh sorry, I wasn't listening. What did he say?'

Julian is brilliant: in one fell swoop, he completely negated everything I'd said.

I wasn't allowed to release my anger on the BBC1 show because I was told not to react if he called me names. He could say anything he liked about me, but I wasn't allowed to say anything personal about him, unless it was to do with dancing.

On the phone-in, I thought, 'Well, I'll mention a few things about him now, while I have the chance,' and it all came out. It was a complete rant.

I don't know if Julian complained, but I was forced to make an apology about that interview. The BBC had thought I was inebriated. I was told sternly, 'Craig, we heard about your phone-in on Julian Clary,' and I was given some very sound advice. 'You are not to get personal about any of the celebrities. Your job is to comment on the dancing and not their careers.'

I was firmly put in my place. I had to say sorry on Claudia's show, although it was an informal retraction.

Unfortunately, backstage Julian and I hadn't got on like the proverbial 'house on fire', as I'd been expecting. That even started to affect my relationship with Erin Boag, his dance partner, because she was, quite rightly, protective of him. I wanted to be able to say to him, 'You're not the world's best dancer, but so what? Let's have a drink and toast your courage.' But the atmosphere wasn't right for that.

I think all the contestants are brave and courageous for taking part in the first place. In my opinion it doesn't matter whether they get knocked out in the first, second or final show. They're still achieving something for themselves and for charity.

One random evening, long after the series had finished and Jill Halfpenny had been crowned queen of the ballroom, I was with some mates in the Black Cap, which is a gay pub in Camden, when Julian and I bumped into each other. There was a drag act on at the time and she said, over the mike, 'You won't believe who is in tonight. Julian Clary and Craig Revel Horwood – sat at the same bar!'

So we greeted each other with a kiss and a 'How are you, darling?' Then we had a drink together and it was all fine.

In fact, I like him as a person very much. During the show, it was hard for both of us to differentiate between criticism of his dancing and a personal attack.

Of course, you could argue that the judges' comments *are* an attack on the celebrities' personalities because dancing is informed by personality. If someone is not confident, or is obstructed in some other way, it's so crystal clear, especially to the four of us who have been watching professional dancing all our lives.

At the time, Julian did say breezily, 'It's all theatre, love,' and in a way I suppose that's true, it is. Nevertheless, it was difficult for me to withstand his personal comments, being the butt of his every joke; and I guess it was difficult for him to take my criticism, especially publicly. I learned a great deal that season.

Strictly certainly relaunched Julian, putting him firmly in the public eye. People had a chance to be reminded of his great wit and dry humour, and warmly accepted him into their homes. He ended up presenting the National Lottery and many other shows. *SCD* works for the contestants in that way, and good luck to them.

Christmas 2004 saw a special version of the *Strictly* format – on ice. *Strictly Ice Dancing* was a one-off programme produced for the festive TV schedule. I thought it was a great idea and was asked to judge it from a dance perspective.

It was said by some that I knew nothing about skating. In fact, I can ice skate and I'm probably up to a grade six or seven – but I would agree that my proficiency is nowhere near polished enough to enable me to judge the skill, by any stretch of the imagination. I certainly couldn't get up and do it any better than the contestants. Consequently, I limited my feedback to the dance aspect and the top line. It was, after all, a dance contest on ice. Like figure skating, you still need to train in ballet and ballroom to enhance your upper body movement. The routines are generally devised with a choreographer first, and then the ice skater works out a way to put those steps on to the ice. Yet it's always the body from the knee upwards that people admire, not the blades below.

Everyone involved expected me to be vile, but I couldn't be nasty about people skating because I didn't know anything about that. Nevertheless, backstage, as soon as I walked in, the fear of God was put into everybody. In make-up, the contestants were all saying, 'Please be kind.' Some of them just froze in terror. They all thought I was going to slag them off, but I think I was – and am – quite generous.

I still managed to upset Carol Smillie, though. I didn't like much about her performance at all, except her gorgeous beaming smile.

David Seaman won it. He was phenomenal. I went backstage to meet him and he was so tall in his skates, even I was craning my neck. It truly was a wonderful show. It looked beautiful and the people you least expected skated well. Then ITV copied it!

I spent Christmas with Lloyd and my family in Australia. It was lovely to see them all again, and my long-suffering sister Sue helped me with my latest project – writing my first book. It was called *Teach Yourself Ballroom Dancing*. I'd been approached to write such a volume a few times and said no, but then I thought it might do me good. So I told the publisher, 'I'll write three chapters and if you like them, I'll finish the rest.'

I drafted some sample text in Australia and decided to test the first chapter on Sue.

'Read this and then see if you can dance,' I instructed, but she got all confused. Most books on dancing are baffling; you require a PhD to understand *The Ballroom Manual*.

So I rewrote it, and boy, did I struggle. I threw the manuscript out three times: I scattered it all over my bedroom once; composed a second draft and ripped it up; and deleted a third entirely when my Mac went down. After that, I wanted to give up.

I had absolutely no experience of writing a book. What I knew for certain was that the content should be described in layman's terms. I'm not Len Goodman, I'm not from the world of ballroom: I needed to understand it just as much as the reader did. My knowledge of dance is wide, if not deep – I have studied all kinds of movement. Rather than being a specialist in one field, I've worked in many, so I recognized the importance of making the book accessible. I wanted to explain the simple basic steps that I had learned as a kid, without patronizing the reader, so that people could pick up the book and actually learn to dance. The book wasn't intended to replace lessons, but to be something that would arm people with a useful foundation before they went to a proper teacher.

In fact, the book was a project I'd long wanted to do for myself, to overcome the issues I had with ballroom and Latin. There are so many versions around the world, I can't tell you. Everyone has a different opinion about the intricacies of the sport, whether that heel lead was correct, and so on. The rules and regulations are so varied that researching the text became a horrific experience, but it did allow me to get to grips with all the differences between the Australian, American, UK and International rules.

I also turned to Len and his lovely partner Sue for help. I danced a lot with Sue to get things clear in my mind and body. She's a qualified teacher of the Imperial Society of Teachers of

Dancing (ISTD) and runs a dance school with Len, and she was wonderful. She helped me enormously. Initially, I didn't want anyone to know because I thought it would undermine my judgement on *Strictly*. But in truth, writing the book, and learning from Sue, has enabled me to be a fairer judge, both on the technical side of things and on the emotional performance.

Just as well. Some of the dancers, such as Erin Boag, had begun to challenge me on matters of technique. However, despite my improved knowledge, I'm sure my altercations with the professionals will continue – particularly as they fight even amongst themselves about the intricate technicalities. You only have to look at the film *Strictly Ballroom* to see that there is a wide range of variants.

There have been arguments in dance for centuries about notation and the way things should be done; and not only in the ballroom and Latin world, either, but in every dance discipline. I think it's safe to say that there probably always will be.

CHAPTER 16 *Comic Relief Does Peanut Butter*

My next TV challenge was taking on the role of judge on *Comic Relief Does Fame Academy*, in spring 2005. My career in the West End provided ideal grounding for the post. Unfortunately, nobody told the audience that.

There was a lot of bitching on that programme, with people – both viewers and those in the team – saying, 'What the hell does he know about singing?' Having only seen me on *Strictly* commenting on dance, no one knew what my qualifications were, largely because there was no VT introduction (a pre-recorded section shown on a live show) to explain.

As a director and choreographer, I evaluate the talents of around 6,000 people a year; and I studied music for almost a decade, so I know a G sharp from a B flat. I assessed the *Fame Academy* acts as I would any West End audition. *I* knew that I was qualified to judge the show, but, when I joined the programme, the audience and the vocal coaches, David and Carrie Grant, didn't. They were always putting me down and saying, 'What would you know about this?' which drove me nuts.

I'd been told to talk about the dance and movement, but I thought to myself, 'Hang on, most of the time the acts are standing at a microphone, so I'm not here to discuss just the dance aspect of the performance, am I? Why have they got me on here?' I then told the producers that I needed to comment on entertainment value and vocals as well, and movement only if it was required, which of course is what I did.

In the end, I felt I had to defend myself on VT. I recorded a slot, where I said, 'I audition thousands of people every year. I'm a director and choreographer, which doesn't mean I only look after dance. Most of the shows I work on are musicals or operas, so I need singers too.'

However, it wasn't until David and Carrie challenged me to sing on Claudia Winkleman's BBC3 tie-in show that people knew that I could actually hold a tune myself. I will always accept a challenge, even if I fail miserably, so I went for it. I sang 'I Am What I Am'. Even Carrie had to admit that I had good vocals.

Eventually, I found my place – but then David and Carrie were reduced to calling me Mr Orange, in supposed defence of the celebs, which was pathetic. I'd recently been to Australia for Christmas, so, yes, I was very, very tanned and I had make-up to match it. On telly, I looked really orange, but that's beside the point.

David and Carrie would often come up to me after *Fame Academy* to say, 'We think the banter on stage is really good.' And I have to agree, it's very interesting for the audience to hear different opinions. But when slanging matches occur, I generally pull out of them unless I have something profound to say, or disagree entirely and feel the need to make my point clear.

We had a lot of on-screen arguments, but that was fair enough. They were defending people that they were coaching so, of course, they would say I was wrong, because it was their teaching skills on the line. There was a lot more at stake for them.

The jokes and jibes continued to flow. Once, David said something like, 'The future's bright. The future's not orange.' Then, when I went out on the street, everyone was calling me Mr Orange. People would walk behind me saying, 'Can you smell oranges?' It was playground stuff and totally bizarre. I can take a joke and am the first person to laugh at myself, but that just seemed unnecessary.

What I love about *Fame Academy* is that the celebrities come on and act, sing and dance – it's probably closer to my world than judging ballroom is, oddly enough.

In the 2005 show, the celebrities were revolting – in the rebellious sense of the word, of course. Nick Knowles became the spokesperson, saying I was too rude and that I should be reined in. He said they thought it was disgusting that they were all being spoken to so bluntly and that I was making contestants cry because of my comments on their voices. But if their voice sucks, and they're out of tune, I'm going to say that. I was only telling them what was wrong with their performances, but they didn't want to hear it.

My fellow *Fame Academy* judge Richard Parks somehow seems to get away with the most personal insults, largely because he does it more for effect. In comparison, I think that when I make a comment, I try to hit the nail on the head and get right to the heart of the problem, which can sometimes be a little too frank for people's liking.

Richard always tells the audience about the song, for example when it was written, who produced it, or whatever, and then reveals whether he loves the performance or hates it. Our colleague, Lesley Garrett, who completes the panel, is a bit of a fence sitter, though she'll always say if there's a problem with the vocals, but in a nice, encouraging way, which is good. I try to be honest and true to myself. Sometimes, I guess, my comments might come out a little harshly or without feeling, but it's not intentional.

On one occasion, I disagreed with Richard when he told one of the celebs, 'You sang that brilliantly. I loved it.' I was astonished and said, 'That was completely out of tune, from the beginning to the middle and to the end.'

But the next night, Richard backtracked. 'When I listened again to the song you sang last night, it was completely out of tune. It was our monitoring system here. I couldn't hear properly.'

I was glad to be blessed with good sound – and it did make me chuckle a little, because it meant I was right.

Actually, Richard Parks and I get on very well off-screen – I have even been to his kids' school to make speeches and hand out awards and so on. Theirs is in fact not the only one; I make many visits to schools all around the country to promote education. I have also become an ambassador for a charity called Teach First, which addresses educational disadvantage by transforming exceptional graduates into effective and inspirational teachers.

The same year I took on *Fame Academy* for the first time, I was asked to stage and choreograph *Once Upon a Time ... The Life of Hans Christian Andersen* for the 200th anniversary of the great man's birth. The concert was to be staged in Denmark in the 48,000-seater Parken Stadium in Copenhagen on 2 April 2005, and it would be televised, live, around the world.

The job was a real coup because I got to work with Olivia Newton-John, Roger Moore and the wonderful Tina Turner. I studied all Andersen's poems and books, and then tied them together to create a representative show. It was huge fun being able to employ all these strange characters for the chorus, like dancers who were really tall or absolutely tiny, or on the heavy side and with faces full of character. Normally, you have to cast dancers who are similar looking, and that usually means slim and gorgeous. For this, I had to find rat characters, fairies, goblins and giants, which made a refreshing change.

For the design, I worked with my über-creative friend Christopher Woods. He was brilliant at making the costumes come to life. The whole project was fantastical, which is right up Christopher's street. I love doing pieces like that as well because they are rare opportunities in the theatre.

It was a massive spectacle, with Olivia Newton-John singing and presenting, some arty storytelling sequences and then 400 kids from various Danish schools on stage in the finale. Directing hundreds of children from the ages of five to thirteen – who speak only Danish – was a bit of a challenge, while simply trying to organize them, along with their chaperones, was a nightmare. But they were good kids. They had all learned the song 'The Snow Queen' at their schools and they sang it beautifully on the night.

Tina Turner was our special guest and she belted out a few of her famous numbers. It was fabulous having her on board, but trying to tie in why she was there, and what she had to do with Hans Christian Andersen, was tricky. Ultimately, we came up with this mirrored swan idea, inspired by the Ugly Duckling story, and she burst through that set piece for her grand entrance, singing 'Simply the Best'. It was truly phenomenal.

Tina is absolutely lovely, a real star, funny, and not precious at all. I expected her to whirl in with an entourage and say, 'Oh darling, I'm not doing that!' but she was really nice.

We had only a day to rehearse with her, but that was more for the dancers' sake than hers. You don't direct Tina Turner. She does her own thing and she came with her own dancers. She has her own, very famous, strut, which all the dancers emulate. You don't mess around with a legend.

The autumn saw season three of *Strictly* hit the small screen. I particularly remember that series for Darren Gough's freestyle dance, which is one of the all-time highlights of *SCD*.

We were all dab hands at the programme come the third season – so polished, in fact, that ever since we judges have often been accused of being scripted, but we genuinely aren't. Everything that the audience sees is completely improvised.

By that stage in the show's history, it was clear that all the judges had very different opinions. I think that's what makes the panel so interesting. The dynamic between the four of us works really well. If we tried to be anyone that we're not, it wouldn't be a success. Consequently, none of us ever makes comments solely for effect because, in order to have an effective argument, you have to believe in it and be able to qualify it. On some other shows it's just argument for argument's sake, which is silly. I won't enter into a row unless I have a valid point to make. Given that, I find it astonishing how often people come up to me and enquire whether or not I'm asked to be nasty. I wouldn't do the job if that were the case. I simply tell it as I see it.

Honesty is a key part of my nature, and the very reason the BBC chose me as a judge. However, my gob can get me into trouble. The third season of *Strictly* became infamous, at least as far as I was concerned, for the Patsy Palmer incident.

Patsy questioned my credentials as a judge, which infuriated me. So I said, in a moment of temporary insanity and fury, 'That's rich coming from a two-bit actress in a second-rate soap, in a puffa jacket who cries all the time.' It was quite vile of me, I admit. But at the time I was angry.

When my retort was printed in the press, one of the papers changed my phrasing to 'a scrubber in a puffa jacket', while another claimed I had called her 'a chav in a puffa', which I would never have said because I've never used the expression 'chav' in my life; it's a British thing. In fact, I'd never even heard of the word until I apparently said it. I read the article and was outraged. I was saying to anyone who'd listen, 'I didn't call her a chav!'

In my riposte, I'd only used the words that she herself had employed about her character in *EastEnders* when being interviewed by Brucie on the very first programme, so I thought I'd be OK. Apparently not. Patsy was understandably unhappy because of the comments I'd made so I got my wrist slapped, deservedly, and I had to make a national apology. It was a much more formal affair than when I'd retracted my comments about Julian Clary. I truly did regret what I'd said about Patsy.

She and I did eventually 'kiss' and make up; it was put behind us and laid to rest very quickly. The incident actually brought us closer. Patsy is an extremely lovely person. She did warn me you have to be very careful with the press and how you phrase things, as it can be taken out of context. She has probably had to put up with that sort of thing most of her working life. Anyone in the public eye does.

In the midst of that third series of *Strictly*, I learned, with heartbreaking clarity, that all good things come to an end. Lloyd and I had met when we were both relatively young; we'd grown up together as a couple; we'd shared some amazing times and experiences; we loved each other deeply. Then thirteen years of bliss came crashing down around our ears.

Lloyd, I think, hit some sort of mid-life crisis. It proved to be the end for us. He said that I went away too much and he was lonely, but when he was here by himself, well, it transpired that he wasn't alone after all.

In late 2005, a rogue jar of peanut butter finally gave the game away. I'd been working away a lot over the past couple of years, and every time I came home, I'd find a jar of peanut butter in the kitchen cupboard. Lloyd hates peanut butter, as do I, so several times I just chucked it out and didn't think anything of it.

But on one occasion, I came back and was struck by its oddity. This time, I looked at the sell-by date, which I'd never thought to do before. It was obviously a recent jar. I thought, 'This is really strange. Why do all these jars keep appearing?' Then I figured Lloyd must have taken a fancy to it. When he came home from work, I asked him about it.

'Who eats peanut butter?' I said. 'Every time I come back, there's peanut butter in the pantry. Have you started eating it?'

'You know I hate peanut butter,' he replied.

'Then why is there peanut butter in the pantry?' I persisted.

'It must be Abi's,' he answered. 'Abi's been staying here.'

Abi is Lloyd's nephew, who stayed at our place occasionally.

I accepted the answer and put the jar back in the cupboard.

That night, we attended a play in Islington. By coincidence, Abi came with us. During the interval, I said, 'Abi, this may sound weird, but do you like peanut butter?' He responded, 'No, not really.' Then I asked him if he'd ever bought it and whether, when he'd been staying at the house, he had left some in our kitchen. He said, 'No.'

At that moment, I was hit by the horrible realization that Lloyd had lied to me. I didn't know what he was covering up, but I knew he was hiding something. When you trust someone for thirteen years, with your life, you don't expect them to lie to you, so I was understandably in a bit of a state.

I started necking drinks in the interval, and after the play, and I got horribly drunk because I was determined to confront Lloyd. I think I was in shock. I knew that our sex life hadn't been great for a couple of years; it had lost its intensity and become rather routine. Yet Lloyd always blamed the lacklustre display on other things so, until that night, I hadn't suspected anything was wrong between us.

When we came back from the theatre, I walked into the kitchen. Lloyd had done what he always did when he got home: taken off his trousers, opened the fridge and started munching away at a snack. I got the suspect jar out of the cupboard and said, 'Lloyd, I have to ask you one last time. Whose peanut butter is this? You must know. You live in the house.'

He didn't say anything, so I carried on.

'I know it's not Abi's and that he hasn't been staying here. Half a jar has been used and you don't use that in one morning, so who has been staying here while I've been away?'

Silence.

You could have cut the atmosphere with a knife. Absolute silence – and guilt written all over his face.

My heart was in my mouth, but I carried on. I had to know.

'Are you having an affair?' I asked.

Silence and guilt.

'I just have to know. Are you having an affair?'

Didn't speak. Couldn't speak. So I kept on fishing.

Then I remembered that the only person I'd captured on film

with Lloyd, looking all boyfriendish, was Michael, the delivery boy from the shop. I thought back to three years earlier, when I'd taken a photo of them on the roof terrace at the house. They'd come home together on a Saturday afternoon, not knowing that I was on the terrace with my friend Margie and her new baby. Looking back, it struck me as odd that they were at the house when they should have been on deliveries together, so Michael was the first name that I came up with.

'Are you having an affair with Michael?' I asked.

As soon as I mentioned Michael's name, his face dropped, his eyes started welling up and he slowly nodded his head and said, 'Yes.'

'How long has this been going on?'

Lloyd started spluttering, 'It's over, it's over. It doesn't exist any more. It's finished. It was just five weeks.'

I believed him. Every word.

'I always knew this would happen,' I told him. 'Over thirteen years, I knew you'd sleep with someone else.'

Lloyd broke down and cried, sobbing, 'Don't leave me. Don't leave me,' over and over again, like a broken record. I calmed him down and told him I wasn't going to leave him, but we needed to talk about it.

Then I said, 'So all the time I've been away, he's been living here?'

'Yes, but I told you, it's over. He's gone. He's gone back to New Zealand.'

It was a mess, but I said, 'We'll get through this. We'll be fine.'

Of course, I started questioning everything then. He really hadn't told me anything. He wouldn't open up about it, or talk about it at all. He just kept saying, 'It's over.' We tried to work things out, but I kept discovering more and more secrets. I logged on to my computer and looked up that photograph of Michael and Lloyd, and I started thinking about dates.

Then I went through the phone bills, which is something I would never have dreamed of doing before, but I needed confirmation of what was going on.

Lloyd kept insisting it was finished, so we started getting through it and I was more relaxed and calm, but he still wouldn't discuss it. I wanted to know about their relationship, when it had started and how. I wanted the gory details and, above all, I wanted him to be honest with me and tell me the truth. But I knew it was going to take a bit of time for him to open up, so I let it lie.

A few days later, Lloyd's friend James came round. I didn't know him very well because Lloyd tended to see his friends while I was away, but it was through them that I began to discover what had really gone on. Lloyd left the room for some reason and James sighed, 'Phew, I'm really glad you know about that thing with Michael.'

Then he confided that he had tried to pick up Michael two years before, but Michael had knocked him back, saying, 'No, I can't. Lloyd will kill me.'

James said cheerfully, 'I'm glad you know about it all now,' but I thought, 'I didn't know any of that!' So I said, 'Keep talking.'

That's the sort of thing I kept hearing all the time. First, Lloyd had told me it went on for five weeks, and then two years, and I think in fact it was nearer three. I'm still not sure of the truth.

Soon after James's visit, Lloyd's phone beeped and I happened to glance at the text message, which said: 'Missing you. The farmer's wife. Pudsey.' They even had cute little names for each other. Lloyd called him Pudsey Bear and Michael called Lloyd Yogi.

I stood and stared at the message and I felt sick. Lloyd had promised me that he had finished it and this was proof he had done no such thing. It was getting uglier and uglier. I knew there was only one thing I could do, so I left the house. I had to get away. I packed my bags and went to stay with my close friend Christopher Woods.

After a week, I came to my senses. Why was I moving out of the house when he was the one who had been sleeping with his boyfriend in our bed for two or three years?

Enough was enough. I went home and told him, 'This is not fair. You move out. I don't see why I should have to.' I said we needed to talk because we had the jointly owned house and shops to consider. We agreed not to spend Christmas together, so Lloyd went to his family and I went to Paris. We planned to reconvene in London on 6 January to sort things out.

That was the last I saw of him until Valentine's Day. He just disappeared. The only communication I received was a text message on Christmas Eve, which read: 'I'm on a flight to finish it. I have to tell him face to face.' Then nothing.

All the time I was in Paris over Christmas, I was sending texts to him, asking, 'Where are you?' and 'What's going on?' but I got no reply.

It turned out that the reason I couldn't get hold of him was because he was on a farm in New Zealand with Michael and his family; mobile phones didn't work in the area.

Before the break-up, we had scheduled a trip to Australia in the new year to visit my family. Eventually, he did get in touch by text to ask, 'What's your arrival date?' I told him I wasn't coming any more and asked him where he was. He just said, 'I'll meet you in Australia.' He turned up at my sister Susan's house in Melbourne and acted like nothing was going on; Susan had no idea what to do.

He told me he'd spent New Year's Eve just sat in a hotel alone. Doubtful, I rang two friends in Sydney and asked them if they'd happened to see Lloyd out and about during the festivities. One of them told me that Lloyd had paid for Michael to fly to Sydney and spend New Year with him. He hadn't gone out there to finish it at all.

By the time I came back from Paris, I had had enough. I thought, 'Fuck this!' and I decided to book the whole year out of

London. My beautiful sister Diane flew over and came to my rescue. That meant so much to me, to have family around when I was feeling lost and alone. She helped me to pack up the house. I rented it out, then went up to Leeds to work on the Kurt Weill operetta *Arms and the Cow* (*Der Kuhhandel*) for the whole of February.

On Valentine's Day, Lloyd turned up at Leeds train station with a bunch of flowers and a bottle of vodka, begging for forgiveness. I said, 'Where have you been?'

'I had to finish it with Michael,' he said. 'I told you that.'

'But Lloyd, we were supposed to meet on 6 January,' I replied. 'It's now 14 February!'

He tried to kiss me, but I said no. Then he started to cry. He wanted to stay in the flat I was renting, but I wouldn't let him, so he had nowhere to live. I made him stay in a hotel down the road. It was killing me to send him away, absolute torture, but I had to.

I told him we needed a year apart and then we could talk about it. Lloyd said, 'I want you back.' And I replied, 'But you keep lying to me.' I told him I knew about New Year's Eve. The trust was gone.

Over the next few months, I gave him numerous opportunities to come back. I told him we could move on, but only if he could get out of the hideous situation he'd put himself in, where he didn't know what he wanted. I told him to make a decision and we'd take it from there.

I was in absolute turmoil. We would talk, but every time we got close to working things out, he'd fly off to New Zealand to be with Michael. He kept running away from things, so it was hard to get hold of him long enough to have a decent conversation. It gradually reached the point where I thought, 'We're going to have to go our separate ways.'

In spring 2006, we decided to meet up for dinner in London at a local Indian restaurant, which was one of our old haunts, to try to talk about things in a calm and adult manner. By the time the meal had ended, we were both none the wiser about our relationship and what he wanted. As we approached the road outside our house, I was so frustrated that I gave him an ultimatum.

'Lloyd,' I said quietly, 'when I cross that road, I'm going to be on the other side. If you stay on this side, I will know that you don't want to be with me forever. If you cross with me, I will know that you do want to be with me, and you'll finish with Michael and never see him again.'

I crossed the road. He stood there and stood there and, finally, he crossed the street and came to me. Then he said, 'But there's one thing. I've got to see Michael one more time.'

That was the final straw. I said, 'That's it. It is now officially over! I can't take this any more.'

I really was devastated because I'd tried for months to sort it out. We'd set up meetings to talk about our relationship, but every time I tried, I received a glazed-over, non-committal response. He couldn't tell me anything about Michael. He was having real problems with the dilemma and essentially he was going through a breakdown. Sadly, I couldn't help him out of it.

In the end, I knew it just had to finish because the limbo was destroying me. It was agony to know we weren't a couple any more, but from that moment, I could begin to go forward.

CHAPTER 17 *Beautiful But Damned*

Looking back, there had been hints along the way. Just before we split, in autumn 2005, we'd gone to Prague for a romantic break. We were trying to get our sexual relationship back on track and where better than in that romantic city? Lloyd had only been there as a student, so it seemed the perfect place.

Unfortunately, I had to fly back in the middle of the trip to do a snooker challenge with Dennis Taylor. *Strictly Come Dancing* viewers may remember that he had dared me to learn snooker in five days after I criticized his dancing. He said I was being horrible to him and asked, 'Have you ever picked up a snooker cue and tried to learn?' Of course, I was absolutely hopeless. The challenge was to see how many balls I could pot in sixty seconds. The answer was none, so clearly they had the last laugh.

The BBC wanted to include the story directly after Dennis's challenge to me, for continuity, so it had to be filmed for that weekend's show.

As soon as I'd finished working, I flew back to Prague and Lloyd seemed to be annoyed with me. It wasn't ideal, I know, but it was part of my job and there was nothing I could do about it.

The worst part was that it had fallen on the date of our anniversary. It was atrocious timing. We went out for dinner, and things were fine, on the surface at least. There were no fireworks, though, no big celebration. It simply was not the holiday I'd planned.

After Lloyd and I officially broke up, his phone calls and texts continued, but all my friends kept telling me, 'No contact,' and they were right. I had to go cold turkey.

In April, I was summoned home from the Friedrichstadtpalast, Berlin, where I'd been choreographing for a couple of months, following my plan of staying out of London for the year. Lloyd needed money. We had some savings in a shared account, which was only in my name, and he wanted his half.

He had got a place of his own by then, and was renting a flat down the street from our house – which I thought was a little bit close for comfort.

The day I got the cheque out of the account for him, I went round to his new apartment and knocked on the door. He wouldn't open it. I knew he was in there because his bike was visible and so was Michael's. I knocked on the door and the window, and then I kept my finger on the buzzer for a minute or so, but they wouldn't answer the door.

I thought angrily, 'OK, so it's come to this. I'm keeping the money, going back to Berlin and fuck him.' I started off down the street, my brain racing. 'This is going to be a nightmare if we can't even see each other to hand over a cheque,' I mused.

Just as I was thinking this, Lloyd came running after me down the road, shouting, 'Craig! Craig!'

I turned around and said, 'I was only trying to give you the cheque so you could cash it.'

He replied, slightly breathlessly, 'I thought you were going to bash Michael up.'

I was horrified. After all we had shared together, and especially given my family background, he should have known that I would never take that route. I've always been a very peaceful person.

The assumption was completely out of character for Lloyd, and was rooted in no friendship that I recognized. From that moment,

I could clearly see that he was having some sort of breakdown. I told him he should go to see a counsellor, and gave him the name of the person whom I'd been planning to use for our relationship counselling, before the split. Apparently, he went two or three times, but he didn't keep it up.

I handed him the cheque and went back to Berlin. The whole episode made me consider all our financial ties. I started thinking about the house. I didn't want to move back into it if it was partly owned by him. I concluded that we needed to make it all legal and get a proper 'divorce'. So that's what we did – and that's how it ended.

It had been a long time since I'd had my heart broken. But I remembered how I used to get by. The producers of my 2004 Guildford show *Beautiful and Damned*, Charlie Dobson and Laurence Myers, asked me if I would direct it in the West End. Eager to sign up, I insisted on only one condition – that it was rewritten and I was happy with it.

Then we had to figure out who was responsible for that, because there had been a lot of people working on it to begin with. That's where it all went a little bit wrong. Kit Hesketh Harvey had written the original book, Phil Willmott had rewritten some of it and Laurence was contributing as well. The songs were penned by Les Reed and Roger Cook, who also wrote 'I'd Like to Teach the World to Sing' for the New Seekers.

I was disappointed that I wasn't allowed to tell the whole of the Fitzgeralds' tragic tale. The producers didn't want it, so we had to miss out the alleged abortions that Zelda reportedly had, and her lesbian sex sessions. However, there were a lot of anecdotes on record about her amazing life with her husband in the 1930s, when they just squandered money and drank champagne until they dropped. We dramatized that story instead.

The production opened in the West End in May 2006 ... and it was a critical disaster. The reviews were horrific, although the audience at least were swept away. The press decided to go for the jugular – and when that's what they've determined, all the media follow suit. The show was massacred.

The leading lady, Helen Anker, whom I thought was extraordinary, and still do, did a wonderful job. She was playing Zelda, who was completely mad and ended up dying in a fire at a mental institution. Only a truly gifted actress could have taken on the role. We need people like Helen in the theatre and it's a shame when the critics come along and annihilate such talented artists.

Robert Hanks, in the *Independent*, headed his review with 'Fitzgerald musical not beautiful – and must surely be damned,' which was obviously not a great start. It continued: 'Helen Anker's portrayal of insanity is picturesque and stereotyped.'

Just one critic, the *Daily Mirror*'s Kevin O'Sullivan, gave her any credit, writing, 'Helen Anker charismatically makes the entire production sparkle.' He also said that she 'dances like a dream', and commented that the relationship between Fitzgerald and his wife was, 'Not perhaps ideal material for a feel-good night at the theatre. But I promise that feel good you will after this exhilarating show, which triumphantly combines a damned good story with some beautiful songs.'

At least someone liked it.

The experience didn't do me any favours, career-wise, but on a personal level it taught me that you can't always achieve everything you want to – because you need the circumstances to be on your side too.

It was the hardest criticism I'd ever had and it was painful to read. Oddly, though, the direction and staging were really left alone. The music, lyrics and book were roundly attacked and, if reviewers don't like those three things in a musical, there's not much you can do to secure positive comments. It was a shame, because the idea had such potential. I really wasn't expecting the reaction we received.

By the time the reviews came out, I was in France again, this time directing and choreographing *The Legend of the Lion King* for Disneyland Resort Paris. Picking my way through the outpourings of venom in the papers, I felt sick. I felt sorry for the cast because they still had to perform it every night and I felt awful that I wasn't in London to be able to go to them and say, 'Guys, don't worry. Don't listen to the critics.'

The show ran for about four months, but I think that it was heavily supported by Charlie Dobson, who was a lovely man who just wanted to pay homage to Zelda Fitzgerald. My father, incidentally, can't stop watching the show on DVD. He absolutely loves it.

The Legend of the Lion King is a thirty-five-minute truncated version of the film *The Lion King*, and took me two years to complete. I had to go through so much red tape, first with the Americans and then with the French – and even then I didn't foresee everything that could go wrong.

I arrived in Paris to find that the floor of the stage was a total mess. After twenty-four months of meetings, discussing it in intimate detail, the floor arrived and it was undulating and sculpted like desert sand and rock. It covered the whole stage and was utterly impossible to dance on. On the model, it had looked flat, but the computer had misread it and there were lumps and bumps everywhere. We had to cut it all away and redesign at the last minute, which cost thousands.

A happier experience was my first directing stint at the Watermill Theatre in Newbury, Berkshire, later that year. The Watermill is a wonderful venue. I'd love more people to go to see the shows there. It's a gorgeous, tucked-away barn of a watermill, surrounded by a stream, which is home to lots of ducks. The building is set in opulent grounds, where you can have a picnic and a glass of champagne before the performance. It's truly beautiful.

The people behind it are really creative and you get top actors, such as Dame Judi Dench, working for next to nothing to appear there. It's a chance for them to perform the role of their dreams to a live and intimate audience. Roughly five or six shows are staged each year, which gives visionary people an outlet. You don't get paid much; everyone does it for love, which generates a fantastic working environment.

My first production there was *Hot Mikado* in summer 2006. It was an unprecedented success, and played a big part in me subsequently securing a regular slot at the Watermill, which is a tremendous honour.

At the end of July through to September, I was asked to choreograph the BBC's new talent show *How Do You Solve a Problem Like Maria?* Although I was now an old hand at appearing on programmes for the Beeb, this was the first time I had worked for them in that capacity. Zoë Tyler was overseeing the vocals; I was to direct and choreograph the girls, helping them to stage their numbers and develop their characters.

In the early stages of the competition, the girls were whittled down from forty contestants to twenty. That group was then asked to perform in front of influential people from the theatre at Andrew Lloyd Webber's house.

The venue was a deconsecrated church in the grounds of Andrew's Sydmonton estate, which he has had converted into a theatre. He often uses it to premiere his own works, such as *Sunset Boulevard* and *The Phantom of the Opera*, and also accommodates the Sydmonton Arts Festival, which is held there periodically. The festival comprises a variety of exclusive previews, which are presented to a private audience of key players from theatre, television and film in order to gauge the future potential of the works. The showcases feature some of the finest talents in entertainment. That year, the *Maria* contestants were part of it. I travelled to the country house to rehearse the girls before their all-important performances.

It was a blazing hot summer weekend as we created the routines and finalized the running order. There wasn't enough room for everyone in the theatre, so I had all the Marias dancing on the tennis court. The sun was beating down and I was getting burned, so I slathered myself in gallons of sunblock; I looked like a ghost.

Naturally, this was the bit they showed on telly – so the first glimpse the viewing public got of me, without my judge's suit and austere expression, was a sweaty, white creature going '5, 6, 7, 8' on a tennis court. I felt right at home doing that, of course, because that's my proper job.

The concert that I staged at Sydmonton was the girls' only chance to bag a place in the live programmes, so it was my duty to present them in the most positive light. I got to know them, established their strengths and weaknesses, and tried to give each one the best possible chance of becoming Maria.

Once we were into the frantic schedule of the weekly live shows, I rehearsed the remaining contestants through the week for their four group numbers and would also direct their solos. *Maria* was a great experience for me because I'm used to working fast, but this was at breakneck pace. The rushes would head off to the BBC and then I'd get notes back from the programme's director, Nikki Parsons, saying they wanted more of this or less of that, or they wanted to redo a whole number – which happened a lot. They also might suddenly decide on a different song.

The pressure of live television is unbelievable. I don't think people realize how much goes into it. It's one thing turning up as a judge, but choreographing it, being there for the contestants, ensuring everyone is emotionally prepared and knows what they're doing, which camera they should be looking at, and so on, is a humungous task. On top of that, the nature of the show was that the contestants were all amateurs; I'm used to working with professionals.

Some of the Marias took direction better than others, but then that's a skill that either comes naturally or not. If I want to extract more charisma or emotion from a performer, what I will say to someone with training will be completely different to what I would say to an amateur. Someone like the eventual winner, Connie Fisher, who had been to stage school, could understand my language, so I could work economically with her. I always trusted her on stage.

There was a lot of hard work involved, but also a lot of fun. I remember that in one session, we were rehearsing a group routine when I said, 'Take four steps back.' Leanne Dobinson (aka Baby Maria) took four massive steps and just disappeared. She had danced herself off the set and into the orchestra pit! The other girls walked forward for the next phrase and Leanne wasn't in her place in the line-up. Instead, there was the sound of crashing cymbals and this almighty scream. We all howled with laughter.

Connie Fisher stood out from the beginning for me as one of the contestants who had potential, along with Siobhan Dillon, who came third. I thought Siobhan was very good. There was one week when the pressure was getting really intense, and she was having trouble with her rendition of 'Chains' by Tina Arena. The girls trusted me to make them look good on stage, so they would come to me if they were feeling terrible about themselves, or nervous. Siobhan came to see me, very upset, saying, 'I have a problem with the music and I don't know if I can do it.'

I said to her encouragingly, 'Trust yourself, Siobhan, trust your instinct. What you did in rehearsal was great, so don't question it. Go for it even more.'

It was a difficult song, as it demanded a lot emotionally. I'd staged the opening with her on all fours, banging on the floor. She's a beautiful girl and she'd always looked great standing still and singing, but we needed to see another side of her character, which I was trying to bring out. I think we saw it. She did really well.

An interesting observation about being a choreographer on the programme, rather than a judge, was that I was treated more like staff. I didn't get cars to take me to the studio; I had to get the Tube. When I was on set, there was no dressing room for me, so I felt a bit in limbo. I'm used to working in that way backstage in a theatre, of course, because that's my everyday job, but it was strange to be treated so differently at the BBC. I wasn't allowed to sit in the studio and watch the show, either. I had to enjoy it from the green room. In fairness, it would have looked odd, having me in the audience, because my face is so recognizably part of another BBC production.

Speaking of which, the fourth series of *Strictly* was about to kick off. There were more contestants than ever before – fourteen in total – and the likes of Spice Girl Emma Bunton, rugby player Matt Dawson and cricketer Mark Ramprakash were taking part. What's great about *Strictly* is that it's not one of those shows that people only do if their career is limping or failing. It isn't about putting a D-lister back on the A-list. A lot of people used to imagine that's what it was, but it's about human endeavour. The line-up for the new run was the best yet.

Mark Ramprakash, as it turned out, had *the* hottest salsa – so spicy that it has yet to be topped. Mark was extraordinary: definitely the best male celebrity to date. The use of his hips showed such control. He exuded an air of show business and displayed a performance skill the likes of which we had never seen before on *SCD*, and may not see again.

The funny thing about Mark was that nothing kicked in with him until the Thursday of each week. He had terrible trouble on Monday, Tuesday and Wednesday, could never remember it – but he always pulled it together. By Saturday night, he was astounding.

Another particularly memorable contestant from the 2006 crop was actress Claire King. Her rumba with dance partner Brendan Cole was one of the filthiest I've seen in my entire life.

I adored having a drink with Claire after the live programme. She's a wild woman. She's out there, she's on it, she's great

company and she loves to party. She just has incredible spirit –
she goes for it, without a care, and you have to do that to be as
free as a dancer.

For a live show, *Strictly Come Dancing* has been relatively free
of monumental cock-ups, but season four was when our luck
ran out. In week four, a microphone cable got tangled around
Mark Ramprakash and Karen Hardy during their salsa. It was
awful. They were just going into this fantastic routine when the
wire became caught on their embroidered clothing. They
couldn't move apart. Poor Karen was devastated, but Mark
appealed for another go and they were allowed to start again,
which was fair. That's the only time we've had to stop the
show.

We've been told that if someone has an injury or let's say, God
forbid, a heart attack on the dance floor, the cameras will cut to
the judges, the floor team will remove the body – and then we'll
carry on! Thankfully, it's never happened.

The contestants do have medical checks before they start,
reassuringly. Still, you can't really tell how they will fare once they
start dancing. Ballroom is a lot more physical than people realize.
It's a sport and people get injured. People use muscles they didn't
even know they had. Even sportsmen find some of the dances
physically challenging, because they are not used to the moves,
even small ones like the rise and fall, which test different muscles
to the ones they regularly employ. On the *Strictly Come Dancing*
tour in 2008, for example, the performers were dancing every
night and were fine; but we went bowling one night and everyone
woke up with sore buttocks!

Some of the contestants go from doing absolutely no exercise,
like Kate Garraway did in 2007, to doing forty hours a week. She
was pushing her body a lot, so she was very sore to start with. A
lot of the contestants find the same.

Bless Kate. She was a great sport. She was no good at dancing,
but she was all for having a go, and took every bad comment on

the chin. She enjoyed herself and we thought she was magnificent, especially as she had the most punishing schedule. Beyond the physical endurance, what kills most of the celebrities is the arduous twenty to thirty hours of training they have to put in each week, which is a nightmare to maintain, particularly when they have other work on the go at the same time.

On series three, for example, Bill Turnbull had to go into the office at four in the morning to do his job, as did his co-contestant Fiona Phillips, and her co-presenter Kate on series five. I spoke to Kate in make-up once and she was just exhausted. I said to her, 'I don't know how you do this.' I really meant that. She had to be at the *GMTV* studios at 4 a.m. to go through the content of her show, work from 4 a.m. to 11 a.m., and then she had to dance the rest of the time. Plus she had an eighteen-month-old baby to look after when she got home.

I guess it all comes down to passion. On season four, Jan Ravens was certainly passionate about the programme. Jan is known mainly as a comedian and impressionist – but she was taking *Strictly* so seriously that she wasn't making anyone laugh.

Some celebrities are not used to being themselves or 'playing' themselves on TV. It's one thing doing an interview as yourself, but quite another when you are out of your comfort zone in front of millions, live. Jan's career as an actress, and a bloody good one at that, meant that she was always portraying characters or doing impressions of other people. She hadn't had to be just Jan Ravens until the show, and maybe she found that to be too much exposure, though obviously I can't speak for how she felt. The show is very raw and a massive challenge, not only physically but emotionally too. Jan took every little bit of criticism to heart, whereas the sportsmen and women, like Denise Lewis, don't. Denise's attitude was, 'Bring it on! Criticize me so I'm better next week.' That is the only way to accept it, otherwise you can get yourself into a real state.

Jan was knocked out in the fifth show, after dancing the

Viennese waltz with her partner, Anton Du Beke. Her dancing up until then had been pretty ordinary, but I actually thought this particular performance was her personal best, so I said so. I also had a small criticism, as I often do, and said she was 'kicking like a mule' when taking her backward steps. I mentioned it only so it could be corrected the following week if she was kept in. After all, if you're not told what's wrong with your dancing, how on earth are you ever going to be able to fix it? You'll only end up making the same mistakes time and time again, and receiving identical comments.

Jan picked up on my remark about it being her best dance yet and asked, 'Why didn't you give me any more points than last week then?'

I replied with total honesty, 'Because it wasn't worth any more.'

After the result is announced on air, the losing contestants always have a leaving chat with Brucie, where they usually say things like how much fun they've had, their thank yous, how it's changed their lives and so on. Jan decided to be a little different. She came over to the judges' desk and spat, 'I hope you're happy now!' (This, incidentally, has since become one of Graham Norton's favourite impressions.)

I'd given her a general critique of her dancing and while it wasn't always favourable – I can't deny that – it wasn't entirely my fault she lost: there were millions of viewers voting too, and they control 50 per cent of the result. What may have upset her most of all was that the public weren't behind her and voting to keep her in. Being kicked out, especially in the early rounds, is a bitter pill to swallow because it means the nation isn't supporting you. There's nothing you can do about that, though – that's life. You can't win everything. The show's for charity at the end of day, so why not make people laugh, and give us all some entertainment along the way?

To blame the judges is ludicrous, because there are 12 million people who have the option to vote. I was shocked by her outburst, totally taken by surprise. It was the first time we'd had an aggressive reaction on the show following elimination, and I felt she was being a bad sport. But I brushed it off and thought nothing more of it. She did her final dance, the credits rolled and it seemed everyone was back on an even keel.

After the live programme wound up, I made my way as usual to the BBC bar, where we always go post-show to chill out and talk about the evening's events.

I was strolling along the corridor on level four, towards the bar, when I spotted Jan standing outside, engrossed in conversation. As I walked towards her, I began to feel slightly nervous and found myself avoiding eye contact. I didn't know what to say because of her obvious antipathy towards me. Her comments had definitely been directed at me, and that line – 'I hope you're happy now!' – kept going through my head.

'I shouldn't go past her and smile,' I thought as I drew closer. 'That will look horrible. But if I choose to ignore her, that would be even worse. I have to say something.'

The BBC corridor is a long, curving walkway, which allows you to see someone who is quite far away. You then have to make a choice about how to behave and what to say as you are moving towards that person. That night, the walk seemed endless, but I made the decision to congratulate her and be pleasant, and pretend she hadn't said what she had.

As I walked, I rehearsed my little speech: 'Congratulations and commiserations,' I would say, 'but you did a great job for charity and well done.'

I began to speak, but Jan turned round and said, 'Not now. Not now,' and brushed me off. I said, 'I just wanted to say you did a great job.' She put her hand up to my face and was backing away, saying, 'Leave me alone.'

Perhaps foolishly, I carried on. 'There's no need to take this so personally,' I shouted, as she was backing even further away.

'Just leave it!' she yelled.

She was retreating from me as if I was trying to attack her, which of course I wasn't. I was thinking, 'This is mad,' but I went after her anyway to try to calm her down.

The BBC bar has double doors and one of them was open. Jan's husband Max spotted what was happening and flew out of the bar, just as I'd had enough and turned to walk away. He started effing and blinding at me, saying, 'Leave her alone. You've done enough already. Keep away from her!'

Then he shoved me in the chest, three times. He's half my size, which made it quite comical, but it was shocking at the time. He just went crazy.

I was extremely embarrassed by the whole incident because it happened in front of five of my friends, who were following me to the bar. They couldn't believe it. They were saying, 'Oh my God! Does this happen every time someone goes out?'

Of course, the answer is no. Generally, people are gracious and will say, 'No hard feelings. It's just a show, love,' or something along those lines. And that's what it is. It's entertainment, pure and simple.

The next morning, I was on *Something for the Weekend*, a TV chat show framed around a delicious Sunday lunch, and they asked me what I thought about the previous night's *SCD*.

'The BBC bar was exciting, darling,' I replied. And I told them the story, live on air. The presenter, Tim Lovejoy, was completely flummoxed. He was speechless.

The following Monday, the story exploded and the aftermath went on for weeks. In retrospect, I should have said nothing, but it had happened and we had about thirty witnesses. I was mortified that someone had taken this so much to heart that their husband felt the need to jump to their defence.

On Mondays, I always appear on Claudia Winkleman's show, *It Takes Two*, with the person who went out of *Strictly Come Dancing* the Saturday before. You can imagine the tension in the air when we all arrived at the studio.

By this time, Jan knew what I had been saying, because it was plastered all over the papers. The problem was that it was all true. Normally, these things are blown up out of all proportion, but this was completely accurate.

She had managed to smother it a little bit. She responded by saying something like, 'How can you believe that? My husband's only little. Can you imagine him pushing that 6-foot-2 judge about? I don't think so.'

They tried to keep us apart by putting us on separate floors, but when I walked into make-up, who should be there but Jan Ravens? We spoke and she mentioned that she was going to talk about the incident on air. She said, 'I will have something to say about it, don't you worry.'

The show's itinerary scheduled Jan's appearance after mine. Of course, Claudia had to ask her about it. Jan twisted it and turned it around as expected and had the final say, which is fine, as we are all entitled to tell our own side of the story. That was the end of it. I was told not to speak about it again and that seemed a good idea.

After Claudia's show, we went upstairs and had a glass of champagne together to finish it. Otherwise, the row was going to go on and on. We both agreed that we needed to be professional about it and stop talking about it in the media, or it would be handbags at dawn and the incident would plague us both for a year. It's not worth it. I was happy to go clink, clink, and forget all about it.

In November 2006, my latest theatrical show opened. *Six Dance Lessons in Six Weeks* was a two-hander about a gay dance teacher who is employed to teach the finer points of ballroom to the ageing wife of a Baptist minister. It starred Claire Bloom and Billy Zane; I was the choreographer.

I had a slight altercation with Billy during rehearsals. We clashed over the basic steps: ever the maverick, he wanted to do his own thing, jive it up a bit and be less formal. In the end, we agreed that we would cover the basic points of Latin and ballroom every morning, so that we could practise technique, before we began experimenting with fancier choreography. From then on, it all calmed down. The routines ended up looking great; Billy can actually dance really well.

The *Six Dance Lessons* producers thought that it might be an idea for Billy to appear on *Strictly Come Dancing* as a one-off guest, to drum up a bit of publicity for the West End play, but Billy declined. He said that that type of reality show was not really for him, which I could completely appreciate. Of course, as it turned out, his girlfriend Kelly Brook was on it the following year.

On opening night, I looked out into the audience and there were the other three *Strictly* judges – Bruno, Arlene and Len – so I now know what it's like being on the receiving end of their judgement. Ooh, they are a scary lot, all sat in a row in the stalls, waiting to criticize my work! Actually, they were nice about it afterwards. Opening night went without a hitch. Sadly, the rest of the run didn't and the production eventually closed a month early.

In December 2006, the BBC filmed *A Day in the Life of Craig Revel Horwood* for BBC2. I thought it was an excellent concept because it showed the world what I actually do for a living, and also plugged dancing, encouraging others to take up the sport. Billy Zane kindly appeared on that show, which may have helped to boost the flagging ticket sales of *Six Dance Lessons* for a short while.

A Day in the Life took a surprisingly long time to film. It was in fact one of my busiest days in reality, which might have been useful for content, but it was a little hairy living through it. It started to bug me towards the end of the shoot, having a camera in my face 24/7. Berry, who was filming me, kept asking me to do everything at least twice, like walking through doors or putting a sausage in my mouth at the local cafe. That particular task did have at least one advantage, in that Mario from the cafe provided me with the nicest and best quality sausages that morning, but by the end of the day, the frequent repetition had become tiresome. I was pleased to get home that night and shut the door on the world.

Come Christmas, in the spirit of the season, I wedged the door open again. I decided to invite both Lloyd and Michael over on Boxing Day, to re-establish the friendship and to show Lloyd that I was OK with him being with someone else. I wanted to get accustomed to being just friends so that they could be together, Lloyd could be happy and I could be free to look for someone else.

We all sat in my house, drinking and partying, and I talked to Michael as though nothing had happened. It was all a bit weird, but I needed to see them as a couple to reassure me that theirs was a relationship worth leaving me for. It wasn't to torture myself, but rather to know that it was a solid partnership that might turn out for the good – instead of Lloyd throwing away everything we'd built up together on some sheep-shearer shag!

Getting over Lloyd wasn't easy. I started to read loads of self-help books to get me through it. Very slowly, I began to deal with it.

Despite my progress, I was still in love with him. I don't think you ever fall totally out of love with someone; you just learn how to make it smaller so you can put it into a neat little box. Then you can shelve it and it doesn't take over your life. I hated Lloyd for not being honest, but I still loved him. That will never go away, I believe, but you can reduce the affection so that your capacity to love someone else grows larger.

I felt very lucky to have had those years with him. He had been an undeniable support. Without having someone, who at least appears to be solid, in the background, I don't think you can make as many mad choices in life. Lloyd gave me the freedom and security to pursue all my crazy dreams and I'll be forever grateful for that.

I've always been a person who likes to be in love and in a

loving relationship. After Lloyd and I split, I had to learn to be happy with myself and to make myself happy. Eventually, I achieved that, possibly for the first time ever. I think it's important that you create your own happiness and don't rely on other people to generate it for you.

As it turns out – to quote Linda Creed's lyrics in Lavish's favourite number – 'learning to love yourself' truly is the 'Greatest Love of All'.

CHAPTER 18 *A Road Less Strictly Travelled*

New year, new job. The Christmas decorations weren't even down when I staged *Just the Two of Us* for the BBC in January 2007. The show teamed celebrities with famous singers in a musical variant of the *Strictly* format.

One of the non-singers was Gregg Wallace, who would later be my judge on *Celebrity Masterchef*. I had no idea I would be facing him in that capacity when I was trying to get him to dance, of course. Sadly, he was the first one out.

Actress Hannah Waterman and Marti Pellow won the series. I couldn't wait to meet Marti when I signed up to the show because I remembered him being desperately cute in Wet Wet Wet.

He knew what he wanted straight from the beginning and had a vision for each song. It was my job to get as much emotional commitment out of Hannah as I could. Often, when actors and actresses try to sing, they forget to act, so I just needed to help the two of them work on their connection.

Having said that, they didn't need much input from me. Once they'd established an emotional bond, about halfway through the series, they were wonderful. Marti was a trooper and an excellent teacher; he looked after Hannah really well. Not all the stars were willing to spend that much time with their celebrity because, unlike on *Strictly*, both were famous before they came into the programme. We had to work with a lot of big egos. Some of the singers didn't want to bother, which upset their celebrity partners, so there was tension backstage. Luckily, I'm quite good at mediating and nurturing. No sniggering at the back.

Comic Relief Does Fame Academy returned in March 2007 and once again I was in the firing line on the panel. The insane Tara Palmer-Tomkinson, whom I adore, enlivened the competition that year. The first time I met TPT, I thought she was off her head. It was on press day, before the series kicked off, when we as a cast give hundreds of interviews in groups of five, talking to ten journalists at a time, moving from table to table. Tara was in my group and you couldn't get a word in edgeways. She was crying during the interviews, then recovering. She was talking about her sex life, then changing the subject. She was discussing her nose job, then she wasn't. She was chattering about her cocaine addiction and then she kept saying, 'I'm so tired. I'm so tired.'

We'd go to the next table and the same thing would happen again – the tears, the confessions and the constant chant of 'I'm so tired'. She was so over the top. She's a bit scary on first meeting and I wondered what we'd let ourselves in for. I felt especially sorry for the people who had to live with her, because all the contestants sleep at the Academy and have to get up at 6.30 in the morning to do kung fu with the choreographer.

As I got to know her, however, she became more and more human. I grew to love her.

Tara gets nervous as hell and then sweats horribly, just like me. Consequently, the papers assumed she was on drugs during the show. But there was no way she could have smuggled charlie into the mansion, which has as many cameras as the *Big Brother* house. Even the toilets have got cameras in them, so we'd have seen her if she'd been chop, chop, chopping in there. It did cross everyone's mind at one point, but she's just naturally wired.

Then she went and won the bloody thing, which was largely down to personality and the fact she let rip emotionally and didn't bar us from seeing her tears. Crying does win votes, it seems. Actually, I would have voted for her every time myself because she was so endearing, particularly when she sat at the piano and sang songs. She's a brilliant pianist and gave some mesmerizing performances. As I've said before in this book, you can be a non-singer and get away with a musical number, if you only act it. Tara's singing came from her heart and soul, and that became the most important thing. The audience felt like they'd been let into a private moment. That's why people loved her. Rather than going for the big voice of someone like Shaun Williamson, the public supported a contestant who couldn't carry a tune particularly well, but always told a good story.

I got on well with Shaun Williamson. He did have a fabulous voice, especially when he performed the rock numbers like Meatloaf. When you compare his voice to Tara's, it seems ridiculous that she won, but she's hilarious to watch and she had such bravado. I loved that. I hate it when people are too reserved to throw themselves into experiences, so it was wonderful to see someone be natural and just go for it.

After the series had finished, Tara generously hosted a thank-you party for everyone, the whole cast and crew. My designer friend Christopher Woods and I went along. I also invited my mate Stu, who was quite down back then and having a terrible time. He lived in Brighton, but I thought he needed cheering up so I said to him, 'Why don't you come to London and TPT's party?' He was beside himself. He'd never been to a celeb bash before and it was gratifying to hear his excited reaction.

The soirée was held in a beautiful penthouse in Mayfair. Everyone from *Fame Academy* was there – Jon Culshaw, Shaun Williamson, Tricia Penrose. There were paparazzi everywhere, as there always are when TPT is involved. When we got inside, the cocktails were flowing and everyone was having a magnificent time.

At three in the morning, we were all rather hammered, but we weren't quite ready to call it a night. A small group of us were saying, 'Where shall we go now?'

Tara responded, 'Come with me.'

So the three of us chaps – Christopher, Stu and I – TPT and Tricia Penrose walked out the door. The photographers' flashes went mad. It was crazy. Stuart had never seen anything like it in his life. We all piled into a black cab, and the snappers were knocking on the windows and chasing us down the street, as Tara was trying to put a shopping bag over her head.

TPT gave the cabbie an address round the corner, which turned out to be her real penthouse. She'd only hired the one we were having the party in – as you do.

The place was amazing. It's a three-storey property in the middle of Mayfair, with a huge roof terrace, a lovely, big, open-plan kitchen and a massive living room, dominated by a grand piano. She has a long staircase going up all three floors and every single step has a pair of shoes on it. She has more shoes than Imelda Marcos. She also has a dedicated room that is just for footwear.

Tara and Tricia decided that they wanted to get changed out of their ball gowns into something more comfortable. The next thing we knew, they were coming up the stairs: TPT was wearing the boots that she wore on the show for 'These Boots Are Made For Walkin'', with nothing else on but a bra and knickers; Tricia was in a borrowed baby doll and a pair of high fluffy mules. Stuart couldn't believe his eyes.

They had resolved to put on a show. TPT sat at the piano and Tricia sang a song. I got up to croon as well. Then we all had a big singalong. It was harmless, fabulous fun. We finally left at around 6 a.m. It was so surreal, such a fantastic night.

I was proud to be asked to become a judge on *Dancing with the Stars* in New Zealand later that spring. They'd already done two series of their version of *Strictly*, and invited me to join them for the third. Brendan Cole, who of course is one of the professional dancers on the UK programme, was also on the panel. That made for plenty of fireworks. Brendan and I get on fine socially, but we never seem to see eye to eye professionally, on either side of the world.

There's a strange crossover with him being a judge in NZ, because I'm so used to critiquing him and him answering back like the loudmouth he is. Brendan winds people up so much that it's hard not to get personal with him, although I never have. On the New Zealand show, we had some huge rows – and have done so in subsequent series too. Afterwards, we choose not to talk about it, otherwise the antagonism would just keep rumbling on.

The other judges in my first year were the dancer Carol-Ann Hickmore and Alison Leonard, a dancer turned broadcaster. Since then, Carol-Ann has been replaced by *Strictly Ballroom* star Paul Mercurio, who also adjudicates the Australian version of the show. But not one of my fellow judges has come close to wrenching the 'Mr Nasty' tiara from my head.

Indeed, during the first New Zealand series in which I was involved, I managed to offend the whole country. The public wanted me out. They thought I was vile to Michael Laws, the Mayor of Wanganui.

Of course, I was only being honest, as usual. If someone's mouth is gaping open for the whole performance, and they're on the wrong foot throughout, I'm going to comment on that. All Michael's routines were awful, but his cha-cha-cha was particularly offensive. I committed the cardinal sin of telling the Mayor of Wanganui that his dancing left a lot to be desired – and the people of New Zealand were up in arms.

Because I don't know the personalities of the celebrities there, I see only the dancing, not the star. But they're really quite a conservative crowd; I think the celebs are treated with kid gloves by the other judges. When I blasted my way on to the

TV and started talking brutally, they weren't happy. Brendan is used to me, but the other judges were shocked.

The headlines were horrendous. One said: 'Visiting judge mauls Laws!' People were asking for me to be chucked off the show. Oh, they hated me. The TV station was bombarded with emails from viewers, saying that they wouldn't watch if I continued to be employed as a judge. Then the ratings went up the following week as everyone who said they weren't going to switch on did, and so did a few more.

What's fun about the New Zealand version is that they don't have the wealth of big soaps that we have here in the UK, so there's no *EastEnders*, *Corrie* or *Holby City* to provide celebrity dancers. The producers rely heavily on politicians, basketball players and rugby players. They have the All Blacks, of course, but you can't have an entire rugby team doing *Dancing with the Stars*, let's face it. On second thoughts, could you? That would be a vision. The NZ production values are the same as in the British version, although they are on a tighter budget, but there just isn't the international recognition of celebrity.

In fact, the woman who won my first series was from Leeds! Her name was Suzanne Paul. She came over to New Zealand to establish her fortune on a make-up range, which she did, but then she launched a tourism business, which went belly up. She lost everybody's money and ended up millions of dollars in debt, so she was trying to pay everybody back.

The programme goes out on a Tuesday and is immediately followed by the results show, so every week we have a big party afterwards. We all watch the episode back with the friends and families of the contestants, while drinking free booze and getting absolutely pie-eyed. It's a nice idea because the loser makes a speech and you celebrate the person who is leaving, and then take in the show, laughing at the judges' comments and the dances alike. It gives the whole thing a family feel and people don't take the criticism personally like they can seem to in the UK.

Mad things happen at every bash. There is always someone falling over or flirting outrageously with another member of the team, snogging people they shouldn't or getting drunk and disorderly.

For example, at one post-show party, we were making merry at a pub called The Establishment. One of the judges, Alison Leonard, had just brought a fresh round of drinks to the table. It was the usual enormous array – pints of lager, glasses of red wine, a couple of bottles of savvy blanc, spritzers and mixers.

Sitting at the bar table on a high stool was the celeb who had just been eliminated. She was so wasted that she went to put her drink on the table, missed it completely, and then tried to save herself from falling forward by placing all her weight on the table with her free hand. At the same moment, she toppled backwards off the stool, flipped the entire table up and landed on her back on the floor, legs akimbo with her dress up around her navel. To add insult to injury, she was now wearing all the booze that had just been purchased. She was absolutely saturated and ended up smelling like a brewery for the rest of the night. It was truly a sight for sore eyes.

On the evening of the final, Alison Leonard was a little bit emotional and cried practically the whole night. Tears of joy, perhaps, that the season had ended, or maybe tears of sadness that she wouldn't be seeing me any more – I'm not sure which, if either. Something had upset her anyway. When she came out of the club, she had massive panda eyes, with mascara smudged all around them, and looked like she'd been dragged through the wringer. Naturally, that was the moment she was papped by a huge pack of waiting photographers. The resulting picture made the front page of the paper the next day. Poor Alison must have hated it.

Candy Lane is the Tess Daly of the show and she's hilarious, a real wild child. At one of our shindigs, she was dancing on the tables and then decided to strut along the bar and jump off it into the crowd. The people in the bar loved it because she's a total star over there.

All this made its way into the press, of course. In the end, they had to find us private clubs to go to after the live programmes, so that we weren't in public when we misbehaved. New Zealand is a small country: there are only 4 million people, and 1 million of them watch the show. When you look at it like that, it's likely that a quarter of the general public know who we are, so you can appreciate the need for a bit of privacy.

The parties never finish until seven or eight in the morning. We do all have such a good time. It's a far cry from what you see on the telly, where everyone is dressed up, looking beautiful and performing sedate waltzes. You would never imagine that in a few hours' time the cast and crew would be out on the town wearing next to nothing, slaughtered and sweaty, and enthusiastically jumping into rows of men.

Speaking of which, while I was in New Zealand I decided it was time to get back on the dating horse. Trying to find love after Lloyd was actually a very dark period. I was over forty and the thought of having to go to a bar and chat people up was horrific. I wasn't used to the dating game anyway, having been in a relationship for so many years – but I was now famous, too, so that put a whole new spin on the situation.

For a single celebrity of forty-plus to go out to pubs and clubs to meet men is awful. People only want to speak to you because they've seen you on the telly. I couldn't face going into a bar by myself, only to sit there like a sad Billy-no-mates, sipping at my drink, waiting for somebody to approach me. I bit the bullet and went out a couple of times on the pull, but the men who came up for a chat were all aged between twenty and twenty-three, which was far too young for me. There was nobody older in those places. Those that did come up weren't interested in me as a person, either, which was discouraging. As I'd anticipated, they just wanted to be seen out with 'Mr

Nasty' or get hold of invitations to opening nights and red-carpet dos.

My next mistake was turning to the Internet.

I had a few friends who were hooked on Gaydar, a gay chat site; two of my mates had even met that way. I thought it might be worth a try, even though I didn't know much about it. I signed up – and quickly regretted it. I had a false identity, but I put my picture up, which was not the smartest move I've ever made. Disaster! After just two hours, I had to take myself off because it was a nightmare. I was bombarded with messages saying, 'Are you Craig Revel Horwood from *Strictly Come Dancing*?' There were a few filthy pictures of certain parts of people's anatomies being sent through too.

It was not exactly what I'd been expecting. I'd been with Lloyd for such a long time that I'd never used these paths to romance before. But the horror didn't end there. I made the schoolboy error of telling someone backstage on *Dancing with the Stars* about my online catastrophe and complained to them that I was sick of meeting young lads. Somehow, it ended up in the paper. It wasn't particularly discreet of me, I know, but I wasn't expecting it to leak out to the press.

The next day, the headline read: 'Gay judge seeks mature man.' I was mortified.

In the last week of my first NZ series, my sister Mel flew over from Melbourne to stay with me in Wellington. We were joined by our brother Trent a couple of days later; he had been delayed as his band had a gig in Australia. I hadn't seen Mel for ages, other than on flying visits to Oz, so it was lovely to spend time together. I felt I could give her my full attention, which had perhaps been lacking over recent years, given the geographical distance between us.

In truth, I find it quite amazing – in view of the two decades that I have spent overseas, separated from my family by that incredible divide called the world – just how close my siblings and

I still are to one another. I sometimes feel guilty about leaving Australia for so long because I think that in some ways it seems selfish of me. But then again, I had to do what I had to do. We've all as a family followed our hearts and dreams: it's made us who we are today. And, on the whole, I think we've turned out all right.

On my return from New Zealand, an off-the-wall opportunity arose – an invitation to appear on that year's *Celebrity Masterchef.* What with my extensive Ballarat catering experience and my love of cooking in my own kitchen, I thought, 'Why not?' At home, I'm a good cook and I enjoy it. I can have a nice glass of wine and I potter around at my leisure. Of course, I haven't got a clock ticking on me – and that turned out to be a source of major tension on the TV show. I was really calm before the cameras started rolling, but as soon as I heard, 'Your time starts now,' I was a mess. I was just so nervous. The unforgivable pressure of passing time and a paralysing fear of failure really affected me.

There were five sections to each programme and I went all the way to the final, though Nadia Sawalha ultimately pipped me to the post to take the prize. I wasn't as panicked as I had been in the Ballarat restaurants, possibly because the team were a hell of a lot friendlier than my old head chef. Nevertheless, when they are filming you in close up and you know you have just two minutes left, but your dish takes four minutes to complete, it can throw you. Also, it was hard being judged – as I'm sure the contestants of *Strictly* would agree.

I was shitting myself in the preliminary show, as well as in the final. It was absolutely awful. People don't realize how difficult it is. You don't even know what you're cooking the first time. You have no clue what the ingredients might be and there are no recipes. Whatever they give you, you have to use to create something delicious – in a kitchen where you've no idea where anything is, or how to use the equipment. Plus you're trying to time delicate concoctions in ovens with which you're unfamiliar. It was horrible.

In the first episode, I was supplied with smoked bacon, minced beef and loads of different types of vegetables, as well as fresh herbs and stock cubes. Then I was told, 'We want a main course. You have fifty minutes and your time starts now.'

I made a spaghetti bolognese. It's a family classic that's deceptively complex: some people can do it well and some can't. It had to be very tasty to win over the judges. It did come out just as I'd hoped, in the end, but beforehand I was trying to pick out the ingredients and I went blank with panic.

The producer came over to me and said, 'Craig, you've got to calm down.'

I replied, 'I know. I'm trying to breathe, but I haven't got time. Too much to do.'

As I progressed through the programme's stages, I became more and more adventurous. It was when I tried to whip up the oysters and lobster thermidor that I got the real shakes. I'd never attempted such a recipe before and it was so hard.

That night, they had the food critics in. One of them said that my oysters looked like duck droppings. Tasting a little of my own medicine was, I suppose, a good thing for the viewers to see, but I felt really vulnerable.

The whole experience was nerve-racking: an endurance test for which I never felt prepared. Nonetheless, I went all out on the show because that's my nature – I don't like losing. Indeed, I've always had a huge fear of failure. In truth, though, I shouldn't be afraid because it's simply another part of life.

As I was getting to grips with garnish, I received an unexpected phone call from the Ballet Boyz, Michael Nunn and Billy Trevitt. They asked if I would be interested in creating a new work for them. The brief was that it should be something to do with tango and would open the refurbished Royal Festival Hall in London that summer.

The proposal was right up my street. The challenge of mixing ballet with tango was one for which I'd long been waiting. I immediately set to work on the project, almost as if my life depended on it. Soon, I'd come up with a concept and storyline for the piece. But I had to search high and low for the right music to complement it. I required a distinctive score that would drive the narrative I'd envisaged. In my quest, I stumbled across a recording by two incredible composers, Osvaldo Pugliese and Astor Piazzolla, performed live in Amsterdam. I immediately knew that this was the one.

Two giants from the tango world, Pugliese and Piazzolla, meet two titans from the classical dance world, Nunn and Trevitt, in a unique amalgamation of two of the best and most famous tango compositions, *La Yumba* (Pugliese) and *Adiós Nonino* (Piazzolla). I decided to call my new work *Yumba vs. Nonino*. It would tell the story of two composers fighting for supremacy, who would merge their genius into one extraordinary opus.

Michael Nunn represented Pugliese's *La Yumba*, while Billy Trevitt danced the long and sweeping lines of Piazzolla's classic. The dance style created for the piece was inspired by many disciplines, not strictly tango and not precisely ballet: a fusion in itself, like the music. It was my hope that the audience would understand and enjoy a unique and thrilling coalescence between four talented legends.

The boys were an absolute dream to work with, generous and willing to try fresh and interesting things. It was a hard slog in the rehearsal room, as neither of them had had any tango experience, let alone ballroom training, so we were forced to start from scratch and then embellish it all at the end.

We had a very limited time to rehearse, too, as I was also busy with my second production for the Watermill Theatre, *Martin Guerre*. The Ballet Boyz and I rehearsed every Saturday for about five weeks, and then did a major overhaul of our creation as opening night drew near.

The piece itself required a daunting amount of stamina and discipline. It crossed my mind on more than one occasion that I had undertaken something I wasn't sure I could pull off. That was a big deal for me, as I have a high regard and respect for the boys' work and I didn't want to let them down.

We all imagined the critics would pan it, but we knew in our hearts that the audience would take it the right way and like it. Somehow, we got it on ... and it was a triumph. As well as playing at the Royal Festival Hall, *Yumba vs. Nonino* went on to be showcased at the Royal Opera House and Sadler's Wells to great acclaim. I've never been as proud as when I saw those guys up there, absolutely nailing the routine from beginning to end. I loved working with them and I know we will continue to create together in the future.

Martin Guerre was another satisfying moment that summer. It was odd going back to a show that had played a role in my early career. Eleven years after I'd worked under Bob Avian on the original West End production, I returned to the musical to direct and choreograph it for the Watermill Theatre.

I took the decision to pare it right down. I stripped away everything that was unnecessary, and turned it into a chamber opera. The story is very complicated because it's based on mistaken identity, but I made it as simple as I could. I also remembered my discussion with Shirley MacLaine in the stairwell at the Prince Edward Theatre and tackled the thorny issue of the subtext. I had to make it clear that the two leads were close friends who really did love one another, but not in a sexual fashion; rather in a male-bonded way. I worked with the actors to communicate the subtleties and intensity of that relationship: they would lay their lives down for each other, and we had to convey that fire.

The Watermill seats only around 200 people, so it's fairly intimate, and the audience felt that they were part of the story. My restaging worked really well and, for the first time, *Martin Guerre* garnered rave reviews.

Clive Davis of *The Times*, for instance, wrote: 'Small is beautiful, and in this revised, chamber version of the ill-starred

Boublil and Schönberg melodrama, you catch an authentic whiff of a cramped, grubby and culturally claustrophobic sixteenth-century village.'

The *Daily Telegraph*'s Dominic Cavendish, meanwhile, announced it was 'as good a showing as the work will ever get'. You can't ask for more than that.

All this time, I was juggling my work balls, so to speak, with balls of an altogether different nature. Despite my dating disasters in New Zealand, I was determined to continue my quest for love. My sister Diane came over for a visit, and she and I went out on the prowl one night. Bingo! I hooked up with a hunk in a bar in Soho, and he became the first guy I dated seriously after Lloyd.

He was very nice – but, I discovered, not very faithful. It seemed he had a boyfriend already, so that fling didn't work out.

Not long after that, I encountered thirty-year-old 'Little Big Dick' (short man, sizeable package). We met at a friend's fiftieth birthday party, through my good pals David and Michelle. He was a really genuine, honest and loving man. I felt very lucky to have met him.

We went on a marvellous trip to Berlin together and our affair lasted for about four months. However, I was only just beginning to stretch my wings in my newly single life, and I discovered that I wasn't quite ready for another intense, full-on relationship. It was such a shame as we got on like a house on fire. He really made me laugh and had a glorious sense of humour, but the timing wasn't right.

Instead, I turned my attention to assessing men in rhinestone-studded suits, as a judge on *The World's Greatest Elvis*, a one-off talent competition to find the best Elvis impersonator from across the globe.

Elvis used his body in dance all the time, and choreographers often use his unique gestures in certain steps, so my West End background again provided the perfect foundation from which to evaluate the performers. In fact, I had recently choreographed a play called *Martha, Josie and the Chinese Elvis*, which had starred Maureen Lipman and included an Elvis impersonator played by Paul Hyu (with whom, oddly enough, I'd been in *Miss Saigon* a million years ago), so I'd had to study Elvis's moves in close detail and had become intimately aware of all his idiosyncrasies. The BBC were aware of the production and had therefore asked me to adjudicate the show – alongside my old 'pudding pal' Suzi Quatro, who was appraising the vocals, and Joe Esposito, a close friend of Elvis, who had actually been the one to find him dead, and who was there as an expert on the King's personality and the different eras of his act.

I so enjoyed sharing with Suzi my memory of the time I had made her dessert when I was an apprentice chef in Ballarat. She was incredibly down to earth. She would lean over to me and say, 'Craig, I can't wait to get out of these leathers!' Elvis truly was her idol; on his comeback tour in the sixties, he had worn the black leather and gone for the heavy rock sound, and that was what had inspired her. I loved that after filming she would go home and put on her fleecy, teddy-bear pyjamas, which she endearingly told me were what she wore in bed.

This might sound obvious, but *The World's Greatest Elvis* was the weirdest show with respect to the sheer amount of Elvises on set, all looking the same. Each one had been handpicked to represent their country, so there was a Japanese Elvis, a Thai Elvis and a Brazilian Elvis, among others. It was all very peculiar.

Before the competition started, I asked the creative team what was expected of me. I was told to be honest – because we were, after all, talking about a legend. If you are going to be named as the world's greatest impersonator of the world's most exalted star, then you should earn the title and be phenomenal.

For me, there was one contestant who looked nothing like Elvis, sounded nothing like Elvis and moved nothing like Elvis. In fact, I didn't know why he was even up there – so I told him that. He was furious and stormed backstage in tears.

At the interval, I was taken aside and told, 'We're just going to re-record one of your comments.'

I leaned across to Suzi Quatro and whispered, 'What do you think about him?'

She murmured back, 'I agree. He's nothing like him.'

Nonetheless, I had to do a re-take and replace my original comments with less offensive ones. I suppose I was being a little harsh on the poor guy. It was his entire career at stake.

What I found strange, though, was that he was wearing the GI outfit – and, in my opinion, looked more like Judy Garland than the King of Rock and Roll!

CHAPTER 19 *In Strictest Confidence*

On 6 October 2007, fourteen nervous celebrities squared their shoulders, pasted on a grin and swept grandly (or so they hoped) on to the dance floor of *Strictly Come Dancing* for its fifth season.

As usual, the other judges and I had had to negotiate the tricky process of meeting the fresh crop of contestants for the first time. As the in-house 'villains', it's more difficult than you might think. We are never formally introduced to the celebs; instead, before the series starts, we are handed a press pack, with brief biographies of them all. We know as much as the media do and no more. Personally, I think it would be nicer if we had a meet and greet, like I would with a new theatre company.

I generally encounter the celebrities for the first time as I walk past them in a corridor. I always make an effort to say, 'Hi, my name's Craig.'

They usually respond, 'Yes, I know who you are,' very warily.

Occasionally, we judges might run into our new colleagues in make-up, but once they're done up in their cha-cha outfits with sparkly faces, it's often hard to tell who some of them are. If our paths haven't crossed in the make-up room or in the corridors, then the first time we see them is when they walk down the stairs on to the dance floor.

Only a week after the new series started, Stephanie Beacham was walking back up that staircase and out of the competition.

She gave a masterclass in how to go out gracefully when she became the first female celebrity to leave the contest. She made everyone smile because she said, 'Thank God! I can't thank everybody enough for voting me out.'

It was absolutely brilliant and had all of us in stitches. She was fantastic backstage because she played up to the Hollywood superstar role, a real diva. Underneath the airy grace, I suspect she may have been quite hurt that she'd been eliminated so early, because she was in fact a very good dancer and she had a lot more to offer, but that's the way it goes on *Strictly*.

Some of the decisions – both the public's and my fellow judges' – can be really annoying. Any irritation I express on the show in that regard is always genuine. At times, I think that we judges approach our marking from such disparate starting points that I almost can't see the point in us scoring. I watch these high marks appear for what I consider to be substandard performances, and I just think, 'That's crazy.'

In the quarter-final of that season, for example, when Matt Di Angelo forgot the routine entirely and gave up halfway through to sit on the stairs, Len and Bruno both gave him an eight, which was ridiculously excessive. As I said on the night, the first part of the dance wasn't particularly good and the fact that he just stopped and sat down was appalling. His fear of failure got to him. Matt's problem was that he judged himself from the outside, rather than experiencing the movement from the inside, so he was not really in the performance.

It's what I call a Shirley moment: having an out-of-body experience, where you leave your physical self and watch yourself externally. I named them after Shirley MacLaine because in her book, *Out on a Limb*, she claims she's had out-of-body episodes and describes them. Actors suffer them all the time. That's when they stop looking natural and look like they're acting. I handed Matt a four for his efforts – and even that seems generous.

I tend to score low and Len tends to grade high, so it's always a bone of contention between us. Bruno is too generous, whereas Arlene can be too harsh, marking a contestant down for a small thing. Overall, I think I'm the fairest – but then, I would say that.

As each series develops, you grow used to certain ways of scoring – for instance, our starting points in series five were much higher than they'd ever been before. The season was an interesting one because the dancing was of a much higher standard. Every year, the talent has improved, so there is less for me to be critical about. I'm not going to say it's bad if it isn't.

Nevertheless, I provoked a lot of complaints that year. People wrote, 'How can you be so opinionated? How dare you tell us who to vote for?' But I don't mind who they vote for – it's their money. It's my job to give them a professional opinion so they can make informed choices.

Actors and actresses are usually the ones who take the criticism to heart the most. That's because they are already sensitive – and they're used to having a character to hide behind. Letitia Dean, whom I adore, was quite upset with some of the comments she received in feedback and found it quite hard going. The two of us had got off to an uneasy start as it was, because some shared history initially lodged itself in the way.

Three years before her appearance on *Strictly* in 2007, Letitia went through a well-publicized split from her husband, Jason Pethers. My assistant, Heather, is now with him, so this was a sensitive issue between us. Letitia and Jason had been apart for three years, and Heather had been with him for two years. Typically, however, when the papers got hold of the connection after Letitia was announced as a contestant on the show, they made the whole thing sound like it had just happened and she was miserable because of it. The coverage hurt her, even though she had moved on.

She and I went through three very difficult weeks. The situation was too close to home. I was in a position to judge her, while my assistant, with whom I had worked for seven years, was in love with her ex-husband. The episode put a strain on Heather and Jason's relationship as well, because every time he went out in public, he was papped. Suddenly, they were in the papers every day.

The stories in the press created an understandable confidence issue for Letitia. She had got over the break-up, yet the media 'exposé' brought it all back. I felt roped into the scenario because I guessed she was always worried about what was going to come out of my mouth on the judging panel and, possibly, she may have thought that I had something against her, which wasn't true at all. Naturally, I would never bring anyone else's private life or mine into comment on the show. That would be completely unprofessional, not to mention rather ludicrous.

For almost a month, there was a slight atmosphere between us. Finally, we got together in the BBC bar one night and said, 'Right, we're going to talk about this.'

So we did, and I'm glad we had that chat because it completely cleared the air. We've been on the *SCD* tour together since, so thank goodness we're now great friends. Tish is loads of fun at a party. There's a girl who knows how to let her hair down!

Another fabulous contestant that season was the beautiful Kelly Brook. I knew Kelly already by the time she appeared on *Strictly*, through her boyfriend Billy Zane and the ill-fated *Six Dance Lessons in Six Weeks*. During the West End show, she and I used to sit in the auditorium together and watch Billy on stage. Conversely, during Kelly's run on *SCD*, Billy was on set every day. He was a wonderful support to her and I did become very fond of him again.

Kelly is a blooming good dancer. It was a terrible shame she had to leave the show early, following the sad news of her father's death, because she was amazing. She would have made it to the final, I'm sure – as long as her dance partner Brendan Cole was kept in check. Their American Smooth could have been stunning if it wasn't for the illegal lift that Brendan included. He has done that far too often.

I loved their dancing, but I thought that they should have been disqualified for that particular piece of choreography. They both knew the rules – and there are reasons for them. If everyone decided to be anarchists on the dance floor, there's no point in a judging panel and no point in our scores. How would an Olympic athlete feel if a rival won a gold medal when they should have been banned? I felt Bruno giving them a ten was frankly irresponsible.

People always assume that Bruno and I don't get on because of our arguments on the show, but they are about dance, because we see dance in a very different way: I love things that he sometimes hates. Our job on stage is separate to our life backstage; despite our on-screen disagreements, Bruno and I are true mates.

When we first started doing *Strictly*, Bruno wanted to get into theatrical choreography, rather than continuing with his usual work in film, TV and pop videos, so we shared some elaborate discussions about my trade. He was very keen to move to theatre, but I explained that it's very difficult to get into and can be quite brutal if you're not flavour of the month. As soon as someone new comes along, all the old choreographers get chucked out. They say TV is fickle, but I think it applies to all aspects of show business. Every producer thinks there's someone better – and cheaper – round the corner.

During the first three series of *SCD*, Bruno and I used to go out together all the time. The dynamics changed when he started judging the American show *Dancing with the Stars*, but when Bruno's in town and not shuttling back and forth to the States, he and I often have lunch together. Sometimes he cooks, and I can tell you that he serves up a mean roast chicken. Afterwards, we'll go out and about for the afternoon and will regularly end up at my mate's place for dinner.

After one such day, we got absolutely hammered and flagged a black cab in St Pancras to get us home. The car door opened and Bruno completely missed the step. He was lying face down with his top half inside the taxi and his knees splayed in the middle of the road outside. Very Patsy in *Ab Fab*. He looked hysterical with his butt sticking out of the cab. Oh, I wish I'd had a camera that night. Where are the paps when you need them?

Bruno swears like a trooper. Every second word is an F-word, but somehow it's less offensive with the beautiful Italian accent. Gordon Ramsay and Bruno would make a great double act. He does make me laugh because his *Strictly* comments are so floral, but, if you listen carefully, you'll realize that they are never really that much to do with dance technique, instead he focuses more on the emotional, 'tiger-in-the-wild' side of the performance.

In series four, his expletives got him into trouble when he swore on live TV and had to make a public apology. He was contradicting some comment Arlene had made and flamboyantly announced, 'The hills are alive with the sound of bullshit.' He also got told off for mentioning God in one comment. There's a clause in our contract that says we can't swear, blaspheme or make sexual references because of the watershed. It is quite difficult to control if you swear a lot like Bruno does, off-screen. It's not easy to switch it off.

When we first started working on the programme, the three male judges shared one dressing room, which was a laugh. Bruno can't wait to take his clothes off, so he would slop around in his pants the whole time. Len, on the other hand – who used to be a stand-up comedian, which not many people know – would entertain the life out of us. He is completely mad and utterly hilarious: I was frequently in stitches with him backstage.

Len can get grouchy sometimes, particularly after he's been travelling. He'll be all 'cheeky chappy' – cheerful smile and sparkling teeth – on set, but then turn into a real old grump when the cameras stop rolling. Sometimes, this can affect the programme. If he's doing the show in America and the UK at the same time, for example, it changes the way he is. Consequently, that influences Arlene's mood and mine too. Nevertheless, I still get on really well with him, and with Arlene – who is also slightly nutty, to tell the truth. In fact, I often feel like the sanest one on the panel!

Just like Len, Arlene is funny. I have the most fantastic memory of her from when we went up to Edinburgh to judge a special *Strictly*, with TV executives as contestants. It was part of an industry awards ceremony and execs from all channels were taking part.

For the event, as on the live show, we had those wretched paddles that display the scores, which are stored underneath our desk in boxes; one set each. When we've decided on our mark, we have to rummage through and choose the one we want. I'm always first up, and then Arlene. On this occasion, I'd just got mine out when I saw that Arlene had knocked over her box and the paddles had gone everywhere. I have never seen her so flummoxed in all my life. She disappeared underneath the desk and the announcement went, 'Judges, your scores please.'

So I got mine ready, thinking, 'Oh my God, she's never going to make it.' They called my name and I gave my score of seven, trying to keep a very straight face. Then the voice said, 'Arlene Phillips.'

She was still under the table, scrabbling around. The camera shot to absolutely no one sat at the desk. Suddenly, she popped up, looked at the paddle she had in her hand, to see which number was on it, and went 'Ten!' She'd grabbed the first one she could find and accidentally gave a perfect score. It was so amusing; she was totally panic-stricken and Bruno and I couldn't stop laughing. Arlene is such a character, always in control, so I love it when she gets flustered and lost for words. She starts embellishing and goes on and on. I can always tell when she's lost the plot a bit because she starts rambling inanely.

Arlene writes a book of notes for every dance when she's judging *Strictly*. It's pages and pages. I note down three things. I either love or hate it, and that's the angle I start from. Once I've decided that, I write down three words that describe the performance or three points that I want to mention, so I might scribble 'arms', 'footwork', 'top line' or whatever else strikes me.

It's useful to have the notes – not only to focus the feedback and make it concise and articulate, but also so that I have a range of aspects to discuss. I listen to my fellow judges' comments and very rarely repeat any element of what they've said. If Len talks about the footwork, I will remark on top line or emotion or something else. It's better in my view to flag up a new perspective for the audience to think about than to rehash the same response; the dancers gain more that way too.

Len, or Len 'Goody' Goodman as I often refer to him, approaches his judging from a teaching point of view; he's quite technical and he tends to love, embrace, nurture and not really hurt anyone's feelings.

As a choreographer, I too love, embrace and nurture; you might find that hard to believe, but it's true. When it comes to judging the contestants, I tackle it in the capacity of a director/choreographer, searching for what may need attention choreographically or dramatically. Is the dance telling a story? Who may need a push to catch up with the rest of the cast? Who's not pulling their weight on stage? Who's overworking the choreography? Are they in sync? I'm always looking for the wrong – but only so that it can be righted. In my own work in the theatre, I have to be supercritical, because I'll have critics analysing my dancers' performances and writing about it in the papers the next day. If the reviews prove unfavourable, that could put me out of work.

Midway through season five, I gave what I thought was a charming interview to a tabloid newspaper. I was horrified by what they printed. In black and white, the bare words read: 'The acid-tongued Aussie said Penny Lancaster looked like a SWINGER, Letitia Dean was FAT and injured Kate Garraway was a HUMILIATION.'

None of it was true. To clarify, I had said that Letitia had some self-assurance issues – but who wouldn't lose confidence dancing next to Amazons like Kelly Brook, Penny Lancaster-Stewart and Gabby Logan? I'd commented that I thought the audience were being brutal keeping Kate in, when she was humiliated each week. Finally, I had remarked that Penny's outfit made her look like she was at a swingers' party. Not the same thing at all.

Dominic Littlewood was voted off the show around this time. In the week following his departure, the *Daily Mirror*, among other media, published his claim that the judges prejudged the scores. That's absolute rubbish. I don't see how you can prejudge anyone in a live competition. Even if we saw the rehearsal, which we very, very rarely do, that's not the dance we pronounce upon.

We judges can never discuss the show's content ahead of time because we honestly don't know anything about it. The *Strictly* team keeps us in the dark until just before the live programme, when the producer comes in to give us a quick briefing. We might be told then that someone is injured, for example, but it doesn't mean we should go easy on them; it's just to keep us in the loop.

At any rate, we don't let those titbits of information alter our opinions. Even injury doesn't cut any ice with me because I would say that if you're badly injured, you shouldn't dance. If you go ahead, I will judge the routine and nothing else. We grade on the performance and the viewers can vote with their emotions. We always see more than the viewing public does, of course, because the TV audience watch pretty cutaway shots, which don't necessarily expose the bent leg or sickle foot.

The rumour mill went into overdrive about Matt Di Angelo and Flavia Cacace during the fifth series. They obviously had a very close relationship. If you are dancing eight hours a day with someone, that changes your personal space and the barriers come down.

My work on *Strictly* wasn't stopping me from lowering barriers of my own, either. As the show continued apace, I was making progress in my love life. On the prowl again, I snagged a third catch: Mr M. He was twenty-three, but very tall and extremely cute, so my age rule went west.

I met him at a fashion show called *The Cambridge Catwalk*, which had been arranged, bizarrely enough, by my ex-wife Jane. Mr M was sitting opposite me. He clocked me and came rushing up, asking for my phone number.

'Sorry, I'm not in the habit of handing out phone numbers to perfect strangers,' I said, before adding charmingly, 'but I do accept them.'

Mr M gave me his details. The next morning, I rang him – and woke him up.

'Who is this?' he demanded, rather crossly.

'It's Craig Revel Horwood,' I said.

He was beside himself – well, he lived in Cambridge. I asked him if he wanted to come down to London and see the TV programme, which he did.

As soon as he arrived, I asked him if he was in a relationship. I think I was paranoid about that sort of thing after my previous experiences.

It was just as well I asked. He said boldly, 'Yes, I am.' He told me that he lived with his boyfriend.

For me, that was the end of that, so it never got off the ground. We stayed in touch, though; he's a nice lad.

Soon afterwards, my friends David and Michelle asked me to judge a drag fashion show for charity at a nightclub called Horse Meat, in Vauxhall. David and Michelle have both been in my life for years and always look after me, rustling up delicious dinners. They are both very house-proud and fantastic cooks, and they were brilliant during my split with Lloyd. So, I was happy to help them out.

(Plus, David told me there was a free bar and a VIP room, and it sounded quite fun, so I said I would certainly do it.)

I turned up in my nice Givenchy suit to judge this contest,

which was really quite tragic, and this bright-blue drag queen – I kid you not – walked down the catwalk and then fell off the end of the runway, into the crowd. Everything was blue – her wig, her dress and even her skin.

Having slipped off the catwalk, she fought her way through the crowd and stood in front of me, yelling, 'What did you give me? What did you bloody give me?' in a broad Welsh Valleys accent. Then she demanded to know how old I was, so I said forty-two, and she plonked herself down next to me on the judging panel and demanded, 'Feel my thighs! Feel my thighs! I'm a rugby player.'

Then, suddenly, she leapt up and said, 'I'll be back in ten minutes,' and she rushed off. I thought she was a complete nutter, so I beat a hasty retreat to the VIP area. I sat there chatting to David. In time, a security guy came up and said, 'There's a man downstairs who says he has your mobile phone.'

'I've got my mobile phone,' I said. 'He's a mad, blue Welshman; don't let him anywhere near me.' So they didn't.

An hour or two later, as I was leaving, after a very pleasant night I might add, he came up to me again as I was collecting my coat and bag from the cloakroom. I didn't recognize him, because he wasn't blue and he wasn't wearing a dress. I simply thought, 'Oh my God. He's gorgeous.'

Then he revealed, 'I'm the blue drag. Kiss me!'

So I did. Then I gave him my phone number.

After all that drama, he lost his mobile that very same night. I didn't hear from him for a month. But he was persistent – as I might have anticipated.

One day, my agent, Gavin Barker, received an email from the blue drag – let's call him DHG – explaining what had happened and including his phone number. So, I rang him, and we agreed to meet up, which was the beginning of the weirdest relationship I have ever had. Although he had been pushy on that first night, he didn't want to have sex. We became lovers without the sexual relationship. Even when he stayed overnight, nothing serious happened.

After three months, I confronted him about it and said, 'Look, I really like you, but can you please tell me if anything is ever going to happen between us because, if not, I don't want you here.'

I was being blunt, but I wanted to know if the relationship was worth pursuing.

He answered, 'I'm into muscles ...'

So I thought that was quite obviously the end of that.

DHG left, and then, a week later, he started texting me again, saying he was coming round. I told him, 'Don't,' and expected to hear nothing more from him.

The following morning, at 3 a.m., I received a text, which said: 'I'm outside.'

The next thing I know, someone is singing a love song, very loudly, outside my house. I went downstairs and opened the door to hiss 'Fuck off!' at him. He was ready for me. He slammed the door wide open, threw me against the wall and started snogging and undressing me at the same time. Then he dragged me upstairs.

Despite his newfound passion, we didn't actually get back together after that. I'd realized that he wasn't the guy for me.

After DHG came Walshy, whom I met on Jake, a website for professional gay men. He was twenty-nine, and we had a lot of fun together. We went clubbing in Ibiza and stayed together, off and on, for about three months. He was witty, charming, honest, dependable and everything I wanted. In one of those cruel twists of fate, though, it somehow wasn't working for me. I had to be honest and tell him. I would never lead someone on if I thought it wasn't going to last; I'd rather split sooner than later.

Not long after Walshy and I broke up, I met Doctor D, whom I thought was perfect. He was gorgeous and he was a psychiatrist – now, I could do with one of those. At thirty-five, he was the right age, too. We shared similar tastes in furniture, decor and so on, and we were both at a place in our lives where we were sorted, but looking for love. It was all rather promising.

Doctor D lived in Bristol, so it took us ages to arrange a meeting. Three months after the first contact by email, we finally went for a beer. He was a laugh a minute, the funniest person I have ever been out with. However, distance meant we couldn't see each other much. A month later, I went to Bristol and we had a lovely meal together.

Sadly, it turned out that we weren't compatible after all. He eventually dumped me because – wait for it – he said the relationship was going too fast, too soon, and it was all too much for him. He wanted to slow things down. I'd thought that seeing each other once a month was sluggish enough. The whole affair lasted about four months, yet it could have been over and done with in less than a week, given the number of dates we actually had.

My next assignation was a rather special one. I met Grant through the same Internet site one Tuesday and our relationship developed at a breakneck pace in comparison. We arranged to meet the very next day, 21 November 2007, after my Wednesday filming for *It Takes Two* at The Hospital – a private members' club in Covent Garden, not A & E!

The club has a TV studio downstairs, from where Claudia's show is broadcast. Upstairs, there is a lovely restaurant, which serves delicious sausage and mash. After the tie-in show finishes, at about 7 p.m., all the *Strictly* gang involved that day often have a drink and some food together. It's a lovely way to spend a weekday evening, eating sausage and mash with people like Penny Lancaster-Stewart and Rod Stewart.

On this particular Wednesday, I'd finished filming my contribution to the programme (during which – as she does every week of the run – Claudia had interviewed me about how the contestants were getting on at rehearsals and I had commented on their training footage), and I was sitting on a corner seat in The Hospital when Grant walked in. I thought, 'He's gorgeous,' and then, 'He'll take one look at me and run.' He was the spitting image of Tom Cruise.

Grant sat next to me and we sheepishly murmured, 'Hello.' Then we got chatting over a couple of mojitos.

It was all going so smoothly and naturally that I said, 'Do you want to go out for some dinner? I know this restaurant called Gilgamesh in Camden, which decor-wise has an ugly opulence, but it's completely over the top and I love the food. Do you fancy that?'

To my surprise, he said he did and we went out for a meal.

There was an obvious mutual attraction, which grew throughout the evening. When it was time to say our goodbyes, we arranged another date. We haven't left each other alone since. I am totally in love with Grant.

He's a pharmacist at a Harley Street clinic, so it's quite appropriate that we met at The Hospital. Grant works with cancer patients, helping to save lives on a daily basis, while I entertain. It does rather bring home the superficial nature of my career, I must admit.

In the blink of an eye, or so it seemed, the finale of season five came around and it was time to crown another king or queen of the ballroom. Alesha Dixon was a delightful winner. She came to us at rock bottom, following her very public marriage breakdown when her husband MC Harvey left her for singer Javine. She admitted she'd been suicidal. Alesha is the most wonderful character, the most beautiful person backstage and, on stage, she's a dream. To think that someone like her can be treated so badly in their private life is awful.

On *Strictly*, she was a real inspiration, to millions. Alesha's survival offered hope to those in similar situations. She extricated herself from her dark days and subsequently triumphed. I think it's positive that people know about such hardship because it encourages them to pull themselves out of their own dreadful scenarios. I don't mean just by attending ballroom lessons; there's often more to it than that. But, without being facile, they are at least a start, because you can meet new people and begin to feel good about yourself again. I don't think we should ever underestimate the power of doing something for ourselves.

I'm often asked whom I judge to be the best and worst contestants in *Strictly* history. Alesha Dixon was a stunning dancer, and the best female all-rounder we've had to date, while the undulating hips of Mark Ramprakash seal his place at the top of my personal leader board.

At the bottom of the scale, Christopher Parker's paso doble from season one will stay in my memory for many more bad reasons than good. Yet it was not Chris but Quentin Willson whom I christened Britain's worst dancer, in series two, and I still stand by that.

On *Strictly*, I have to be honest and critical. Not just with the contestants, but also with myself. That has always been how I've got through life: if I lied to myself, it would reflect in my work. The critiques you see me deliver on *Strictly* come straight from the heart.

If they didn't, I'd simply be playing a TV character – and then I'm no better than a pantomime villain. And I hate panto.

Until I'm offered one, that is.

CHAPTER 20 *The Greatest Love of All*

At the beginning of 2008, *Strictly Come Dancing* embarked on a UK tour, playing forty dates in seven cities. Kate Thornton, who was fabulous, presented each show. As Bruno was working on the US version of *Dance X* (renamed *Dance Wars* in America), it was judged by just three of us: Len, Arlene and myself.

The timing was tricky given my burgeoning relationship with Grant. For in addition to the hectic UK tour, I was booked on a flight to New Zealand, just two days after the last gig, to film my second series of *Dancing with the Stars*. I wasn't due back until May. It's hard to get to know someone when you're not even in the same country, so I had serious questions about how we could make it work. I feel sorry for anyone I meet because there's not much I can do about the nature of my job and the amount of travelling it entails. I'm always open and honest about the situation with anyone I'm romancing; I have to explain to them that my job is my priority, because I love it, and I won't give it up for anybody. It's what I do and what I adore doing.

Grant, thankfully, understood that, and we agreed to give it a go. We called each other every day, wherever we were.

I wasn't exactly sure how the live tour format of *Strictly* would work, but it was a real smash. It was pure entertainment and each audience got to vote, which meant that we had a different winner every night.

It was weird judging the same routines time after time. We had to look at them with fresh eyes, otherwise all the feedback would be the same and our responses would grow stale. The dancers improved as the tour went on, but there remained room for error. Occasionally, some of them would forget a bit of the choreography or perform the wrong step, which was quite lucky for us judges because it gave us something new to comment on.

Chris Parker and Matt Di Angelo had a running dare going, where they'd challenge each other to add strange moves into their choreography. Chris would perform an extra hip thrust in his paso doble, and I'd say, 'I believe there was a superfluous thrust in that routine.'

The contestants conspired on these things backstage to see if we were watching. Of course we were: we had eagle eyes out there. They were doing the same dance every night, so a different move stood out like a sore thumb. On the TV show it's much more difficult to appreciate such nuances because you have only ninety seconds to see what's going on.

Without the judges, the whole show would be simply a presentation piece. It's the competitive nature of the format that people love the most. And, boy, are they competitive! The tour had a slightly different atmosphere, however, because some contestants – namely Chris Parker – took part even though they knew they were never going to win.

Chris is a star, because he just doesn't care what we think about him. I would love him to improve, but he really hasn't. As much as I get upset with the situation, because I don't believe his interpretations are really dance, he is a good sport. His notorious paso was chosen as his Latin dance for the tour because he was so hilariously bad at it on TV. At some of the gigs, when he got a good reaction, he did a lap of honour with his cape flowing behind him. He was the highlight of the evening.

Len gave him an extraordinarily generous ten in Manchester, which the crowd loved. The audience like to see our reactions to the less talented celebrities like Chris because they wonder what the hell we can say about something as bad as that, without being horrifically rude or personal. Len really felt for him, because Chris put his heart and soul into it and really had a go, so Len marked him up for entertainment value. My argument, of course, is that it is still a ballroom competition and we are meant to mark contestants on their ability to dance.

Chris did well on both the programme and the tour because people empathize with him and can see themselves in him. They also love people like James Martin because, as much as his cooking is fantastic, his Latin sucks. Yet his ballroom is magnificent. It just goes to show that you can't always be good at everything.

James, I'm quite sure, was not fond of the tour at the start because of the judges' negative reaction to his Latin number. If you imagine that you have to dance the same routine every night, and you already know what the reaction is likely to be, when you consistently receive just a five or six in the scores every time, it is a difficult prospect.

But James is no fool. He played the game and entertained the crowd, wiggling his bottom to get them on his side, and at the end of his cha-cha-cha, he made no bones about the fact that he finds that particular dance style challenging. He has a laugh with the audience and they adore him. James is a savvy guy and he realizes that any situation can be turned around to your advantage, so he transformed his approach. He has a charming personality and is a great communicator, which is why he's on telly and is so successful.

Tours always bring out mischief in performers. In the midst of the run, some of the lads displayed their childish side – with good old Len joining in too. The set-up backstage was that all the male dancers and celebs were put into a single dressing room, while Len and I got one to ourselves. The judges are never off set during the evening, so it seemed very unfair on everyone else. The boys needed to be together because it made it easier for the wardrobe stylists, but they were always jealous of our opulent dressing rooms. They would have no sofas, no chairs, and there would be ten of them sharing one space; we always got these really posh rooms with TVs, sofas and tables, as did Arlene and Kate Thornton. At one venue, we had a marvellous room with lovely furniture … and the next night the furniture was gone. The boys had moved it.

Len decided to take revenge, so he went and hid all their dance shoes. He didn't give them up until the last minute, just as they were about to go on. After that, war was declared. It lasted for weeks, with everyone trying to get one up on each other, hiding one another's stuff backstage. It was ridiculous, but very funny.

There was a great deal of partying with the team after each gig. One night in Manchester, I got horribly drunk. I'd been out for a boozy lunch with Len and then met the others for dinner – and more wine. On the way back to the hotel, I was shouting marks out of ten out the cab window at everyone I saw, so I probably insulted half of Manchester.

Then I fell over on top of Stuart, the warm-up man, and we ended up rolling around in the gutter outside the hotel. Not only that, but I went in and bought another bottle of rosé, which the others hid from me after the first glass to prevent me from drinking it. I was on a mission that night.

The next morning, everyone was exclaiming, 'What were you *like* last night?'

Oh, it was heinous. I had the hangover from hell and felt awful.

Chris Parker has the management take away the contents of the minibars in his room in every hotel, because he knows he'll go through them. By the time you've eaten the chocolate, nuts and crisps and had a few drinks, you've spent your entire wage.

Chris is a really sweet boy and he does love to party. A couple of years after he was in *Strictly*, he kept being photographed falling out of nightclubs and into gutters looking tragic, but I didn't see any of that on the tour. He's a lot more controlled now.

I always think *EastEnders*, and all the other soaps, must be a hard place to come down from for young actors like Chris. These artists are put on a pedestal and become famous overnight. Fifteen million viewers watch them. They can't walk down the street, or be treated normally, and they're papped constantly, so it changes their life immediately. When that finishes and no one offers them another job, they must wonder what the hell to do next. One minute they're famous and flying high, and the next they are just ordinary people again, but with the added problem of fame.

Fame is a funny thing. People somehow find it odd to see celebrities in the flesh – and they think it even stranger to see a group of them together. When we judges venture out in public as a gang, or even as a duo, there are a lot of double takes. I went to the Trafford Centre in Manchester with Len one afternoon and our fellow shoppers kept stopping us and talking to us. One lady came up to Len on the street outside and said, 'You're brilliant on that show – the *Antiques Roadshow*.' Oh, that made me chuckle.

Every night on tour, during the finale, Len, Arlene and I would stand on a raised platform above the stage, sidestepping and doing a little bopping. One evening, as we were busting our moves, a woman from the audience staggered from the opposite end of the stadium and began dancing into the centre of the stage in a very bizarre fashion. Len saw what was happening and went down to intercept her and dance her off. Then he came back, laughing like a drain, to boogie with us again.

It all got too much for him. He slipped and fell down the steep stairs to the stage and hit the deck. He lay there in a crumpled heap for the longest time. I looked at Darren Gough, and the pair of us corpsed with laughter, then Christopher Parker got the giggles. Len was lying with his legs in the air like an upturned turtle! I reached out to grab him in an attempt to get him on his feet, without success. It was the most hilarious thing I have ever seen. I did feel sorry for him, but backstage we must have chortled for about half an hour. He came off complaining that everyone had just laughed and no bugger had helped him up.

In fact, those same stairs caused me a lot more damage in a much less dramatic incident. The band struck up the familiar *Strictly* theme tune as the show opened one night. Kate came down the stairs, followed by me, with Arlene and Len behind. It's a long staircase and I was walking down carefully, with the cameras on me, waving and smiling to the crowd – who were booing, of course. On the second to last step, I heard a ping go in my leg and I thought, 'Oh no, I've done something awful.'

I couldn't shriek in pain and collapse theatrically in a heap. Instead, I had to dance across the stage and go into a little swirl with Arlene before we sat down. That night, I did the most peculiar travelling step to reach her because I was limping in agony. I had no idea exactly what the injury was, but I knew my leg muscle had gone somehow because I'd actually heard it crack. All I'd done was walk down the stairs, but my calf had ripped – a total freak of nature.

We reached our seats at long last. Arlene was waving and smiling next to me. I carried on smiling, but through gritted teeth I hissed, 'Arlene, I have ripped my calf muscle from the bone and I need ice, immediately.' We were in close-up on camera and I was clutching my calf under the table. Speaking through her own broad smile, she said, 'Oh my God, are you all right?' I had to sit there for about seven minutes while Kate presented all the dancers, who were coming down the stairs one by one, each with their own introduction, and it seemed to take forever.

As soon as the lights went down, Arlene ran off stage, bless her, and fetched some ice, which I strapped to my leg. I spent the next two hours in torment with water dripping down my leg. Nightmare.

Backstage, everyone had heard about it, because Arlene had informed the team that I needed instant attention, but there was nothing they could do for forty-five minutes or so. I couldn't move. I had to stay where I was until the interval. The physios are fantastic, so they strapped me up temporarily during the break, and the next day built up my heel for me and strapped my leg properly, so I could at least walk.

The evening after it happened, there was an announcement to say, 'Craig fell down the stairs last night.' For a whole week of the tour, I couldn't make my entrance on that staircase. I had to walk in at the side, limping over as if nothing had happened, and the dance with Arlene had to go. She did a twirl around me instead.

I was on crutches after that, with a huge bandage on my leg. The amount of people laughing at me was hideous. Chris Parker and a few others I'd been vile to were giggling with glee. Actually, I have to say it healed really well and was starting to bind after only a week and a half. That was due to the fact that the physios looked after it so competently.

One of the aspects of the tour that I adored was working in front of a live audience. It makes all the difference. In the studio, the audience is usually around 200 people, but on tour we had over 10,000 in some venues, all of them screaming and booing me. It was murderous.

In truth, I'm OK with the catcalls because I think people enjoy it. I don't have to like it on a personal level (and who would?), but a character has been born that people love to hate. One would hope they don't really mean it. It's just the audience getting involved with the show and voicing their opinion. I think everyone is entitled to their own point of view and that's why *Strictly* is so exciting because, although you could liken it to a pantomime, it's a truly interactive event. The audience have the chance to affect the outcome. If you took that tool away from them, they wouldn't bother cheering or heckling.

The boos are all good-natured and affectionate, I like to

think. One lady came up to me on tour and said, 'Craig, you're fantastic. I know you get booed and I was the loudest in the audience, but I love your comments.'

I believe I often voice what the viewers are really thinking. Len represents what people would say in public, as you tend not to criticize others then, but you can bet your bottom dollar that everyone sits at home saying, 'Ooh, come and look at this, dear. Have you seen that bloke dance? He's terrible.'

In February 2008, I got the chance to meet an icon, thanks to Bruce Forsyth's eightieth-birthday celebration. The BBC was recording a special show to mark the occasion and asked all four *Strictly* judges to take part. All we had to do was get up and ice a cake, as part of a *Generation Game* segment, but they called us in early so we were sitting around filing our nails for about five hours before anything happened. Arlene was grumbling all the way through because it was taking so long.

People often get restless in situations like that, and start finding things to whinge about, like costumes and jewellery, or they moan that they were called too soon. Those sorts of things don't bother me. I just keep quiet, or I'll go to my dressing room and lie down. I can think of worse jobs to be doing than turning up and icing a cake for Bruce's eightieth. In fact, I consider it an honour to have been asked.

It was star-studded event, with Jonathan Ross, Richard and Judy, Paul O'Grady and even some musical royalty, in the shape of Liza Minnelli, in attendance.

Liza was lovely. She told me that she was a huge fan of *Strictly*. She knew exactly who we were. It was a huge moment for me because Liza and Barbra Streisand are the two people whom I've been dying to meet all my life, and I adored her. She was so sweet and generous.

We watched Liza rehearse with no fancy costume, no make-up and with her hair not done. It was great to see her au naturel and then, later, to see the Liza Minnelli we all know and love in 'performance mode'. It was a real insight to observe the contrast because one – the 'Liza with a Zee' persona – was outwardly confident, while the other was vulnerable, a bit like a scared rabbit. She switches it on for a show and she's an absolute star.

At these pre-recorded, televised events, a singer will perform a routine and then the producer will run the tape back and usually ask them to do it again, so they can cut out glitches or nail a better cutaway shot. I felt sorry for Liza, though, because she belted out 'New York, New York', which is a huge number, and then immediately had to do it again. She really works like a dancer would and gives it 150 per cent, so she was sweating like a diva. The studio was also very hot with all the lighting and so on. I just wanted to take her into a cool room with a big fan, sit her down, and say, 'Let's chill for fifteen minutes, then do it again.'

She'd already performed on Jools Holland's show in another studio before she'd even arrived at Bruce's. To do that and then come to us and sing 'New York, New York' twice ... She was a true professional: absolutely breathtaking.

Afterwards, Liza went up to Arlene and said, 'I love your work.'

What a compliment. Arlene was so beside herself, she had to sit down.

Len's a bit of an autograph hunter on the quiet, so he knocked on Liza's dressing-room door to ask her to sign something. She wrote, 'To Len, love from Liza Minnelli – you're worth a ten.'

To tell the truth, Len even asks people who come on *Strictly* for their autograph.

I do occasionally get star-struck myself. I loved it when Beyoncé came up to me on *SCD* and said my name. We were backstage and she walked over and said, 'Hi Craig. I think you're great on the show.'

I nearly had a heart attack – oh my God, Beyoncé knows who I am!

Kylie Minogue was on the programme too, and she was lovely

and genuine. It's weird to think that these huge stars watch the series. You know you've made it when Beyoncé and Kylie know your name. And for Liza Minnelli to tell us she was a fan was simply incredible.

Another lifelong ambition fulfilled. Only Barbra left now ...

I was bowled over at the end of February because Grant managed to get time off work to come to New Zealand with me for the whole two months that I'd be filming *Dancing with the Stars*. It was wonderful. His company encouraged me to challenge myself in all sorts of new ways.

Consequently, I found myself jumping out of a plane over Queenstown at 15,000 feet. This was my, admittedly extreme, attempt to overcome my fear of heights.

I have always suffered from vertigo. I once tried to scale Sydney Harbour Bridge and freaked out halfway. I struggled on and got there in the end, but just as our group arrived at the summit, a huge thunderstorm hit: cue lightning, thunderclaps, the works. We couldn't see a thing through the fog and were forced to endure an emergency evacuation. Is it any wonder I have an issue with heights? Funnily enough, both my brother Trent and sister Diane suffer from the same phobia. We all freeze as if we are paralysed.

At 15,000 feet, the air is thinner so you need oxygen, which was making me quite dizzy to start with. I was the first one to jump. The sound of the door, as it slid back to reveal the huge space that I was about to hurl myself into, was the worst thing. I looked down and felt violently ill.

Nevertheless, I forced myself to make the jump – and had the most exhilarating experience of my life. You freefall for about a minute and a half, which I felt really comfortable with, although I couldn't breathe because the air was rushing against my face so much. It fills your mouth and nose and your face blows up to twice its normal size: not a good look.

I would recommend skydiving to anyone who has a fear of

heights. Once you're out of the plane, you've got nothing to lose, so you abandon yourself to it. If the parachute doesn't open then you're screwed, true, but you will have had an amazing experience on your way out.

There aren't many places in the world where you can jump from that height. The standard distance is between 9,000 and 12,000 feet, but the additional elevation allows you just a little bit longer in freefall. It has helped me with my fear, although it hasn't conquered it entirely. I still get the panicky feeling. Nonetheless, I feel it's made me a braver person.

As a case in point, Grant and I also tried parasailing in New Zealand, which turned out to be more frightening than the skydive. These great, big, glorious mountains surround Queenstown and there's one particular place where the landscape enables you to catch the wind perfectly. You just run and jump off the mountain with a parachute: below you is a pine forest and then a schoolyard, where you land. Some people touched down on a nearby beach instead.

I found that the taking off and landing was a nightmare, but the bit in between was wonderful. Parasails are quite easy to steer because if you want to go left, you just pull left – which is fine if you know your left from right, of course, but tricky for those of us who don't. To add to my difficulties, the wind threatens to throw you off course if you're not sure what you're doing. Fortunately, I had an instructor with me, which was a godsend. If I'd done it on my own, I don't think I'd have lived to tell the tale.

I loved the entire escapade, although I found it scary that your feet hang so close to the tops of the trees. Then there's the fact that you're running off a cliff. On the skydive, when you're 15,000 feet in the air, the world looks so far away, like a view, that it doesn't feel real until you get closer. Throwing yourself off the side of a mountain, however, feels like you could crash a lot more easily, because you can clearly pick out all the details below. You imagine that you might smash into trees, or break your legs on people's houses.

As it turned out, I did crash-land and nearly broke both my legs. There was a gust of wind that hit us just as we came down and we landed so heavily that my lower body went completely numb. I really thought I'd broken something. Grant helped me to recover by supplying a nice glass of wine to get me over the pain.

When we returned from New Zealand, Grant moved in with me, and my happiness was complete. He is the perfect man for me. He's sensible, charming, loving, funny, wants identical things to me and has had similar life experiences. It's already been an adventure. I don't know what the future holds, but, in the words of Liza Minnelli in *Cabaret*, maybe this time …

Back on British soil, in May 2008 I was asked to present the Villain of the Year prize at the British Soap Awards. I can't imagine why they picked me for that one. Jack P. Shepherd from *Coronation Street* was the winner.

It was a terrifying night. Everyone else could have fun, but I couldn't let my hair down until I'd done my bit. I was panicking about getting the name wrong, after looking at the video of the shortlist and then coming back to the autocue.

It was strange having to present. I'd never done that sort of thing before. People assume that because you're on television you can do it automatically, but on *Strictly* I work organically, in that I watch something and then comment on it. Put a script in my hand, place me in front of an autocue, and I am a fish out of water. It's not as easy as it may look. Indeed, many full-time presenters specifically train for it. I knew it would be a challenge for me, but I said yes because I wanted to try it. I don't think I made a complete fool of myself.

Soon after that, I appeared on ITV's *An Audience with Neil Diamond*, and was invited to ask a question. I knew he had once danced with Diana, Princess of Wales, so I wanted to know what that had been like. Back in Ballarat when I was growing up, my mum always had Neil Diamond playing in the house. 'Beautiful Noise' was her favourite song. She would have loved to have met him, but sadly she wasn't there. The fact that I got a dialogue with him was amazing. I was able to tell him that his music had inspired me to dance, and that my first ever *pas de deux* had been performed to 'Love on the Rocks'.

In early summer 2008, my schedule became dominated by my latest Watermill Theatre production, *Sunset Boulevard*. It was another extraordinary task, as all the musicals I have had the pleasure to direct at the Watermill have been.

The casting for this show was critical. Kathryn Evans was my first thought for the role of the faded film star Norma Desmond. I had seen her in numerous productions and always thought her the underdog of West End leading ladies. She had a voice and range that were ideal for the role; she could still dance any of her contemporaries off the stage; and, of course, she was an actress of the highest order.

In short, she was perfect, but she had been out of the business for a while. A couple of years before, Kathryn had suffered a terrible car accident in Ipswich, not far from where she lives with her husband, Peter Purves of *Blue Peter* fame, in Suffolk. She broke her leg in two places, as well as her collarbone, and she wasn't sure if she would ever get back on stage again.

It was my job to convince her to do it, because I knew she was the only one who could – who had the craftsmanship as an actor and a vocal musician, understood the character, was the right age … and would consider working, initially, for a lot less money than usual at the Watermill. To my delight, she said yes.

Kathryn came in with great trepidation. After her time away from the stage, I hoped the experience would give her a platform from which to relaunch herself, as with Gloria Swanson in the movie version of *Sunset*. There was a sense of life imitating art in that, although Kathryn's personality is very different from

Norma's. Kathryn is actually quite shy, which is such a contradiction because on stage she's so out there, and shockingly believable.

Next in the casting came the leading man, who would play opposite Norma as the young writer, Joe Gillis. So who would a film star of fifty fall in love with?

Ben Goddard, who had been my leading man in *Martin Guerre* the year before, sprang to mind. Not only was he stunning in that part with a fabulous singing voice, but he also played the piano, flute, guitar, saxophone, double bass, bass guitar, drums, banjo, classical organ and mandolin. Such multiple talents were essential for my vision of the musical.

Remembering him from *Martin Guerre*, I basically offered him the job, without seeing him. We arranged to meet for a drink in a London bar to discuss it further. When he walked in, it turned out that he was 5 stone overweight, with a waist measuring 42 inches. I couldn't believe it. As tactfully as I could, I broached the subject with a question.

'You do realize, darling, that the character of Joe Gillis opens act two in a pair of Speedos, sitting round a swimming pool?' I enquired.

It wasn't subtle and he knew exactly what I was getting at.

'Don't worry, Craig,' he told me. 'I'll turn up for rehearsals and I'll be trim.'

And he was. He put his mind to it, went running every morning, and by the time the show opened at the Watermill, he looked amazing and had lost 10 inches from his waist. He's a driving force in any company, a true leading man.

It was the first time I had ever directed any of Andrew Lloyd Webber's material. I was slightly apprehensive about making the show smaller, reducing his score unashamedly and placing it in the hands of twelve multi-talented actor/musicians in a space the size of my living room. Thankfully, it worked out brilliantly. I even received a phone call from 'the Lord' himself to congratulate us on our achievement.

Andrew and I were no strangers, as we'd worked together on the *Maria* show for the BBC. In fact, I can remember singing 'Greatest Love of All' in an impromptu karaoke evening at Andrew's home during filming, which was, I'm sure, an unforgettable experience for all concerned.

Andrew wanted to come to see *Sunset*, and for me to sit with him and chat about it afterwards. Naturally, I was a nervous wreck, but I tried to hide it. The show is only a couple of hours long, but every second of that performance was terrifying. I felt I was holding my breath for the entire time, from the moment the curtain went up right through to the curtain calls.

It was a great relief when, at the end, Andrew turned to me and said, 'Congratulations, Craig, you've done a wonderful job.' I could finally exhale.

Generously, Andrew took Grant and me out for dinner that evening and we stayed overnight at his opulent country home, which is not very far from the Watermill. It was filled with the most incredible pre-Raphaelite oil paintings and beautiful furniture. We had a fabulous night's sleep after some delicious wine, and then awoke to a breakfast that was fit only for a king – or queen in my case. Andrew is a very charming man and lots of fun to be around.

Summer 2008 also saw me attend the Caudwell Children's Legend Ball. The people behind it run a marvellous charity, which provides specialist wheelchairs for disabled children. They even have chairs that lift the kids up and help them to dance, which I think is brilliant. Thanks to the popularity of *Strictly Come Dancing*, I'm fortunate to have the opportunity to help all sorts of charities. As well as supporting Children in Need, which is the fundamental backbone of *SCD*, and pursuing my ambassadorship with Teach First, I'm also involved in Performing Arts Workshops summer schools in Milton Keynes and have worked with Dr Miriam Stoppard of the 'Love Your Bones' campaign. This drive aims to increase awareness and understanding of osteoporosis; I created a 'Boogie For Your Bones' dance for the National Osteoporosis Society for World Osteoporosis Day. Without *SCD*, none of this would be possible.

All the children at the Caudwell event were *Strictly Come Dancing* fans. They were thrilled that some of the dancers and judges were there. I was thrilled because Whitney Houston was performing. It meant so much to me that I was literally rendered speechless. It was so good to see her back on track again as she's been through some terrible times; we all saw that publicly. It must have been difficult for someone who is that huge a star to have been seen like that.

All the ladies from *Loose Women* were on my table. It was a fabulous night. I was having a wonderful time with people like Ronan Keating and Louis Walsh, with whom I get on very well.

Then I went backstage to meet Whitney. Suddenly, I became all dumb and stupid. I was awestruck – and filled with memories. I wanted to tell her about Lavish singing 'Greatest Love of All', how I'd used that as my audition song; to describe the drag circuits of Melbourne and Sydney and Lavish's rapturous reception. I wanted to explain that the song had helped me through the break-up with Lloyd and put me on a happier path. But – for once in my life – I said nothing.

CHAPTER 21 *Dancing Pigs and Elephants*

Series six of *Strictly Come Dancing*, which began on 20 September 2008, proved to be something of a rollercoaster ride. Once again, fourteen celebrities were competing, but the competition seemed to focus – at least as far as the press were concerned – on just one man: the now notorious John Sergeant. To this day, everyone remembers his horrendous/hilarious paso doble, when he was Neanderthal man dragging his poor partner Kristina Rihanoff across the floor; he may as well have had her by the hair and danced with a club in his hand.

Yet after the public continued to vote him in, despite his technically challenged dancing, he cut his losses and did a runner in week ten, announcing to a press conference on 19 November that he was pulling out 'in case he won'.

As far as I'm concerned, John Sergeant was lacking courage and determination: a gutless wonder, to use an old Aussie term. I don't think he had the strength to stay. I believe he should have honoured his contract, because he knew what he was getting himself into when he signed up. It's not as if it was the first series we'd ever done.

He also knew that if he danced badly he would be ridiculed, naturally – but for his dance alone. Len touched slightly on the personal when he mentioned John's weight, but Arlene never called him the 'dancing pig', as the media reported. In fact, it was the press that labelled him that, but the story went round the world.

My dad was listening to the radio in Australia and heard: 'The judges of *Strictly Come Dancing*, the UK's equivalent to *Dancing with the Stars*, have called a political journalist a "dancing pig". Do you think this is fair? Should they be sacked?' This was in my home town of Ballarat, which struck me as bizarre. Who cares about John Sergeant?

The answer to that, unfortunately, is that everybody cared about John Sergeant because he made it that way. What other country in the world backs a quitter? Only in Britain would people say, 'Poor John Sergeant. Imagine how terrible he would feel if he had won.'

At the time, a lot of people were calling for our heads. Mind you, we're used to that. There hasn't been a season without someone screaming: 'Get him off our television!'

With everyone baying for our blood, the frustrating thing was that it seemed as though John Sergeant's was the only voice being heard. The BBC didn't want us to expand on the situation – and quite rightly, because it would only make a ridiculous story drag on. (In my opinion, there wasn't a story in the first place. A journalist had left a game show. So what?)

Yet the media turned it into the biggest splash ever, even in the broadsheets. Len Goodman was on the front page of the *Telegraph*, for goodness' sake. I couldn't believe it. When I saw that, I said wryly, 'Look, darling, you've finally made it.'

John's abrupt departure was soon overtaken in dramatic terms, however, by a logistical problem that nobody saw coming. On 13 December, the semi-final, the top two couples – Rachel Stevens and Vincent Simone, and Lisa Snowdon and Brendan Cole – received exactly the same judges' score ... with the consequence that Tom Chambers would be in the dance-off whatever happened: the viewers' votes couldn't save him.

The first sign of the controversy was when Tess Daly announced, live on TV, 'There's a problem with the voting and we'll be coming back.' The judges were as bemused as the rest of the world. The four of us were saying to each other, 'What's going on? What's happening?' We had no clue whatsoever.

Then Bruce and Tess revealed that all three couples were going through and we thought, 'How is that possible?' Clearly Tom had the lowest score. Yet it was the fairest solution – and because we would normally have had three couples in the final anyway, it rebalanced the outcome.

The incredible thing is that the flaw in the system had always been there, but it had never cropped up before because we had never had two couples ranking the same at that stage. It took six series for the possibility to come to light.

I was confused at the time, and I still am. The following week, I was on breakfast television and the presenter said, 'Craig, you're the sensible one. What is going on with the voting?'

I replied, 'Darling, I haven't a clue. I'm still in the dark, and we're coming up to the final.'

Eventually, the decision was made that if the same thing happened in the final, Len, as the head judge, would have the last word on the couples' ranking. In a professional competition, the judges watch several couples at once, confer, and then the head judge decides who should win.

In ours, because the contestants dance individually, the scores are based entirely on our own opinions. I have no idea what marks the others are going to give until they hit their buzzers and start to pick up their paddles. We can't rig it in any way. But in real judging, if there's a tie, the head judge makes a decision.

In fact, that had to happen in the 2008 Christmas special – we had a four-way tie at the top of the leader board, so we had to stop filming for an hour while Len ranked them all. Luckily, that show was pre-recorded and didn't involve viewer voting, just votes from members of the studio audience, so it wasn't quite such a drama as the semi-final.

The BBC cut the backstage green room for series six. It used to be great having guests chilling out in a VIP green room, where you could visit them between the filming of the Saturday and Sunday shows.

Instead, we judges had our own little green room – because the producers had come up with the idea of filming us backstage between the programmes. In the Sunday episode, they'd show us relaxing over a glass of wine and talking about the contestants, airing our dirty laundry.

In general, the 2008 season had a really different atmosphere behind the scenes, because it was more fun-loving than most years. The only spanner in the works was John Sergeant, who, in my opinion, wasn't the most loved or embraced person backstage – but that may have been because the rest of the contestants were all luvvies, and he wasn't. Unlike actors who give up their identities, and sportspeople who are known as themselves, journalists never reveal who they really are. They can be cunning in order to extract information from you and may pretend to be your best friend, then they go away and write something vile.

My own experience with journalists has not always been good. There was one, Petronella Wyatt, who came to do an article for the *Daily Mail* and befriended me, but only to encourage me to say something she could use as a headline – which turned out to be: 'I hate ballroom – and the judges love make-up.' What I actually said was that I hate the rules and regulations that ballroom has, in comparison to my theatre choreography.

One of her sentences started out really nicely and then stabbed me in the back. 'One on one, Craig is charming, friendly and has an attractive face, with cobalt eyes full of puckish mischief. But Stalin could be charming, too.' Nice!

I always call *Strictly* 'my Saturday girl job', but the more high profile it makes me, the more I can do for different organizations. That autumn, I became heavily involved with the National Osteoporosis Society (NOS). The reason I got involved initially was because my mum suffers from arthritis and bone trouble – although those problems are not directly related to osteoporosis. I'd also thought that it would be an extremely worthy charity, especially considering my line of work.

The NOS love having me on board because I really believe in the cause and I'm up there gunning for it. As well as creating the 'Boogie For Your Bones' routine, which promoted dance to kids nationwide as an ideal form of exercise to strengthen bones, I was also Mr September in the charity's Really Naked Calendar 2009. Joanna Lumley, Michael Parkinson, Bruce Forsyth and loads of other celebs participated – but don't worry, I didn't strip off. It was an X-ray calendar with a lovely picture of my hip bone!

I also rubbed shoulders on countless occasions with the charity's president, Her Royal Highness The Duchess of Cornwall (oh, the circles I move in!). Grant and I had dinner at Clarence House at the beginning of December. It was one of the busiest days of my life, but it was quite typical of my schedule at the time. I had interviews with the press for *Strictly* in the morning, rehearsals for *Sunset* in the afternoon (which was midway through its West End transfer, having been such a smash at the Watermill), then I had to change into my suit at 4.30 to do Claudia's show *It Takes Two*, and then on to the charity event in the evening.

I have to say, it was fab-u-lous: I was on the top table with all the people who had donated millions to the NOS, including businesswoman Ann Gloag, who owns a whole train company! Camilla was absolutely adorable: gracious, witty and great fun.

I had the pleasure of her company again only a short while later. Three days before *Sunset* opened in the West End, I presented a snippet from the musical *Jersey Boys* at the Royal Variety Performance. Afterwards, during the line-up backstage, where the Royal Family meet all the performers, the Duchess leaned over to me and joked, 'We have to stop meeting like this.' I replied, 'I know, darling, twice in two weeks. It's too much!'

Less than 72 hours later, *Sunset Boulevard* opened at the Comedy Theatre on 15 December 2008. The opening night was fantastic. Loads of people from *Strictly* came. Bruno and Arlene were there, as well as contestant Mark Foster and professionals Ian Waite and Karen Hardy. The performance went amazingly well: there was a standing ovation and people just raved. When I stood up in the box, suddenly the whole theatre turned towards me and started clapping. I couldn't believe it. I felt like the Queen! Straight afterwards, I was mobbed by the audience, and the reviews the next day were glowing. It got four stars in every paper and everyone loved it.

Time Out commented: 'Craig Revel Horwood's small-scale revival is a distinct improvement on the original.' And Michael Billington, in *The Guardian*, said, 'The main discovery is that inside Lloyd Webber's big belter of a musical, there is a smaller, more dramatic show that has been waiting for years to be let out.'

David Willetts, who used to play the Phantom in *The Phantom of the Opera*, took on the role of Norma's manservant Max in the West End. He was superb ... so much so that he was nominated for Best Supporting Actor at the Olivier Awards. In addition, our wonderful leading lady, Kathryn Evans, was nominated as Best Actress. I was so pleased for her. What a comeback!

We also received nominations for Best Musical Revival and Best Company Performance. It was gratifying to get such a stamp of approval on the show. We were all absolutely delighted with the recognition.

Sunset led to a new and exciting venture when the musical director, Sarah Travis, and I decided to set up our own company,

Acid Clutch Productions. Our intention is to take the actor/ musician genre to new levels and to make shows accessible to everyone. In these difficult financial times, it makes sense to pare down, without compromising the integrity or quality of the productions we wish to present. The enterprise is scary because we are investing our own money, which is a big risk, but I've always said: if you don't risk, you don't gain. I'm prepared to risk a lot because I know I have talent; if I end up in the gutter, I will always claw my way back somehow.

Just five days after *Sunset*'s incredible first night, it was the last night of *Strictly Come Dancing* 2008. The bizarre thing about the semi-final voting cock-up was that Tom Chambers, who was guaranteed to be in the dance-off in the semis, emerged as the triumphant champion in the final. He thoroughly deserved it, though, on the night.

If you judged from beginning to end that season, and factored in who'd danced the best over the whole period, and who was the most consistent and technically the best dancer, then Rachel Stevens should have won. In my professional opinion, Rachel was the better dancer – but she did a not-so-hot show number as her final dance, whereas Tom's was a real show-stopper. For merit, on the night of the final, the best person was undoubtedly Tom.

The new year saw a new *Strictly* tour beginning. Taking part was my old sparring partner Julian Clary, about which I was slightly nervous.

As it turned out, however, I had a blast touring with Julian. We had started to patch up our differences when we'd bumped into each other in Camden a few years before, but it took the tour for us to become firm friends.

In one of the hotels we stayed in, we were given a VIP bar, where we could go for free drinks in a private setting, and while we were there, I said to Julian, 'Let's have a drink tonight.' There we had our first proper, social get-together and we found each other really rather interesting. He's now on my dinner-party guest list!

Of course, in front of the audience, we had to keep up appearances as the feuding, bitching queens ... and the crowd loved it. The trouble was that I was trying to keep a straight face the whole time, but Julian would crack me up to the point of uncontrollable giggles.

In the show, I would call him 'limp, lame, lacklustre' as I had on the TV programme – only this time, when it came to his samba, I added 'ludicrous', because that's exactly what it was. Julian would always come back with something hilarious. At one point, he said, 'That's rich coming from an Australian drag queen.' He'd read this book and then used everything against me!

Julian is really quiet backstage, but once he gets out there, there's no stopping him. He had the audience in hysterics. His dance partner, Lilia Kopylova, was also amazing. When they made their entrance each night, he used to do a little mime to suggest she'd been on the vodka. She acted brilliantly as his foil and I saw a completely different side to her. They should do a double act.

Also on the tour were Kenny Logan, Gethin Jones, Jodie Kidd, Tom Chambers, Rachel Stevens, series-two winner Jill Halfpenny, and Cherie Lunghi. Cherie loves the dancing and we love her. She's professional to the core and really funny: she comes out with some sparkling one-liners. Bruno came with us too this time, because there was no *Dance Wars*, so all four judges were there.

The tour really brought home how well known the judges' catchphrases are. The audiences were so responsive. I would say, 'I have one word for it and it starts with "F",' and 16,000 people would say, 'Fab-u-lous!' I nearly died the first time that happened. Oh, the power of television! It's bizarre. Scary. Len's 'SeVEN!' is always a winner too. Len brought the house down on tour with that score, because he always saved it until last – for Julian Clary. 'Seven' used to get booed, but everyone adores it now.

Camilla Dallerup resigned from *Strictly* after series six. Her last dance was while we were on tour. Everyone gave her a ten, except me; I awarded a nine. I thought nothing of it until after the show, when Len came up to me backstage and gave me a massive bollocking for being so mean. He went on to remind me that it was her last night on *Strictly* ever and the least I could have done was give her a ten.

My heart sank. I felt so bad, as it would have been such a great score for her to go out on: a perfect 40. The situation had completely slipped my mind when I was out there on the stage judging. *C'est la vie.* She danced wonderfully, and did so throughout the many series. I will miss her courageous choreography on the show and her bubbly personality.

As a result of the voting cock-up in the TV series, the BBC changed the voting system for the tour. The judges' scores served as a guide, but had no impact on who won or lost. The audience had the ultimate power.

I always find it incredible how tightly scrutinized the voting is. There's always an official to oversee the counting. I don't think people realize how serious a business it is backstage. It's a humungous operation.

On tour, Rachel won the most shows, Gethin won about six times and Kenny won six times too. Even Julian Clary won on a couple of occasions. He used the most outrageous ruses to win over the audiences, saying that he was from Glasgow, his mother was ill and that he'd never won anything in his life, ever. Whenever he won, after begging for votes, he would make this horrendously long speech.

'I'd like to thank wardrobe, I'd like to thank Swarovski crystals, the team behind me, catering; I'd like to thank my agent, Lilia's agent; I'd like to thank the band…' (he went on to name them all individually). Then he ended on, 'But ultimately, I'd like to thank Kate Winslet.' He was brilliantly funny.

When we played in Glasgow, Kenny, of course, won every single show, even though he was the second worst dancer next to Julian. The Scots are very patriotic and the booing and screaming had never been so loud. We had a piper on stage as a special treat, and he played 'Flower of Scotland' for Kenny's waltz. That brought the house down.

I hated his waltz, naturally, and I despised his paso doble, which I gave a three because he stomped around like a lunatic and was pulling his kilt up the whole time, showing off his legs. I commented, 'That sort of lascivious behaviour may be acceptable in the Scottish Highlands, but it's hardly acceptable on the ballroom floor.' The boos were deafening.

While in Glasgow, the *Strictly* gang decided that we would go for a night on the razz. I turned up at this bar to find Kenny armed with two bottles of vodka, with pouring spouts, freepouring down everybody's throats. He sat me down, pushed my head back and started pouring Grey Goose down my neck – I felt a bit like a force-fed goose myself.

Everyone was on the Grey Goose and it just got messy, messy, messy. My lovely cousin Logan and his wife Angela, who now live in Edinburgh, came along to meet everyone, and brought their friends, David and Katie, along too. Katie has, shall I say, a fairly ample bosom. At one point, I filled her cleavage up with vodka and then stuck my head in there and drank it all out. My whole face was covered in vodka; her whole dress was saturated. Thank God for the smoking ban – Lord only knows what would have happened if someone had lit a match!

We were all dancing, everyone was snogging everyone, and it was one of those insane nights. Kenny was doing this power lift with Ola and spinning her around – and then Gethin tried to do it with Lilia, but dropped her. Gethin's other half Katherine Jenkins was there too; she was taking photographs of this outrageous behaviour as we all crashed towards four in the morning, when a few of us ended up in McDonald's to soak up some of the vodka.

Katherine proceeded to miss her plane home the next morning – because she had put the camera film in for developing at the Boots in the airport, and the pictures hadn't come back by the time her flight was called. She decided she couldn't possibly leave evidence of our debauched evening in the chemist, so she valiantly missed her plane to protect our honour!

The next morning, however – to my horror – I discovered all these pictures of that night on Facebook. I nearly died. I was straight on the phone to the perpetrator, saying, 'Take those down *now*. They could end up in the *News of the World*!'

A month or so later, on the other side of the world, another vodka night ended in disaster. I was judging on the New Zealand show *Dancing with the Stars* again. As is my habit, I had picked up two litres of vodka when I flew into the country. On this particular night, I invited the presenters, Jason Gunn and Candy Lane, the assistant producer Erina Ellis and the producer Debra Kelleher round to my flat. After a few vodkas (not many, I hasten to add), we decided to go into town.

We were walking past a supermarket car park when poor Erina tripped over not one, but two, concrete blocks. After the first one, she saved herself, but the second one sent her sprawling and she landed flat on her face. There was blood gushing everywhere. Because she was flailing about after the first trip, she didn't get her arms out to break her fall and she cut her face and nearly broke her nose.

As we sat in the gutter trying to deal with this emergency, people all around us started shouting, 'Oh my God, it's Craig Revel Horwood from *Dancing with the Stars!*' and before we knew it, there was a crowd gathering. The programme's popularity really soared that series – the ratings shot up to 1.3 million, which is a massive third of the population – so my profile was higher than ever. It was the last thing we needed that night. Luckily, Erina made a full recovery, although she did look like she'd gone twelve rounds with Mike Tyson when all the bruising came out.

Having survived the John Sergeant debacle in the UK, I experienced a similar situation in NZ, when an entertainer called

John Rowles decided to leave *Dancing with the Stars* due to ill health. When they told me, I said, 'Oh no, I've just been through one of these!' John Rowles is very famous in NZ, so he was a high-profile person to have on the show and it was disappointing to hear that he was dropping out.

His doctor said he was suffering from exhaustion and wasn't fit enough to continue – but I don't think he took kindly to the judges' comments as his routines weren't going well. However, he made a miraculous recovery just in time for his own tour. I'm not saying his doctor didn't advise him to drop out – just that he should have got a second opinion!

I got into trouble again for one of my comments about another contestant during the series. There was a full-figured actress called Geraldine Brophy competing, and I said her waltz 'reminded me of the dancing elephants in *Fantasia* – absolutely beautiful'. The audience went completely silent, all jaws dropped to the ground – but it really wasn't a backhanded compliment. Those who have seen the dancing elephants in *Fantasia* will know that they are absolutely gorgeous. They do a beautiful, graceful waltz and then the hippos take over. There was no disguising the fact that this was a large lady, and her lovely waltz simply reminded me of that scene! The press were down on me like a ton of bricks for calling her a dancing elephant, but it wasn't intended as an insult.

My fellow judge Brendan Cole was also up to his usual tricks, goading me constantly to get a reaction, so we had a good few rows. During one programme, I told him he needed a CAT scan and was two sheep short of a sweater.

I was really pleased to get back to the southern hemisphere – and not just for work. Most importantly, I had a chance to see my family again. I'm going to try to see them more often in the future because I feel now, as I get older, that I'm missing out. I'm starting to feel the distance, yet the busier I get in London, the less able I am to go off and see people, so I have to make the decision either to knock something on the head, or to find work that will take me to Australia.

While I always miss my relatives, I was particularly pleased to catch up with them that year, as in February their lives had been threatened by the ferocious bush fires that swept Australia for a whole month. Ballarat was near the bush fires, and so was Melbourne. My sister Susan lives in Lower Plenty, Melbourne, surrounded by trees, and the bush fires were thirty minutes away from them.

At the time, they were ringing me and saying that they didn't know what to do. Everything was so dry; it was hideous. They had packed their car, ready to go at a moment's notice – but people were getting caught as they fled.

You can't understand how bad it is until you are actually there and you hear the trees exploding. It's terrifying; the sound of exploding gum trees in particular is awful. I remember that sound as a child.

Bush fires are normal, you see, but not on this scale. Regular bush fires burn the trees to ashes and enrich the soil: that's how Australia works. It's natural and there are normally firebreaks, where the ground has been bulldozed, so that a fire can be contained. But if a fire spreads all around you, there's nothing you can do.

I wrote desperate emails to my sister, saying, 'Just leave! Now! Take a holiday for two weeks, pack the kids up and go.' I was desperately worried and felt particularly powerless, but they stayed put despite my pleas. Fortunately, they came out unscathed.

I was therefore delighted that Sue came over to stay with Grant and me in New Zealand while we were there. Grant's mum, Gail – who is only six years older than me – and my mum came along too.

This visit to NZ was completely different to the previous year because Grant and my relationship had developed now, so we weren't still wondering about one another. We'd been together well over a year, and I'd given Grant a gorgeous ring on Valentine's Day – a simple band with ten diamonds – to show how much I loved him and wanted to be with him.

It was sort of like an engagement ring, but marriage is still a question mark in my mind, because of all I've been through with Jane and Lloyd and everybody else in my life. When I think of all the opportunities I've had that haven't worked out, it makes me nervous. If you want to share your love with someone, I don't believe you need a piece of paper to prove it. A ring signifies the same: that you want to be with that person, you belong to them and you will remain faithful. I'm not religious, but I believe in symbolism, and that's why I chose the ring.

The lovely thing is that all my friends and family adore Grant too. My friend Amber has just made him godfather to her second son Digby. This honour gave Grant a brand-new nickname – 'Auntie Grantie'.

Funnily enough, people think my accent is rubbing off on Grant when they meet him – but just for the record, he gained his qualification for pharmacy in Australia, studying there for seven years from the age of twenty-one, so he has a bona fide Aussie accent. That at least is not my bad influence!

In New Zealand, I hired the same penthouse apartment as I had the year before. This time, we discovered that it had an extra floor. When we arrived, Sue went off to explore, then came down the stairs and said, 'There's an open door up there which goes into a whole other apartment.'

'I don't think that's for us,' I said, but when I looked, I found plates of welcome food and drink laid out and a note saying, 'Welcome back, Craig, there's champagne in the fridge and crudités.' I couldn't believe it. I was screaming. The place was huge! Just a shame I didn't know that the year before …

The apartment is stuffed full of expensive paintings and ornaments worth hundreds of thousands. It overlooks the harbour where the ferries come in from Wellington. My friend Ross kindly took us out on his yacht around the Marlborough Sounds, which was absolutely gorgeous. The water was deep blue and crystal clear so we could see all the blue cod swimming around. It was breathtaking.

As a special treat, Grant and I took Mum, Sue and Gail to Wharekauhau, on the North Island, for dinner. Wharekauhau is an estate on a sheep station that's been done up to the most amazing spec for private fine dining. You pay about NZ$500, which is about £200, to get a helicopter over to the estate and then enjoy mouth-watering food in a unique setting.

The trip was one of the hairiest journeys of my life. That day, the weather conditions were the windiest in which you could possibly be permitted to fly. The helicopter was only a tiny little craft and, as we went over the mountains, we were blown sideways. I'm a nervous flyer anyway, as is my mum, so we were both yelling our heads off. Gail was the only one loving it, but then she's a bit of an adrenaline junkie.

Once we got over the mountains, the weather cleared up and we had beautiful sunshine, a wonderful meal and the day couldn't have been better. We got back on the helicopter, slightly tipsy, to learn that it had to go around the peninsula because of the wind, so on the way home we got a brilliant view of the coastline. It was just a-maz-ing.

From New Zealand, I flew to Australia, while Grant flew home. My sister Diane and I went to see my father's side of the family in Perth, which was excellent as I managed to get to my grandfather's grave for the first time. That was weird – because I was looking at a grave that almost has my name on it. He was Revel C. Horwood instead of C. Revel Horwood. It felt very spooky.

I hadn't seen that side of the family for twenty-two years, since I was in *Sugar Babies*, and there were lots of lovely memories there for me. My aunt gave me a special photo of Mozza and myself in the bush: I'm standing on a rock, doing an arabesque, while he tries to emulate me.

They also showed me an old 8 mm film shot before our family moved to England. There was lots of footage of me aged three, Sue aged four and Di as a young toddler. It was remarkable seeing moving colour footage of us, because we have only stills from that era and it was the first time I'd seen myself in action as a child. It was a bizarre thing to watch.

I was in Perth for Mother's Day. I spent it with my grandmother Phonse. She's ninety-two now and still giving it large. I got a lot of family recipes from her as I'm hoping to put together a book of the dishes I grew up with, my family's favourites and the ones I cooked on *Celebrity Masterchef*. Talking to Phonse was, as ever, fascinating. Who knows if I'll get the chance again? I made the most of every moment.

As my visit to Oz drew to a close, I just had time for a whistle-stop trip to Ballarat. I had one day there with my mum and we crammed everything in. I caught up with my ex-girlfriend Deanne; she's married with kids now, but still as mad as ever. We stayed up talking into the very early hours, getting to bed around six in the morning. I also got together with some of the people from Ballarat Lyric Theatre, and managed to squeeze in a meeting with the Ballarat Arts Foundation to discuss setting up the Craig Revel Horwood Award for Contemporary Dance and Choreography.

This annual award will go towards helping a young student achieve their dream of becoming a dancer or choreographer. It feels very special to give back to the very town that gave me that opportunity in the first place, and to give someone new a helping hand.

The last thing I did was to go to the trout farm to see Dad. He's got six sheep now, as well as the fish. They're all called Dorothy – yet only one of them is a ewe. He opens the gate and they come flooding into the garden to nibble at the windows.

Dad is still drinking copious amounts. Every waking moment, he's cracking open a beer, but that's just the way it's going to be now. I've had to learn to accept that about him, because that will not change. If you accept it, it makes life a whole lot easier to deal with. Otherwise you torture yourself, and what's the point of that?

We talked about this book, and he said he had been quite taken aback by it in the beginning, but once he read through it again, in a sober light, he understood a little bit more about himself, about me and about our relationship. It has really calmed things down between us. Now, everything is out in the open, which helps the two of us to put the past behind us.

I was back in London by the middle of May to do a photo shoot in drag. Lavish wasn't rearing her beautiful head again – far from it. Rather, the photo shoot was staged to launch a new venture, as I had agreed to take on the role of the Wicked Queen in *Snow White and the Seven Dwarfs* over Christmas 2009 at the Venue Cymru in Llandudno, Wales.

I'd always thought that panto was something I never wanted to direct or be involved with … until I was offered this headlining job. I think the on-screen perception of me as 'Mr Nasty' makes me naturally suited to the role! The production will give the public an opportunity to have a good old go at booing me, which will be fun. The gig will be hard work too, however, with two shows a day right through the Christmas calendar. And I have to say that the thought of wearing heels again doesn't entirely thrill me – but a girl's gotta do what a girl's gotta do …

More pressing than the panto in summer 2009 was my next production at the Watermill Theatre. I was going back to my roots: *Spend Spend Spend* presented an array of challenges when I began to rehearse it in June 2009 as an actor/muso show, my fourth to date. I was very much looking forward to staging the musical in a smaller space – and setting the entire evening in a Yorkshire pub. The scenes would unfold within that great British tradition.

The most difficult thing for me was forgetting what I'd previously choreographed ten years earlier. I had to come up with fresh ways to tell the story. I suffered countless moments of déjà vu as we worked through the numbers, recalling the great times I'd had creating the original show. It was a wonderful adventure.

I discovered how much I'd grown, not only as a director, but also as a person. There's nothing like life experience to help inform scenes. This time around, I felt like I really understood the piece, and could really get my teeth into the story and tell it as honestly as was humanly possible. There's something about revisiting the past: if only on reflection, you tend to see things as they truly are.

From Ballarat to the Beeb, my life, so far, has been a varied dance. In parts, a sexy salsa or a dramatic explosive tango. Occasionally, a sedate waltz. It's been out of time and wobbly in places, but sometimes it has achieved the perfect steps.

Overall, it's been an entertaining, show-stopping … nine.

One thing it has certainly never been is dull, dull, dull!

Index